THE CHRISTIAN MYTH

THE CHRISTIAN MYTH
Origins, Logic, and Legacy

Burton L. Mack

CONTINUUM
NEW YORK • LONDON

2001

The Continuum International Publishing Group Inc
370 Lexington Avenue, New York, NY 10017

The Continuum International Publishing Group Ltd
The Tower Building, 11 York Road, London SE1 7NX

Printed in the United States of America

Library of Congress Cataloging-in-Publication Data

Mack, Burton L.
   The Christian myth : origins, logic, and legacy / by Burton L.
Mack.

      p. cm.
   Includes bibliographical references.
   ISBN 0-8264-1355-2 (alk. paper)
   1. Christianity—Origin.   2. Christianity and culture.   I. Title.
BR129 .M33 2001
   270.1—dc21

                                        2001032495

For
BJ and Barbara
who have already redefined religion

CONTENTS

PROLOG

All peoples tell stories about their past that set the stage for their own time and place in a larger world. This world expands the horizons of memory and imagination beyond the borders of their contemporary world and becomes populated with images, agents, and events that account for the environment, set precedents for social relations and practices, and intrude upon the daily round in odd and surprising ways. These agents and images usually have some features that are recognizably human, but are frequently combinations of figures that do not normally appear in the real world and they can also be grotesque. Most peoples have not found it necessary or even interesting to reflect on the "truth" of their stories or grade them according to their degree of fantasy as has been the case in modern Western societies. When asked about such things by modern ethnographers, the answers have been a smile and a frown. As a story-teller for the Hopi indians of the southwestern United States said, when asked how he knew their stories were true, "Because they are told."

There does seem to have been a measure of curiosity about the stories of other peoples as contacts have been made throughout human history. But the stories of another people will probably not have been the first features to catch attention. Behavior, dress, and language have usually been the features of another people that register difference and call for explanation. However, when the contacts are close and the threat of conflict or cultural competition is felt, the stories and the ways in which the stories are cultivated by a people take on added significance. But even then, the range of critical responses to another people's stories, from finding them curious and interesting to worthy of satire and disparaging humor, does not seem to have included questioning their rationality or "truth."

From antiquity there are many examples of what might be called friendly intellectual curiosity about other peoples' stories and cultures as well as attempts to explain them. The Greeks especially turned their curiosity about other cultures into research projects and produced explanations for the differences they encountered when compared with their own stories and systems of philosophy and thought. They produced vast collections of data about other peoples, such as we have in the works of Herodotus, and they looked for ways to understand the stories of other peoples by noting similarities with their own and often assuming that they therefore meant the same things as Plutarch's treatise on Isis and Osiris shows.

Pausanius lets us see that the Greeks were capable of focusing curiosity upon their own stories, and Cornutus provides us with a remarkable documentation of the way in which the Stoics made sense of Homer's stories by means of allegory. This means that the Greeks had taken note of the figures and events storied in their world of the imagination and had wondered about their difference from the way in which people and activities appeared in the real world. They had learned to call the agents of that imaginary world "gods" and "heroes" and were starting to ask questions about them. At first they did not bother to give the stories about the gods and heroes a special name, referring to them just as they would refer to any story *(mythos)* or report *(logos)*. But eventually they tried to distinguish between "myths," "histories," and "fables." And since they had developed many systems of logic, science, and philosophy to account for the real world, translating the stories of the gods and heroes into allegories of the real world was not too difficult to imagine. They also came up with other explanations. Euhemerus, for instance, argued that the gods and heroes had once been real people and their stories real historical events. It was in the process of venerating them and retelling their stories that they became gods and the events became fantastic. Thus the Greeks are an early example of thinking about both their own stories and the stories of others, and developing theories in order to make sense of them.

One might have thought that the early Christians, living in the worlds of hellenistic thought and cultural mergers, would have learned from the Greeks how to accommodate the stories of the gods of other peoples in their desire to imagine the world as a single "house" *(oikoumene)* in which all peoples would live together as children of the one god. But no. For some reason early Christians came to think of their own stories of the God of Israel and father of Jesus as true in a way that made all of the stories of other peoples false and dangerous. It was not long before Christians used the term "belief" to express their acceptance of the truth of the gospel story. As for the many other stories that did not recognize and agree with the purposes of the god and hero of the gospel story, they eventually were banned, if not burned. The reasons for being so adamant about the "truth" of the gospel story are very complex, but one factor seems to have been the way in which the Christian myth was set in history. That it was a story of the gods, in some ways like other stories of the gods and heroes known to all in the Greco-Roman age, is clear. But one of its features that Christians were expected to believe was that the high god of the gospel had plans to expand his kingdom and rule over the whole world, and that the inaugural event happened "under Pontius Pilate." This introduced a combination of *mythos* and *historia* which is very tight, and especially so in that the event of importance was definitely dated and of recent, not archaic history. This is an exceptionally odd feature of the Christian myth, and Christian apologists have always used it to claim that the gospel is not "myth," but "history." However, as will become clear in the course of this book, the "setting in history" of the gospel story is one of its more obvious mythic features.

One can trace the effects of this story and its claim to be the truth throughout the long history of Christian dogmatics with its focus upon "heresy" and "orthodoxy." One can also trace the effects of the story's claim to reveal the truth about the one true God destined to rule the world throughout the histories of Christian societies and their encounters with other peoples. It helps to explain features of the emergence of Christendom in the time of Constantine (fourth century), the Roman era missions (fourth to sixth centuries), the encounter with Islam (seventh to ninth centuries), the crusades (eleventh and twelfth centuries), the period of European empires (twelfth to fourteenth centuries), the so-called age of discovery (fifteenth to seventeenth centuries), the era of colonization (seventeenth to nineteenth centuries), and the modern period of globalization (twentieth and twenty-first centuries). For the first several centuries of the Christian era there was little friendly curiosity about the stories of other peoples or questions raised about the "truth" of the gospel story.

Of some interest to our theme of the Christian gospel and the concept of myth is the change in attitude occasioned by the Enlightenment and the era of colonization. The Enlightenment introduced a rational critique of the basic tenets of Christianity and encouraged intellectual curiosity not only about the natural world but also about human history and the overlooked texts from antiquity. The era of colonization had produced intriguing reports of "primitive" peoples and their "beliefs" that explorers and missionaries brought back from Africa, Asia and the Americas. What happened was that the reports of other peoples and their stories began to merge with the now burgeoning archives of textual information about the pasts of many ancient Near-Eastern and European peoples. Scholars pored over older texts from the classical period of Greece and from the later Greco-Roman world. North European sagas, epics, rituals, and folktales were collected, published, and studied. The texts available to scholars from the ancient Near East and India were published in 51 volumes by Max Müller as *The Sacred Books of the East*. And the modern study of myths began.

The first phase of the modern study of myths was largely an academic and textual exercise. The written accounts of what other peoples "believed" and/or had believed were translated, compared with other texts, and studied. The Enlightenment had taken the edge off the sharp and unthinking rejection of other cultures and made it possible for intellectual curiosity to explore the rationales and logics of other peoples' stories, ways and thinking. But the Enlightenment critique of Christianity, the substitution of "reason" for "faith," and the shift from metaphysical theologies to Deism did not dismantle an essentially Christian mentality in the approach taken to the study of myth. Myths were thought of as systems of "belief," and the underlying questions had to do with the "reasons" for thinking that the myths were "true." "What were these people thinking?" and "How could they possibly have believed these stories they told?" were the questions driving scholarly curiosity.

14

A first approach was to classify stories by type and distinguish the lot from essays, treatises, manuals, and the "sacred texts" of high culture "priests" (such as Brahmins). Stories were divided into fairy tales, fables, sagas, legends (with "heroes" as protagonists), and myths (with "gods" as agents). The assignment of a particular story to one of these classes was frequently uncertain, but the concepts associated with the classes were quite clear. That is because the principles of distinction had to do with the "nature" of the principal protagonists and the problems they encountered. In fairy tales, smallish, fanciful "little people" appeared as helpers to children and youth who had gotten themselves into trouble. In fables, animate characters turned the surprising consequences of their actions into morals. Sagas told of leaders-to-be on extended quests for the establishment and rule of a place and a people. Legends told of heroes tested under assignment to combat the external forces that were threatening a people. And in myths, superhuman agents of a cosmic or transcendent order of reality created the world and controlled human destiny.

Naturally, the focus fell upon myths. While there was some interest in the other types of story, and though the interest sometimes registered as questions about the social and psychological "meanings" of these stories, only myths created problems that required cognitive theories of explanation. That is because, with myths having to do with stories about the "gods," the questions of "truth," "reason," and "belief" immediately surfaced, their relationship to "ritual" had to be explained, and the "religion" they were assumed to support had to be assessed. In retrospect it is not difficult to see that the assumptions underlying the very problem that myths created for the Enlightenment intellectual were the result of centuries-old familiarity with the Christian system of myth and ritual and its theological and philosophical rationalizations. There was, to be sure, a backlash to the rationalism of the Enlightenment. But the backlash, especially that of Romanticism, only succeeded in making the comparison and explanation of myths more difficult. With notions of symbolism and revelatory religious experience used to "appreciate" all myths, there was no way to account for their differences.

Many studies of myth and schools of myth theory developed from the eighteenth to the early twentieth centuries, most based on the assumption that myths were attempts to explain the material world or rationalize historical events of dramatic significance to a society. That myths imagined gods in order to render such explanations was thought to be a mark of the pre-enlightenment stage of human intelligence and mentality. Some myths were mistaken accounts of such things as the creation of the world, the emergence of animals and human beings, the astrophysical functions of the sun and moon, the reason for the round of seasons, the fertility of the crops, and the causes of natural disasters. Other myths were fanciful attempts to express the significance of social practices such as the enthronement of kings, New Year's celebrations, May Day games, and the harvest festivals. Since myths rendered obviously poor explanations, they were evidence for a "disease of language," the confused state of thinking at earlier stages of human evolution in which ignorances of causes and the lack of proper names resulted in faulty reasoning. All of these theories are now reviewed in retrospect by scholars as versions of a common explanation of myth based on a rationalist critique. The rationalist theory was still quite strong at the end of the nineteenth century when ethnography began to change the data base, and other theories of myth began to be developed. There was, however, a legacy of this first phase of myth studies that determined the way in which scholars and ethnographers would look at myth throughout the twentieth century. That legacy was the way in which the concept of *myth* had been linked to *ritual* and both to the emergent concepts of *religion* and *culture*. Ethnographers and historians of religion would record and discuss the myths of a people as parts of a larger pattern of thinking, activity, and cultural production.

The reason ethnography made a change in the study of myths is because of the way in which the descriptions of myths were recorded. Fieldwork as the method for doing ethnography meant that the researcher was "reading" and recording the entire round of activities that defined the life of a people, not just a text from a distant time and place about a myth or a ritual divorced from its life context. Myths were part of the life of the people, as were rituals, and though "religion" was rather quickly seen as an unhelpful concept, the notion of culture easily took its place. Thus the data base changed in myth studies. The number of myths available for study increased exponentially. The familiar themes and "types" of myth were compounded.

The occasions on which myths were told or evoked, as well as the social roles responsible for protecting and rehearsing them, hardly fit the older notions of "ritual" and "priest." And the depictions of mythic figures and the images used on ritual occasions started to blend into what ethnographers began to call *cultural* symbols. Thus the second phase of myth studies had to develop new theories.

If the first phase of myth studies was quite content to explain myth away, or at least to explain why the older, archaic and "primitive" myths were now passé, the second phase sought to understand myth as essential for the creation and maintenance of a society. Functionalist theories looked for ways in which myths inculcated values and attitudes. Symbolic theories emphasized the contribution myths made to images and symbols of importance for the definition, identity, and celebration of a society. Structuralist theories analyzed the way in which myths were put together in order to get at the logic of the story and the mode of thinking of a people. And so, in the hands of ethnographers, myths became essential ingredients in social description and analysis. And in the hands of cultural anthropologists, myths became windows into the otherwise unexpressed ways in which a people imagined themselves, thought about themselves, and negotiated their plans and values.

One might have thought that scholars interested in Christian origins and cultural history would turn their attention to the Christian myth and explore its social functions and rationale in keeping with modern myth theory. That has not happened. The Christian myth has not been an object of scholarly investigation. The very idea of the gospel story being called a myth has been anathema to Christians and scholars alike. Although the gospel was the Christians' story of the gods, and although it was always in mind when scholars were working with the stories of the gods of other peoples, only the stories of the gods of other peoples were called myths. The gospel story, by contrast, was referred to as the gospel and it was imagined as "true" in ways that other myths were not. That means that a study of the Christian gospel as the Christian myth will have to chart new territory. It also means that, since the gospel is well known as the story that documents the "origins," reveals the "logic," and constitutes the "legacy" of the Christian faith, asking the reader to see it differently presents the author with a threefold challenge.

The first challenge is that, in order to consider the gospel as myth and to account for *its* origin, the customary direction of cause and effect at the beginning of Christianity will have to be turned around. The gospel will no longer be the document that accounts for (records, attests, tells the story of) Christian origins *generated by the historical Jesus*. The portrayal of Jesus in the gospels will have to be seen as myth and accounted for as mythmaking. It is the origin of the gospel as the myth created by early Christians that needs to be explained. The second challenge has to do with the need for developing a theory of religion that runs counter to the way in which religion is understood by most Christians. If we want to see the logic of the gospel as myth we will have to reconstruct the social situations in which it first came together, look for the reasons early Christians had for imagining things as they did, and apply a bit of *social* theory about myth and social interests in order to see that logic at work.

And as for the legacy of the Christian myth, a sweep through two-thousand years of history will have to be imagined in order to ask about the way it has worked and continues to work at the beginning of the twenty-first century. This is the third challenge, and in some ways it is the most difficult of all. That is because current scholarly investigation of religion and culture has learned to be cautious with respect to generalizations held to be definitional for a religion or a culture conceptualized as a single system with organic functions. It is also the case that scholars have learned about the importance of social practices and behavior when describing a society. They have also learned that discourse always needs to be related to practice in order to see the dynamics of planning, rationalization, contestation and negotiation that characterize social life. To promise a reflection upon "the legacy" of "the Christian myth" is therefore brash and easily mistaken for a reification of the history of an idea. However, what I have in mind is a composite of many myths that were created, considered, compared, sorted, and arranged during the first 300 years of Christian history. The result was the formation of the New Testament with its focus upon the narrative gospels, and the Christian Bible with its rationale as Christian epic. Naturally, I will have to be careful to acknowledge the changes in the tenor, scope, and character of the gospel story in the course of 1700 years of Christian cultivation, and include the social circumstances and social reasons for the various appeals to the Bible in the history of the United States. Thus the "legacy" of "the Christian myth" is actually the story of its repeated rehearsals, replications, and reinterpretations, not the story of an impingement upon the human imagination driving human history from without.

Part I is about the scholars' quest for the historical Jesus and the notion of Christian origins that it assumes. That notion is the traditional Christian persuasion that something about the specialness of Jesus and the events of his life and death inaugurated the Christian faith. The earliest texual layers of the Jesus traditions project an image of Jesus that is quite unlike that portrayed in the gospel story. In this respect "The Case for a Cynic-like Jesus" (Chapter 2) is similar to the portrayals of the historical Jesus by other scholars (Chapter 1). But in contrast to all other pictures of the historical Jesus presented by scholars of the quest, the point will be made that neither a Cynic-like Jesus nor any other portrayals of the historical Jesus can account for Christian origins. The argument will be made that even the earliest layers of the "teachings of Jesus" do not contain the "authentic" sayings of the historical Jesus or project a true picture of what he must have been like. Thus the process of "mythmaking" had already begun, a process that eventually produced the narrative gospels and "the Christian myth." That being the case, a serious critique of the traditional scholarly quest for the historical Jesus, together with its assumptions and aims, is justified and presented. It is instead the process of social formation and mythmaking that needs full description and theoretical grounding if we want to redescribe and explain Christian origins. Part I ends with the challenge of redescription, given the state of New Testament studies, the contours of the traditional "map" of Christian origins now in place, and the fact that the discipline of New Testament studies has apparently not found it necessary to question the notions of divine intervention and miracle at the fountainhead of Christianity.

Part II is devoted to a social theory of religion and myth. These chapters are necessary lest the project of redescription be seen as an attempt to forge a "new hermeneutic." The project in Christian origins called for in Chapter 3, and undertaken by the national seminar described in the Annex, is not being pursued as a new hermeneutic with contemporary theological interests in mind. It is being pursued in the interest of explaining Christianity in terms appropriate to the academy and with potential for explaining the effective difference Christianity makes in our time. Those terms will have to be derived from academic disciplines in which social theories of myth, ritual, and religion have been generated. New Testament scholars have not thought it necessary to discuss theories of religion. As hermeneuts familiar with the Christian religion and trained in theological disciplines, New Testament scholars have been more or less unaware that a particular theory of religion has implicitly been at work in the discipline of New Testament studies. Thus the theory is unacknowledged and unexamined. It is the popular view of religion taken from the long history of Christianity as the prime example of religion and standard for the study of other religions. This book will challenge that view of Christianity by analyzing the reasons for the construction of its myth at the beginning of the Christian era and by offering another theory of religion to explain it.

Part III presents analyses of two variants of the Christian myth, the Gospel of Mark (Chapter 6) and the New Testament as a whole (Chapter 7), plus a brief history of a social affect of the Christian myth in the United States (Chapter 8). The analyses focus on the social logic of the myth that is quite different from the customary theological interpretations of the gospel, and question its helpfulness at the turn of the twenty-first century. Chapter 8 is a reflection on the way in which the Christian myth has influenced political and social practices in the United States. The reader will know that the myth is alive and well at the beginning of the twenty-first century, but may not have thought of its legacy in contemporary terms. Thus these chapters are examples of the cultural critique made possible by the design of the redescription project. The same theory of religion used to question the "origins" of the Christian myth will be used to reflect upon the "logic" and "legacy" of the myth in American society and culture.

The critique of American society and culture with which the book ends is basic to this study. Though it is grounded in a purely academic approach to the New Testament and Christian origins, the critique of its continuing influence is not merely a matter of academic interest. Both the Gospel of Mark and the New Testament are what Harold Bloom would call "strong texts" that continue to be read as standards for image formation and imitation. Their long histories and social logics have contemporary relevance in ways that are profound and largely unexamined. By analyzing them and the ways in which they continue to be viewed and manipulated, it is possible to ask questions about the effective difference Christianity is making in our world. The Christian myth and the Christian mentality that continues to cultivate it affect everyone in American society regardless of personal views and religious orientation. Thus the study of Christian origins is crucial, and a thoroughly academic approach to the social logic of the Christian myth at the beginnings of the era will call for a thorough investigation of the social role Christianity continues to play.

In the Epilog, it will come as no surprise to see that an analysis of the "origins," "logic," and "legacy" of the Christian myth will make it possible to call for diligent thinking about the social structures of the democratic society we are trying to construct.

In the Annex, a national seminar project currently under way is described as a concerted effort to meet the challenge of redescribing Christian origins. Its theoretical foundations, methods, and approach to early Christian texts are described, and a brief look at the "new map" envisioned is given. It will be argued that Christian beginnings should be located in the experimental social formations produced by the early Jesus movements, including their debates, claims, social interests, and mythmaking. Colleagues in the fields of biblical studies will be interested in this account of the work of the seminar, and the general reader may well find it helpful to catch a glimpse of these scholars at their work.

PART ONE

Setting Aside the Gospels

CHAPTER ONE

The Historical Jesus Hoopla

The Continental Quest

New Testament scholars have been preoccupied with the quest of the historical Jesus for over two hundred years. The first sign appeared in Germany in the late eighteenth century with the publication of the Reimarus fragment by G. E. Lessing, "The Aims of Jesus and His Disciples" (1778). The twists and turns of the first 125 years were traced by Albert Schweitzer in his book *The Quest of the Historical Jesus*, published in 1906. Schweitzer's study created consternation at the time, for the picture of Jesus he presented at the end of that history was not that of the sane humanitarian imagined by liberal scholars at the end of the nineteenth century, but that of an apocalyptic visionary bordering on insanity. According to Schweitzer, Jesus went to his death in the mistaken conviction that he was the messiah and that his being put to death would surely usher in the kingdom of God. Schweitzer's interest in probing a dark psychology for Jesus did not survive, but his portrayal of Jesus as an apocalyptic preacher did. It was eventually accepted by scholars in England and America, at first rubbing uncomfortably against deeply unreceptive cultural sensibilities, but finally becoming the standard account of the nineteenth century quest. It is well worth reading for it relentlessly explores the motivations for this scholarship at every turn. It soon becomes clear that the motivations driving the search for Jesus were no different from those that have been driving the entire discipline of New Testament study from its beginning, namely to determine what started the Christian religion.

One can see that the discipline emerged as one of the principle applications of the new and powerful intellectual development known as rationalism. Applied to early Christian texts, rationalist thinking quickly set the agenda for the new discipline of historical-critical investigation. The discipline was said to have two major objectives. One was the attempt to separate "history" from "myth," whereby "history" was understood as the rendering of a plausible account of events in contrast to the imaginary and mythic constructions early Christians put upon them. The other objective was to identify the earliest events of importance for the emergence of Christianity and to account for all subsequent history either as a corruption of those pristine revelations or as a development from them. In retrospect we can see that both of these objectives were motivated by cultural interests of the times. The first objective, getting the history straight, was driven by an Enlightenment mentality. The second, identifying the impulse that started the new religion, was a Protestant preoccupation. Putting the two motivations together, this scholarship soon found itself concerned with the Jesus quest as the way to discover an original event for Christian origins.

Naturally, it was the gospels that caught and centered scholarly attention. At first it was thought possible to set them side by side in columns and produce a single narrative called a "harmony." But then the differences among the four could no longer be overlooked. The gospel of John was eventually set aside because its characterization of Jesus as self-consciously divine could not be merged with the picture presented by the other three gospels. Then the differences among the other three became critical and the so-called "synoptic problem" was seen. The task was to determine which was the first to be written, and thus the most authentic record of the important events. Many of the results of nineteenth century scholarship were related to the quests for Jesus and Christian origins: miracle was seen as the principal feature and problem of early Christian myth; Q was discovered, the source for the sayings of Jesus common to Matthew and Luke; Markan priority among the synoptic gospels eventually prevailed; the influence of the mythologies of the Greco-Roman world, including the apocalyptic world view of contemporary Jewish provenance, was discovered in early Christian writings; the difference between the Jesus of history and Paul's "Christ of faith" was recognized and problematized; and so forth. However, it is very important to see that, for all of the critical acumen invested in these studies, the goal of the quest was never called into question. That goal was to rewrite the gospel story as a plausible "life of Jesus." It was taken for granted that the proper account of Christian origins would be a biography of Jesus. The unexamined assumption was that the gospels were the confused attempts of early Christians to write a biography, and that the task of the modern scholar was to correct their mistakes by critical reconstructions and rearrangements. Thus the nineteenth century filled with "lives of Jesus" that sought to remedy the flaws of the ancient gospels. Schweitzer himself produced a "life of Jesus" at the end of his book as his own contribution to getting the history straight and accounting for Christian origins.

A change took place early in the twentieth century that came to be associated primarily with the name of Rudolf Bultmann. Bultmann was suspicious of the narrative gospels as biographies, as was Karl Ludwig Schmidt and others working in the early 1920s who saw that Mark, the earliest gospel, was composed by piecing together smaller, disparate units of anecdotal material. Since this material must have made its point on its own or in other contexts, before it was taken up to compose a narrative gospel, the task now was to trace the earlier history and significance of these smaller bits of lore about Jesus. It soon became obvious that material of this type had repeatedly been embellished and resignified in the course of its transmission, and Bultmann concluded that only a basket of unconnected fragments remained with any claim to having had a "setting in the life of Jesus." It was therefore not possible, according to Bultmann, to know anything about the historical Jesus except for the fact that (his famous *Dass*) there had been an historical Jesus, and that he had proclaimed the arrival of the kingdom of God. Bultmann's detailed study of the teachings of Jesus and the way in which each saying was given brief narrative settings in the course of early Christian elaboration and interpretation, eventually to be subsumed by the larger narrative gospels, was published as *The History of the Synoptic Tradition* (1921). This book became the standard text for the next period of gospel studies which New Testament scholars called form-criticism.

However, Bultmann's own fascination was not with the gospels, but with the *kerygma*, the "proclamation" that Jesus as the Christ had been crucified and resurrected (or what we now refer to as the *christos* myth). According to Bultmann, it was not and is not the historical Jesus, but the *kerygma* that created and continues to focus the Christian faith. Thus his existentialist hermeneutic and his program of demythologization were launched as theological projects. His importance is legend, and his influence among New Testament theologians is still quite strong. His students, who eventually occupied most of the New Testament chairs in the German University system, did continue to worry about losing the historical basis for the Christian faith by giving up the quest for the historical Jesus, but all they were ever able to do was to render an existentialist interpretation of the voice behind the sayings attributed to Jesus and compare it with Bultmann's existentialist interpretation of the *kerygma*. The odd result of these attempts was that, when the significance of both the *kerygma* and the voice of Jesus were described in existentialist terms, there was little difference between them. Jesus appeared as the first Christian, a conclusion most uncomfortable for all but the most romantic of pietists among the scholars. James Robinson called these attempts *A New Quest of the Historical Jesus* (1959). But the new quest was hardly "historical." The better assessment of this post-Bultmann era of Jesus studies, pursued primarily by Bultmann's own students and other scholars who had been deeply influenced by him, is that it actually wrote *finis* to the old quest for the historical Jesus.

American Hoopla

Not, however, in America. The cultural climate in America was not ready for Bultmann's dictum that we cannot reconstruct the historical Jesus, or for the deeply existentialist interpretations of the "voice" of Jesus by Bultmann's students. As a matter of fact, Americans had never paid much attention to nineteenth century critical, historical, biblical scholarship to begin with. And they have always found it difficult to entertain either an existentialist or a tragic view of life. Protestant Christianity in the United States has been squeamish about the rituals of the Mass and the Lord's Supper, uninterested in meditations on the passion, and unable to grasp the logic of the *kerygma*. It has been the gentle Jesus, meek and mild, the Jesus of Charles Sheldon's novel *In His Steps*, that has fascinated the American imagination and determined its definition of Christianity. *In His*

Steps, a novel about a town that decided to live for an entire year just as Jesus had lived, was published in 1897 and became the next best selling book after the Bible for 60 years, selling over 8 million copies. With such an image so deeply etched in the American popular mind, it is no wonder that the critical edge of continental gospel studies and quests for Christian origins bypassed America.

Thus there are two types of hero in American popular culture. One is Jesus, the absolutely harmless and vulnerable incarnation of selflessness. The other is the cowboy, the incarnation of independence and the ability to master any situation. Both are "good guys," as they say, always on the side of justice, fairness, and the little people. But Jesus is the archetypal victim. He is crushed by his enemies because he will not fight. The cowboy, on the other hand, is the archetypal victor. The cowboy has the power to defend himself against any who get in his way. He fights and always wins. In the American mind there is no need to decide between these heroes. Each is idolized for his own virtues, and that means that Americans can always imagine their heroes being clean and good, whether they win or lose. The popular image of the cowboy was created by *The Virginian*, a western novel published in 1902 by Owen Wister. *The Virginian* became required reading in American public schools for decades, selling more than two million copies before it was eclipsed by its imitations: the dime Western, the radio serial such as *The Lone Ranger*, and the Western movie, all of which burgeoned during the 1920s, 1930s, and 1940s, and the influence of which is still unmistakable in the cinema of violence and apocalyptic that currently marks American entertainment.

So what about the history of New Testament scholarship in America, and the reasons for the rash of Jesus books that has recently caused such a furor? The first thing to notice is that the stage was hardly set for dealing with the critical issues of history and myth introduced into the American academic scene in the forties and early fifties. It was only then that American scholars finally took note of Bultmann, read Kierkegaard, and began trying to catch up with the European history of New Testament scholarship, the history of religions schools, the perennial issues of Christian origins, the various criticisms for controlling the exegesis and interpretation of texts, and the fact that, in Europe, New Testament study had been a rigorous academic discipline for over 150 years. During the fifties, Europeans and American scholars trained in Europe were invited to leading positions in graduate schools in the States, bringing with them the lore, rules, and rudiments of European intellectual traditions. It required, however, another fifteen or twenty years before scholars trained and working in America found a way to focus their newly learned critical skills upon questions appropriate to the American scene. One of the big questions that bothered American scholars was the negative conclusions of the European quest for the historical Jesus. Surely Bultmann had gone too far in erasing the face of the historical Jesus. Surely Schweitzer was wrong in his view of Jesus as a mistaken apocalyptic visionary. Surely it must be possible to know what Jesus had said or done that started the Christian religion. Don't we need to ask whether he knew what he was doing? And so, not having worked through all of the critical issues familiar to the older quest, American scholars were not yet sobered by its findings or failures. They decided to work it out for themselves by making a fresh start.

The American quest was launched in the late sixties and early seventies. Robert Funk organized a seminar on the parables of Jesus for the Society of Biblical Literature and provided the first example of a critical approach to their interpretation with his *Language, Hermeneutic and Word of God* in 1966. This was a clever move, for it started with Bultmann's insight about the importance of the teachings of Jesus, and agreed with the post-Bultmannian effort to render an existentialist interpretation of the teachings. But in order to render such an interpretation, Funk used a structuralist analysis of the parables on the model of narrative criticism then current in French thought, and combined it with more than a touch of appreciation for literature as an aesthetic object. The aesthetic object approach to literature, frequently called the new criticism, touched the very heart of American sensibility. And Funk's picture of Jesus as a story-teller whose parables made it possible for a listener to imagine and "enter the kingdom of God" agreed with what Americans already thought it meant to be a Christian. It was a very exciting idea, and it launched the two major projects for which American New Testament scholarship has become rather well-known: parables research and the modern Jesus quest.

The major players in the Jesus quest have been Robert Funk and Dominic Crossan. Others of importance have been the Jesus Seminar and its members, Marcus Borg, Richard Horsley, E. P. Sanders, and Paula Fredriksen. Robert Funk's Jesus told stories with a poet's sensibilities and a preacher's desire to change the way people think about the kingdom of God (a cipher left undefined). His recent book, *Honest to Jesus* (1996), shows that Funk still thinks the parables are the key to the authentic voice of the pre-gospel, pre-mythic, pre-kerygmatic Jesus, and that hearing that voice is sufficient for Christian transformation and guidance. Dom Crossan also started with the parables, but soon expanded his database to include the entire collection of the sayings of Jesus, and eventually took seriously the so-called passion narratives as well. In order to pare down the hundreds of sayings attributed to Jesus from the first three centuries and arrive at the so-called "authentic" sayings, Crossan devised a method which he called "triple attestation." The assumption was that, if a saying was included in three textual traditions independently of one another, it must have been authentic. It sounded good, and few were able to question whether his three textual traditions were always "independent." And so, on the basis of these "authentic" sayings, and with a little help from the narrative gospels, as well as some considerations about Galilee taken from archeological studies, Crossan proposed the picture of a wandering peasant intellectual whose talk of the kingdom was heard as a social critique as well as an invitation to personal transformation.

The Jesus Seminar was Robert Funk's creation, and its work was heavily influenced by Crossan as well. All of the sayings attributed to Jesus in texts from the first three centuries were reviewed over a period of about ten years. Studies were made and votes taken to record scholarly judgments about the authenticity of each saying. The work of the seminar was governed primarily by the notion that Jesus's teachings must have been unique. This meant that sayings and concepts common to the cultures of context would not be considered authentic, nor would sayings from later Christian texts found to be embellishments and interpretive additions to the collections of his teachings. The results, published in *The Five Gospels* (1993), color all of the sayings found in the New Testament plus the Gospel of Thomas according to the following code: Red means authentic; pink means Jesus may have said something like it; gray expresses serious doubt about the authenticity of a saying; and black means that Jesus could not have said it. Of about 500 sayings, the seminar voted 13 red, 77 pink, and the rest gray or black. According to Funk, the red and pink sayings sound as if they were spoken by a "laconic sage." As you might have expected, the Jesus Seminar accomplished a successful merger of Funk's poet and Crossan's peasant preacher.

Marcus Borg did not produce a critical study of sayings and texts to support his picture of Jesus, preferring instead to start with a poll of what liberal scholars have said. The question Borg thought important was whether Jesus had been an apocalyptic visionary or a teacher of wisdom. The consensus of the scholars he polled was that Jesus had been a teacher of wisdom. The kind of wisdom Jesus "taught," according to Borg, must have been divine, a kind of mystical knowledge of God. One of his books is about *Meeting Jesus Again for the First Time*. I include Borg in this roster of scholars only because his books are very popular and because he is regularly mentioned by the media as a scholar of importance for the quest of the historical Jesus. In fact, however, the popularity of his works and their promotion by the media illustrate the difficulty Americans have had in distinguishing between academic scholarship and pious meditations.

Richard Horsley's Jesus is different still. Horsley has not been impressed with parable studies or Q studies, and he has not been interested in promoting a mystical experience of the divine sage Jesus. Instead, he has worked with the portrait of Jesus in the gospels and has tried to fit it into a social history of Palestine. His Jesus is a prophet-messiah who called for the restoration of village life in Galilee on the model of being "Israel," or the "people of God" as Horsley imagined it. The problem, of course, was that Galilee had come under the economic, military, and political domination of other powers, most recently of the Romans. Horsley cannot find any evidence that Jesus actually instigated a peasants' revolt against the Romans, which means that the question of why they killed him becomes troubling. Horsley works this out as best he can in one of his many books about Jesus, *Jesus and the Spiral of Violence* (1987).

E. P. Sanders has also written several books about Jesus and the gospels, including *Jesus and Judasim* (1985). The importance of this book is that Sanders acknowledges one of the embarrassing questions for questers of the historical Jesus. It is that no one has been able to say why Jesus's "teachings," however construed, motivated the Romans to kill him. Sanders argues that, if it was not what Jesus said that mattered, it must have been something Jesus did. He finds it in the story of Jesus in the temple, the episode of provocation in the narrative of the crucifixion. Taking this narrative incident as historically factual, a story others have shown to be a fiction required by the logic of a mythic martyrdom, Sanders works out the reasons that all of the actors must have had for playing the roles they did in Jesus's crucifixion. Thus the "passion narrative" turns out to be "historical."

Paula Fredriksen has received much attention because of her book, *From Jesus to Christ* (1988). She argues that the gospels and the early history of Christianity do not make sense unless Jesus was an apocalyptic visionary. And still others continue to imagine Jesus as having had an eschatological self-consciousness that made it appropriate for him to think of himself as the messiah, or even as a person with a very special relation to God assigned to fulfill the role of the apocalyptic son of man. Thus the tide has risen of scholars and books adding ever more gospel features to the figure of the historical Jesus. Even Helmut Koester, the leading representative of the Bultmann school among American scholars, has said that Jesus must have been a combination of prophet, miracle-worker, and exorcist just as the gospels portray him (1982, p. 78). That is saying quite a bit for a Bultmannian and reveals the influence of the American scene. Is it any wonder, then, that a rather impressive number of major New Testament scholars have joined in presenting accolades to Luke Timothy Johnson's *The Real Jesus* (1996), a book that attacks the very idea of a quest for the historical Jesus? Johnson argues that the Jesus of the gospels *was* the "real" Jesus as "remembered" by the early Christians!

These, then, are the scholars who have caught the attention of the media and the American public. Borg has been given a million dollars to carry on the good work. The results of the Jesus seminar have been published by Macmillan, a major commercial press. The works of Funk and Crossan have been presented to the public as sensational publishing events by HarperSanFrancisco. And media events from talk shows, televised conferences, and book signing tours, to advertised workshops and TV documentaries have turned the scholars' quest for the historical Jesus into a public forum. Journalists and producers usually report on the phenomenon by comparing the views of scholars with those of churchmen, theologians, and the average Christian. The difference between the scholars' historical Jesus and the Christ of the gospels imagined by the average Christian is usually portrayed as radical and sensational. That, of course, has created consternation. And since neither the guild of New Testament scholars nor the media have been able to adjudicate differences among the many profiles of Jesus at the level of historical criticism, the differences are always explained in terms of the personal attitudes of the scholars themselves toward Christianity and the church. Thus all of these views of and about Jesus, including the various scholarly portrayals, are treated as personal opinions if not "faith statements," and there is no way for the American public to know whom to believe or what to think.

At the End of the Quest

I want now to offer four criticisms of the quest for the historical Jesus, especially as it has been pursued in recent American scholarship, and then suggest a better approach to the examination of Christian beginnings. (1) A first criticism is that the quest has not produced any agreement about a textual data base from which to work. The textual units used for this or that profile change from scholar to scholar without any agreed-upon theoretical framework to adjudicate the differences among them. This is a serious indictment of the guild of New Testament scholarship. The guild pretends to be an academic discipline, but in fact resists the pursuit of a theoretical framework and the accompanying rules of argumentation necessary for coming to agreements about matters of data, method, explanation, and replication of experiments or research projects. These are foundational matters for an academic discipline. To resist them indicates that something else of importance must be driving the energies of the quest for reasons other than academic. Thus it is the case that most reconstructions of the historical Jesus have started with prior assumptions, unexpressed, about the importance of a certain kind of Jesus. With this assumed profile in mind, textual material has then been collected in its support. Thus, in the case of sorting through the sayings of Jesus, the Jesus Seminar used criteria such as the principles of "dissimilarity" and "most difficult reading" on the assumption that sayings coming from Jesus must have been unique, novel, without cultural precedence, and therefore catching, surprising, important, and capable of changing the way people thought (and think!). This means that a certain kind of Jesus was assumed as the measure for distinguishing "authentic" sayings from later attributions. This is clearly circular reasoning, and even if the assumption of Jesus's novelty were correct in some respect, it would require additional argumentation to support that rationale. Crossan's criterion of "triple attestation" requires scholarly agreements about being able to delimit three early, completely independent textual traditions, agreements that are simply not present in the current state of New Testament scholarship. And even Crossan has not been careful about applying his rule of three, as for instance in the privilege granted to the parable of the good Samaritan for which there is only one, very late textual tradition (Luke). In the cases of Horsley, Sanders, Fredriksen, and others, the lack of control over the database requirement is even more egregious. If there is no agreement about what texts count and how to turn them into data for historical reconstructions, it means that the quest cannot be thought of as an academic discourse within a scholarly discipline. There are no rules for conducting research in the quest for the historical Jesus; there is no common, agreed-upon basis for debate about theories of memory and mythmaking. Proposals of all types are brought down to the level of personal opinions, explained by brief personal profiles of the scholars involved and left there. Naturally, those opinions tend to prevail in the popular mind of the guild and the public that are most congenial to the traditional ways of imagining Christian origins.

(2) A second criticism is that none of the profiles proposed for the historical Jesus can account for all of the movements, ideologies, and mythic figures of Jesus that dot the early Christian social-scape. We now have the Jesuses of Q1 (a Cynic-like sage), Q2 (a prophet of apocalyptic judgment), Thomas (a gnostic spirit), the parables (a spinner of tales), the pre-Markan sets of pronouncement stories (a lawyer for the defense), the pre-Markan miracles stories (an exorcist and healer), Paul (a martyred messiah and cosmic lord), Mark (the son of God who appeared as messiah, was crucified, and will return

as the son of man), John (the reflection of God in creation and history), Matthew (a legislator of divine law), Hebrews (a cosmic high priest presiding over his own death as a sacrifice for sins), Luke (a perfect example of the righteous man), and many more. Not only are these ways of imagining Jesus incompatable with one another, they cannot be accounted for as the embellishments of the memories of a single historical person no matter how influential. Thus the link is missing between the historical Jesus as reconstructed by scholars and the many figures of Jesus imagined and produced by early Christians. Since the quest for the historical Jesus has been pursued in the interest of explaining Christian origins, this missing link is a very serious consideration. It means, in fact, that the quest has failed. The object of the quest has purportedly been to remove the fantastic and miraculous features of the Christ myth and gospels from the "real Jesus of history," but the more important problem for explaining Christian origins is to account for the diversity of mythic claims about him. No reconstruction of the historical Jesus has done or can do that.

(3) A third criticism is that the link between the teachings of Jesus on the one hand and the story of his crucifixion on the other is missing. None of the scholars that start with the sayings of Jesus has ever been able to account for the crucifixion of Jesus on the basis of those teachings. This means that something is wrong. The teachings and the crucifixion should make sense when put together, but they do not. This is a very serious criticism of the quest. It is also a very serious criticism of the narrative logic of the gospels where the teachings and the crucifixion are in fact interwoven. Only two of the questers for the historical Jesus have dared to tackle this one. Crossan's study of the "gospel story of the death of Jesus" (*Who Killed Jesus?*, 1995) is a large accumulation of historical and cultural data in the interest of arguing that many details of the crucifixion story, especially those details that suggest Pilate's innocence on the one hand and the complicity of "the Jews" on the other, are *not* history but "Christian propaganda." This looks at first to be a good start toward a recognition of the gospel accounts as mythmaking. But Crossan is not interested in pursuing that question. What interested him were present day hermeneutical issues dealing with Christian anti-Semitism. Thus his study begs the questions of (1) whether the

story of the crucifixion was based on fact, and (2) whether the reasons for killing Jesus had anything to do with his activity as a "peasant preacher," the portrait Crossan had painted earlier in his reconstructions of the historical Jesus. The book is therefore a clever tour de force and a potentially deceitful arrangement of smoke and mirrors. Although it argues against the historical plausibility of detail after detail in the gospel account, the outline of the book follows the gospel story and thus leaves it in place as the narrative account the reader continues to have in mind. The strategy here is similar to that of Crossan's book about *Jesus: A Revolutionary Biography* (1994), a book that marks episode after episode of the gospel story as implausible history, yet leaves the gospel outline in place as the way to imagine Jesus's "biography." Worse yet for the *Who Killed Jesus?* book, even the details held to be implausible are sensationalized by redescriptions taken from the social and cultural histories of the time external to the gospel framework. The "fact" of the crucifixion is left in place as certain even if still in need of explanation (!), and the problem of accounting for the crucifixion is left at the level of the reader's imagination of a temple incident that, though admittedly implausibly provocative, nevertheless must have triggered the entire crucifixion scenario. Thus the reader is left with the impression that *something* of the sort must have happened, crucifixion and "resurrection" included, and that it was these events that generated the Christian religion.

Sanders's book, referred to above, is more honest in that he struggles valiantly to work out the logics of the various rationales and misunderstandings that "must" have converged in the decisions and behaviors of those who played a role in the event as storied in the gospel account. But neither Sanders, nor Crossan, or any other scholar in quest of the historical Jesus, whether working primarily with the teachings traditions or the narrative logic of the gospels, has been able to connect them in a convincing account. This must mean that the textual data for reconstructing the historical Jesus are inadequate or have been wrongly construed, or that the texts available for a reconstruction of the historical crucifixion are inadequate or wrongly construed. What if both sets of data are inadequate and incompatable because they are the products of early Christian mythmaking?

(4) A fourth criticism is that the publication of books about the historical Jesus as well as the public discussion of them has assumed a purpose for the quest that is unreasonable and ill-conceived. That purpose has been to rectify and rejuvenate Christian faith and self-understanding. Christians approach the question of Jesus and Christian origins as a seriously definitive enterprise. That is because Christian mentality, especially in its Protestant variety, locates the message, authority, events, and power upon which the Christian churches draw *precisely* at the moment of origin, and that moment has always been defined by the appearance of Jesus "in human history." The conventional view is that, by recall and ritual, Christians can strike once more the magic flint that ignited and can reignite the Christian vision and faith. The problem for the historian and for the quester of the historical Jesus is that the Jesus of importance for the Christian faith is the Jesus as portrayed in the gospel story.

The scholarly approach to Christian origins is critical with respect to the gospel accounts in the New Testament. The quest for the historical Jesus and his teachings is an attempt to reconstruct the "real" Jesus behind the gospels. Scholars have thought of this effort as a requirement for intellectual honesty in the face of the extravagant and mythic features of the gospels, and therefore as a helpful correction or revision of Christian origins. But Christian mythic mentality is not thereby called into question. It functions still in the hope that the true, originary core of the Christian vision or revelation can be found at the beginning in the person of Jesus before the gospels were written. Many new questers, such as Funk and Borg, have expressly stated that they would like their portraits of Jesus to substitute for the gospel picture and thus make it possible for Christians to be followers of Jesus without the entanglements of conventional Christianity. Many are the Christians who have wanted to believe them. The problem is that it was not and is not the historical Jesus whom scholars are able to reconstruct and imagine that created, creates, and sustains the Christianity that made Jesus such an important figure in the first place. It is the Jesus Christ of the gospels, creeds, myths and rituals of the Christian religion that resides in the collective imagination and that influences social and cultural attitudes. As Kenneth Woodward, editor of *Newsweek*, said in a Reuters news service interview, his concern was that "[The leaders of the historical Jesus movement were] weakening what is remarkable about him. His social teaching is not that remarkable and diluting him into a kind of 1960s revolutionary is not interesting. What is interesting is that he says, 'Not my will but thine be done.' " How is that for putting the Jesus Seminar and company in their places? How is that for the final line on what it was that Jesus said that matters? How is that for the confidence of a major critic and editor in the self-evident truth of the gospel story? It has apparently not dawned on Woodward, or on *any* major journalist I know of, that the quest for the historical Jesus started with and is rooted in a scholarly consensus about the *mythic* aspects of the New Testament gospels. But that apparently does not matter. Reading a book about the historical Jesus is not enough to erase the gospel portrait. The gospel portrait continues to be the narrative source for imagining the historical Jesus even when the reconstruction of the historical Jesus is set to challenge the gospel story.

If we want to render a cultural critique, it is the relationship of the Christ of the gospel story to the cultures that pattern our social constructions that needs to be addressed. Skirting the narrative gospels to get "back" to the historical Jesus will not work. No reconstruction of the historical Jesus can account for the narrative gospel in the first place, or challenge the narrative gospels and the portrayal of Jesus they present in the popular imagination. The current quest for the historical Jesus does *not* raise questions about the supposed reasons for the importance of the historical Jesus. It does *not* raise questions about the effective difference Christianity makes as a social presence and cultural influence in our world. It has *not* asked what it is about the Christian gospel and religion that is inappropriate, inadequate, troubling, or even dangerous as we face the social and cultural issues of our time. New Testament scholars have not found a way to broach, much less discuss questions such as these in public forum. The quest for the historical Jesus actually avoids these questions. It seeks, on the model of the Protestant reformation, to leapfrog over the "wrongheaded" myths and rituals of the Christian churches to land at the beginning where the pure, clean impulse of an uncontaminated Jesus can rectify and rejuvenate Christian faith. That is mythic thinking with an apron-string attachment to Christian mentality. It will not produce a scholarly account of Christian origins. And it will not produce a rejuvenated (Christian) spirituality unbeholden to the gospel accounts.

Changing the Focus

This means that we need to start over with the quest for Christian origins. And the place to start is with the observation that the New Testament texts are not only inadequate for a Jesus quest, they are data for an entirely different phenomenon. They are not the mistaken and embellished memories of the historical person, but the myths of origin imagined by early Christians seriously engaged in their social experiments. They are data for early Christian mythmaking. The questions appropriate to these texts should be about the many Christian groups and movements in evidence, their particular social circumstances and histories, and the various social reasons they had for imagining a teacher in so many different ways. To read these texts only in the interest of the quest to know the historical Jesus has been to misread them, to misuse them. They simply do not contain the secrets of the historical Jesus for which scholars have been searching. Early Christians were not interested in the *historical* Jesus. They were interested in something else. So the question is whether that something else can be identified.

CHAPTER TWO

The Case for a Cynic-like Jesus

Historians of early Christianity distinguish between the Jesus traditions and the mythologies of the death and resurrection of Jesus *christos*. The myth of Jesus *christos* was based on the logic of a martyrdom that merged the Greek notion of the noble death with a hellenistic version of an old Semitic wisdom tale about the trial and vindication of an innocent victim (Mack, 1988, Chapter 4). The *christos* myth was a very early development within a Jesus movement that had spread to northern Syria, as reflected in the letters of Paul, but it does not document the earliest or the most characteristic form of cultivating the memory of Jesus within the Jesus movements in Galilee, northern Palestine, and southern Syria. The earliest traditions consist mainly of the "teachings of Jesus" in the genre of a collection of "sayings" *(gnomologium)* plus snippits of "biographical" material characteristic of the Aristotelian "life" *(bios)*. These included "anecdotes" *(chreiai)* and "reminiscences" *(apomnemoneumata)*. The three collections of major significance for the teachings of Jesus are Q (from *Quelle* meaning "source," i.e., the "source document" for the sayings of Jesus used by the authors of the gospels of Matthew and Luke), the Gospel of Thomas, and sets of chreiai used by Mark in the composition of his gospel. Whereas the *christos* myth imagined and mythologized a martyrdom for Jesus, the Jesus traditions did not. The Jesus traditions were oriented to the teachings of Jesus, and those who belonged to his "school" cultivated his teachings as a sufficient rationale for their movements.

The synoptic gospels can be understood as a late first-century merger of Jesus and *christos* traditions. In the gospels the *christos* myth was given narrative form and historical setting as a dramatic event of Jesus's trial, crucifixion and resurrection, and the Jesus traditions

were recast in such a way as to account for the conflict that precipitated that eventuality. Mark, the first of the narrative gospels, established the basic plot that linked Jesus's crucifixion with the
destruction of the temple and could therefore have been imagined
only after the Roman-Jewish war of 66–73 C.E. Before the war
neither the *christos* myth nor the Jesus traditions needed or produced
a narrative gospel with an historical setting and motivation to account for Jesus's death (Mack, 1988).

A postwar dating for the narrative gospels is an extremely important datum for the reconstruction of Christian origins for it sets the
pregospel Jesus traditions free from the portrayal of Jesus created by
Mark. Mark pictured Jesus as a charismatic and prophetic proclaimer
of an apocalyptic message that included the destruction of the temple
at Jerusalem and the imminent appearance of a new social order
called "the kingdom of God." Mark's picture has been accepted by
everyone, whether Christian by confession or not, mainly because
there has been no other story or portrayal of the "historical Jesus"
with which to compare it, and it does agree with the traditional
Christian imagination.

Recent research in the pregospel Jesus traditions has challenged
this acceptance of the Markan portrait. One approach has focused
upon the pronouncement stories, or elaborated chreiai, in the synoptic gospels. Another has engaged the compositional history of the
pregospel *gnomologium* Q. Both of these currents of research have
identified an earlier stage of memory and imagination in the Jesus
traditions that exhibits features resembling popular Cynic idiom and
behavior. This chapter will describe the data discovered at the bed-
rock of the Jesus traditions, draw the parallels to popular Cynicism
of the time, and discuss the significance of these findings for the
project in Christian origins.

The Earliest Layer of Q

The discovery of Q was made in the course of attempts to solve
the "synoptic problem," or the textual relationships among the gospels of Matthew, Mark, and Luke. The standard solution is called the
two-document hypothesis, namely that Matthew and Luke each used
Mark and Q independently in the composition of their gospels. Mark

provided the narrative outline for both Matthew and Luke, replete with miracle stories, pronouncement stories, plot and passion narrative; Q provided the instructional material common to Matthew and Luke, sayings that do not appear in Mark. The task for scholars has been to reconstruct Q by comparing its citations in Matthew and Luke. This task is now nearing completion (Robinson et al., 2000).

Along the way much has been learned about Q. The genre has been attested in early Christian circles by the discovery of the Gospel of Thomas, another text consisting only of the sayings of Jesus. The compositional design of Q has been identified. And the compositional history of the collection has been determined by paying attention to the coherence of three strata of material. These strata are now being referred to as Q1, Q2, and Q3 (Kloppenborg, 1987; 2000). The Cynic parallels are characteristic for Q1, the earliest stratum of the Q tradition. A comprehensive study of this document and the history of the people who produced it is available in *The Lost Gospel* (Mack, 1993).

Q1 consists of six or seven clusters of sayings material, each of which forms a thematic unit, and all of which are judiciously placed for instructional effect in the larger frame of the text created at the later Q2 level of composition (Mack, 1993, p. 109). These thematic units exhibit various kinds of rhetorical and compositional design, one important type of which is what the hellenistic teachers of rhetoric called an elaboration or a complete argument (Mack and Robbins, 1989, Chapter 2). By paying attention to the rhetoric of these units it is possible to determine core sayings and the direction of their elaboration. There is a high incidence of aphorism in this core material. Consider the following (cited with reference to their incidence in Luke):

> Fortunate the poor; theirs is the kingdom (Luke 6:20).
> The measure you give is the measure you get (Luke 6:38).
> Can the blind lead the blind (Luke 6:39)?
> A pupil is not above his teacher (Luke 6:40).
> No good tree bears bad fruit (Luke 6:43).
> Foxes have holes, birds nests, but "man" has no home (Luke 9:58).
> The one who asks gets (Luke 11:10).
> A kingdom divided will be destroyed (Luke 11:17).
> Nothing is hidden that will not be revealed (Luke 12:2).

Where your treasure, there your heart (Luke 12:34).
The one who exalts himself will be humbled (Luke 14:11).
If salt is saltless, it is good for nothing (Luke 14:34–35).
No one can serve two masters (Luke 16:33).
The one who seeks to save his life will lose it (Luke 17:33).

These sayings are not unusually clever. Many are simply versions of age-old proverbial lore, and all need some life context in which to score their point. But they are pungent, slightly unnerving, and mildly humorous in the sense that insights about human behavior and desire have been pressed to the point of extremes if not absurdity. They illustrate the aphoristic nature of the wisdom attributed to Jesus at the earliest stage of recollection available to us.

If one now looks for aphorisitc sayings that are phrased as imperatives instead of maxims, a somewhat clearer picture of an ethos begins to come into view. Imperatives actually predominate in Q1, many of which function as core injunctions at the heart of small instructional units. The following list illustrates the behavior enjoined in the Jesus movement at this early period:

Rejoice when reproached (Luke 6:20).
Bless those who curse you (Luke 6:27).
If struck on the cheek, offer the other (Luke 6:29).
Give to everyone who begs (Luke 6:30).
Judge not, that you not be judged (Luke 6:37).
First remove the log from your eye (Luke 6:42).
Go out as lambs in the midst of wolves (Luke 10:2).
Carry no money, bag, or sandals (Luke 10:4).
Greet no one on the road (Luke 10:4).
Ask and you will receive (Luke 11:9).
Don't be afraid; you are worth more than sparrows (Luke 12:7).
Do not be anxious about your life, what to eat, what to wear (Luke 12: 22).
Sell your possessions and give alms (Luke 12:33).
Judge for yourself what is right (Luke 12:57).

The public arena is the place of accidental encounter with people who are living by traditional rules. The behavior enjoined is risky, but possible. And there is more than a hint of social critique or countercultural life-style. The advice is to be cautious, but also courageous. One should not respond in kind, but take reproach in stride and with confidence that one is right. If the maxims cited above are read in the context of these instructions, a corpus of sayings begins to emerge that exhibits a distinctly Cynic flavor. Now, by expanding the data base to look for themes that recur throughout Q1, the recommended way of life takes on a profile that is clearly comparable to popular Cynicism:

Critique of riches (Luke 6:20–21; 12:15–21, 33–34)
Critique of hypocrisy (Luke 6:41–42)
Voluntary poverty (Luke 12:15–34)
Renunciation of needs (Luke 6:30; 9:57–60; 12:22–34)
Fearless and carefree attitude (Luke 12:4–7)
Etiquette for begging (Luke 6:30; 10:5–7; 11:9–13)
Etiquette for responding to reproach (Luke 6:22–23, 27–33; 10:10, 37–38)
Severance of family ties (Luke 9:57–60; 14:26)
Sense of vocation (Luke 9:57–60; 10:3–10)
Authentic discipleship (Luke 6:39–40, 46–49; 14:26–27)

These themes cohere in the definition of a life-style that was recognizable as Cynic during the hellenistic and early Roman periods. Most of them are clichés associated with standard descriptions of Cynics, and many have their roots in a Cynic rationale for living "naturally" within a society governed by convention (*nomos*) instead of nature (*physis*). It should come as no surprise, therefore, to find an abundance of analogies taken from the natural order, especially among the arguments used to support the logic of the recommended behavior:

Give and it will be given to you . . . a full measure, pressed down, shaken together, overflowing (Luke 6:38).
You do not get figs from thorns, nor grapes from thistles. And you do not get good people from bad people (Luke 6:44–45).
The one who hears my instruction, but does not practice it, is like a man who built a house on the sand (Luke 6:49).
No one putting his hand to the plow and looking back is fit for the kingdom of God (Luke 9:61).
Foxes . . . birds . . . a human being (Luke 9:58).
The harvest is large; the workers few (Luke 10:2).
Go out as lambs among wolves (Luke 10:3).
Ask each day for bread for the day (Luke 11:3).

If a son asks for bread, will his father give him a stone, or if for fish, a
     snake (Luke 11:11)?
No one lights a lamp and puts it under a bushelbasket (Luke 11:33).
You are worth more than the sparrows (Luke 12:7).
Do not be anxious; consider the ravens (Luke 12:24).
Why be anxious? Look at the lilies (Luke 12:26–27).
If God clothes the grass, how much more you (Luke 12:28)?
God's rule is like a mustard seed (Luke 13:18).
God's rule is like leaven hidden in three measures of flour (Luke 13:
     20).
If salt loses its saltiness . . . (Luke 14:34).

The attempt to undergird the challenge of a Cynic life-style by
such arguments, and especially by appeal to the notion of God's
rule, marks the limits of Cynic correspondence in the early Jesus
movement. In the elaborations of Q1 a Cynic ethos is changing
into an ethic held to be standard for some social formation. This
feature moves away from popular Cynicism with its orientation to
the individual. A note of seriousness about the Jesus movement is
discernable that modifies the humor and playful repartee characteristic of the Cynic's direct engagement of society. A similar élan
for the earlier period of the Jesus people can be imagined by noting the aphoristic quality of the maxims and imperatives listed
above. But the playful spirit of social critique was eroded in the attempt to codify the Cynic's stance toward the world and turn it
into a norm for intergroup relations. We shall return to this point
after a brief discussion of a similar development in another stream
of the Jesus movement documented in the pre-Markan pronouncement stories.

The Pre-Markan Pronouncement Stories

Pronouncement stories were a major building block for the composition of Mark's gospel. A brief scenic description is the setting for
antagonists to question Jesus or object to what he says and does.
Jesus responds, most often by making two or more statements that
answer the charge and silence his questioners. The truncated "dialog"
usually ends with an authoritative statement by Jesus from which
these stories take their name as pronouncement stories. In the Gospel

of Mark there are more than two dozen such stories with important sets of five occurring at the beginning (Mark 2:1–3:6) and at the end (Mark 12).

Formally, the pronouncement stories are elaborated chreiai as recent studies have demonstrated (Mack and Robbins, 1989). In some cases it is possible to reconstruct an original chreia at the core of a pronouncement story and follow the logic that led to its elaboration. Some of these core chreiai are quite similar to chreiai in the Cynic tradition. It is chreiai such as these that must have had their origin in an early pregospel period of the Jesus movement. Consider the following reconstructions:

(1) When asked why he ate with tax collectors and sinners, Jesus replied, "Those who are well have no need of a physician" (Mark 2: 17).

(2) When asked why his students did not fast, Jesus replied, "Can wedding guests fast while the bridegroom is with them?" (Mark 2: 19)

(3) When asked why his followers plucked grain on the sabbath, Jesus replied, "The sabbath was made for people, not people for the sabbath" (Mark 2:27).

(4) When asked why they ate with unclean hands, Jesus replied, "It is not what goes in, but what comes out that makes a person dirty" (Mark 7:15).

(5) When asked who was greatest, Jesus replied, "The least" (Mark 9: 35).

(6) When someone addressed him as "Good teacher," Jesus replied, "Why do you call me good?" (Mark 10:18)

(7) When asked if the rich could get into God's kingdom, Jesus replied, "It is easier for a camel to squeeze through the eye of a needle" (Mark 10:25).

(8) When someone showed him a coin with Caesar's inscription and asked, "Is it lawful to pay taxes to Caesar or not?", Jesus replied, "Give to Caesar Caesar's things, and to God, God's" (Mark 12:17).

And from Q:

(9) When a woman from the crowd raised her voice and said to him, "Blessed is the womb that bore you and the breasts that you sucked!", Jesus replied, "Blessed rather are those who listen to what God says and mind it" (Luke 11:27–28).

(10) When someone from the crowd said to him, "Teacher, tell my brother to divide the inheritance with me," Jesus replied, "Sir, who made me your judge?" (Luke 12:13–14)

These reconstructions are quite similar to large numbers of chreiai characteristic for the Cynic tradition. The Greek penchant for crisp formulation and clever rejoinder was not limited to the Cynics, of course, but chreiai of this type are much more frequent in the Socratic, Cyrenaic, and Cynic traditions than are the ethical maxims and proverbs *(apothegmata)* attributed to teachers in the traditions of the Academy, Stoa, and other schools with more systematic philosophical and ethical interests. This is evident, for instance, in the number and type of chreiai attributed to teachers in Diogenes Laertius's *Lives and Opinions of Eminent Philosophers*.

Though thoroughly popular in form, the chreia was cultivated at the highest levels of intellectual life and became in fact a major means for characterizing philosophers. In Diogenes Laertius even the dour Plato, the deadly serious Zeno, and the dimly remembered primeval seven sages are reported to have tried their hand at such repartee. However, judging from the incidence of attribution in Diogenes Laertius, sayings anthologies from the hellenistic period, and other written materials of the Greco-Roman period, it was the Cynics who were obviously masters of the moment and for whom chreiai were most appropriate.

A game of sorts seems to have been played with the Cynics by those courageous enough to confront them. Since they lived in a kind of negative symbiosis with society, espousing indifference but actually dependent upon it, almost any situation could be turned into a trap. The trick was to catch the Cynic in some inadvertent inconsistency by pointing out his lack of complete independence. The Cynic reveled in these encounters, taking them as opportunities to expose the normal expectations as ridiculous. The chreia was a perfect medium for distilling the nature of such exchanges. In order to win, the Cynic had to put an altogether different construction upon things. Strategies ranged from playful put downs, through erudite observations and insights, and biting sarcasms, to devastating self-deprecations, but always with a sense of humor to ease the blow. Here are some examples:

When asked by someone whether he should marry, Bion answered, "If your wife is ugly she will be your bane, if beautiful you will not be able to keep her to yourself" (Diogenes Laertius IV 48).

When censured for keeping bad company, Antisthenes replied, "Well, physicians attend their patients without catching the fever" (Diogenes Laertius VI 6).

When someone said to Antisthenes, "Many praise you," he replied, "Why, what wrong have I done?" (Diogenes Laertius VI 8)

When someone wanted to study with him, Diogenes gave him a fish to carry and told him to follow him. When for shame the man threw it away and departed, Diogenes laughed and later told him, "Our friendship was broken by a fish" (Diogenes Laertius VI 36).

"Most people," Diogenes said, "are so nearly mad that a finger makes all the difference. If you go about with your middle finger stretched out, people will think you mad, but if it is the little finger, they won't" (Diogenes Laertius VI 35).

When someone reproached him for frequenting unclean places, Diogenes replied that the sun also enters the privies without becoming defiled (Diogenes Laertius VI 63).

When asked why he was begging from a statue, Diogenes replied, "To get practice in being refused" (Diogenes Laertius VI 49).

Crates declared that ignominy and poverty were his native land, a country that fortune could never take captive (Diogenes Laertius VI 93).

When one of his students said to him, "Demonax, let us go to the Asclepium and pray for my son," he replied, "You must think Asclepius very deaf that he cannot hear our prayers from where we are" (Lucian, *Demonax* 27).

The Cynic rejoinder has often been taken by moderns merely as an arrogant display of diffidence. To the Greeks, however, much more than haughtiness was at stake. The Greeks measured response by its humor and cleverness, and a certain logic was involved in getting off the hook unscathed. The French classicists Marcel Detienne and Jean-Pierre Vernant have suggested the term *metis*, or cunning intelligence, for the kind of crafty wisdom required. Whereas sophia was the wisdom appropriate to conceptual systems and stable social orders, metis was the savvy needed for contingent and threatening situations. Metis was the wisdom practiced by rhetors, doctors, navigators, and actors, as well as any who found themselves threatened by stronger forces or opponents. Metis was the skill required to size up the situation, bend to the impinging forces, feign entrapment, then suddenly shift positions in order to escape or, if lucky, turn the tables to come out on top. In the case of net fighting, for instance, the weaker would feign vulnerability, wait for the opponent's over-reach, then grab his net and swing it back upon him. The Cynic chreia is an exellent example of metis in the genre of riposte.

The logic works as follows. A circumstance puts the Cynic on the spot: how can you frequent places that are socially unacceptable (more than likely a euphemism for houses of prostitution)? The first move is to identify the issue underlying the challenge. In this case it is the notion of the socially unacceptable, commonly condensed in the cultural category of things unclean. The second move is to shift orders of discourse and find an example of "entering unclean places" in which contamination does not occur. The sun, for instance, "enters" privies without getting dirty. The clever discorrelation between the two instances of entrance into unclean places creates the humor. Explicit instruction is not the object. The interlocutor may not go away to meditate on theories of things clean or unclean. But he may laugh and let the Cynic go his way, or even catch the point about the limited and arbitrary application of a common category of social classification. As for the Cynic, acceptance of the terms of the challenge, a shift in the orders of application for a category, and a momentary confusion in the logic of the situation results in escape from entrapment.

The chreiai attributed to Jesus operate by the same logic. In every case the Cynic swerve is characteristic of Jesus's rejoinder. The shifts in orders of discourse are easily identified. In number 1, the issue of contamination is scuttled by shifting from meal codes to medical practice. It is similar to the chreia of Antisthenes. In number 2 the discrepancy pertains to times when fasting was appropriate and times when it was inappropriate. Number 3 rides on the distinction between two sabbath rules, one a proscription and the other an allowance. In number 4 the incongruous is created by juxtaposing meal codes and a scatological observation. It is similar to Diogenes's response about social and natural contaminations. The put downs in numbers 5 and 6 ride on the critique of common social values having to do with class. The ambiguity of the terms is used to advantage in statements of contrast, much the same as in the response of Antisthenes when told he was being praised by many. In number 7 there are two twists. One is to shift from the question of ability to a consideration of difficulty, thus appearing to say yes, the rich might be able to enter the kingdom. But the other is to use an example of difficulty so ridiculous as to say no, there is not a chance. In number 8 the political (legal) and the religious (natural) orders are conjoined in a conundrum. As a conundrum the answer is similar to Bion's response to the question about marriage. In 9 two notions of blessedness are set in contrast, but then confused by a shift in the orders of social relationship. And the 10th Jesus chreia is quite like a large number of Cynic chreiai in which a student is sternly corrected for some misperception and thrown back upon his own resources for seeing clearly and taking up the Cynic way.

Were Christians not accustomed to hearing Jesus's words as sharp ethical injunction coming from the imperious founder of Christianity who steps forth in the narrative gospels, the cleverness of these retorts might yet cause a smile or two. They play on the delightful confusion created by the intentional misuse of categories, and they suggest that at some early stage in the Jesus movement playful rejoinder may have been enough to justify an unconventional practice in the face of conventional askance. Support for thinking so is given when this playful mode of discourse is compared with the aphorisms of the earliest layer of Q. But, just as in the Q tradition, it does not appear that good humor of this sort lasted for long. As the elaborations of these chreiai into pronouncement stories show, a mood of seriousness soon set in, rejoinders were turned into principles and rules, and Jesus's words took on the aura of unquestionable authority. Can that history be explained?

The Social Situation

Q1 and the Jesus chreiai are evidence of a very early stage of the Jesus school. The picture that comes into view is quite different from the traditional scenario of Christian origins. Instead, this picture correlates nicely with standard descriptions of popular Cynicism at the time. A particularly significant point of contrast has to do with the nature of the social critique implicit in each view.

The traditional image of Jesus and the beginnings of Christianity are dependent upon the narrative gospels that stem from the period after the Roman-Jewish war. These were myths of origin for Christian communities that took advantage of the Roman destruction of Jerusalem to imagine that Jesus had come for the purpose of confronting and reforming the religious institutions of the Jews. Christians could then see themselves as the rightful heirs of the religious legacy of Israel's illustrious history. This schema of the old versus the new is so basic to subsequent Christian mentality that the image of Christian origins is hardly thinkable without such a challenge to the religion of the Jews and a direct conflict with its leadership. However, Q1 and the Jesus chreiai know nothing of such a conflict or purpose. They paint instead a picture of social critique that is wide ranging and thoroughly compatable with first century Cynicism.

Traits that correspond to a Cynic stance include the public arena, a personal life-style conscious of its rub against the social context, challenging address to individuals, an emphasis upon behavior as the major way to make a critical statement, the ad hoc nature of encounter with the straights, a determined purpose not to be controlled by conventional mores, and a scattershot approach to critique without a program for the structural reform of society at large. There is no indication that Jesus and his early followers had zeroed in on the temple state in Jerusalem as the cause of all society's ills. They were not engaged in an attempt to reform the diaspora synagogue. The Jesus people did eventually run into social codes of purity that were Jewish, but their response to them was similar to the tweaking Cynics gave to any social convention thought to be stuffy and pretentious. Jewish codes were simply part of the Galilean picture along with other obvious manifestations of social stratification, structure, and convention. At this early period the social structures that kept people in their places included the wealthy, the powerful, the Romans, the local courts, and the systems of production and taxation, as well as the presence of Jewish scribes who served as retainers for the Jerusalem establishment.

Galilee was not Judea. It was a land of independent peoples quite capable of sustaining a landed economy in the face of repeated hegemonies by foreign kings. Annexation by the Jewish Hasmoneans in 100 B.C.E. was not a homecoming any more than the destruction of the temple at Samaria in 135 B.C.E. insured Samaritan loyalty to the second temple state in Jerusalem. Galilee at the time of Jesus was the epitome of mixed peoples and cultures characteristic of the hellenistic period. It was ringed with hellenistic cities founded by the Ptolemies and Seleucids, and experienced the rebuilding of Sepphoris and the founding of Tiberius on the hellenistic model by Herod Antipas who ruled as tetrarch under the Romans from 4 B.C.E. to 39 C.E. Greek was spoken as well as the other Semitic languages of the Levant. And the trade routes through Galilee, the little breadbasket of the Levant, ran out in all directions to connect with the major highways of the time.

As for the possibility of Cynic influence in Galilee, one need only call to mind the illustrious history of Gadara, but a day's walk from Nazareth across the Jordan. Like many smaller hellenistic cities, Gadara was justifiably proud of its cultural institutions and produced such famous Cynic philosophers and poets as Meleager (100 B.C.E.), Philodemus (110–40 B.C.E.), and Oenomaus (120 C.E.). As for Meleager, an author of discourses, poems and epigrams who flourished about 100 years before Jesus, he has been credited with the first critical anthology of Greek epigrams. So Galilee was hardly an isolated backwater district, untouched by the cultural currents of its time.

Thus the correspondence between the Cynics and the discourse of the early stages of the Jesus movement can be acknowledged as plausible and appropriate for Galilee in the early first century. But it is also the case that Cynic traits get buried as the Jesus traditions develop. This is true of the Q tradition where Q2 blossoms into prophetic and apocalyptic announcements of judgement upon an evil generation, as it is in the elaboration of the pronouncement stories and their use in the Gospel of Mark where the scribes and Pharisees become the chief antagonists and objectors to the nonconventional behavior of Jesus's disciples. For neither of these developments is a Cynic analogy apt. Do these developments call into question the picture of Jesus as a Cynic-like sage?

The feature that signals the major difference between the Cynics and the early Jesus movements is a social notion that gradually comes into play as the shifts in discourse are tracked. Already in Q1, the odd attempt to elaborate a Cynic style into an ethic as a standard for belonging to a group erodes the playful thrust of an individualized behavior. In Q2 the signs are clear that association with the Jesus people created social stress at the level of family and village relationships. In both Q2 and the elaborations of the chreiai as pronouncement stories the question of loyalty to a movement looms large, and there are indications of boundaries being erected and myths of legitimacy being explored. The emergence of seriousness about the venture is directly related to the shift away from Cynic-style discourse and toward the entertainment of rhetorical forms of judgment and self-justification.

All of the changes in the tenor and contents of the teachings of Jesus documented in this early literature, as well as the shifts in group formation and self-identification reflected in these literary histories, must be ascribed to his followers. There is some indication that the Jesus movements were attractive because of experimentation with strategies for personal well-being, social savvy, ethical integrity, and novel markers for ethnic identity. These social formations took place gradually and the developments in discourse by increments. This is clear from the many different forms of early Jesus schools and *christos* groups for which we have evidence. Thus the fact of social formation is obvious and that fact marks the difference between the Jesus schools and the Cynics. It also marks the point at which the Cynic discourse characteristic for the earliest phases of the Jesus movements yields to language more appropriate for groups defining their borders than for an individual's critical stance toward society at large.

The Cynic Hypothesis

The investigation of the Cynic parallels to various features of the Jesus traditions is a fairly recent interest among New Testament scholars. Nevertheless, these studies have already produced several publications, among them two books by Gerald Downing (1988; 1992), Leif Vaage's *Galilean Upstarts* (1994), my book, *The Lost Gospel* (1993), and many articles. Thus the "Cynic hypothesis" is now a concept in early Christian studies. However, that is not because most New Testament scholars find it an attractive idea. On the contrary, most do not. The very thought of Jesus as a Cynic-like sage has created a furor within the guild, and there have been many reviews, essays, footnotes and remarks invested in the effort to dispense with it before it is taken seriously. For those invested in the gospel's view of Jesus and his importance for Christian origins, the danger is real. A Cynic-like Jesus does not fit their picture. There are no marks of divinity or specialness, much less any suggestion of mission, call and preparation of disciples, or plan for a program to change the way the world works. As for the proclamation of an expected judgment upon Jewish religion and institutions, there is none. And the tenor of the teachings is hardly a good example of strictly Jewish idiom, mentality, and interests untarnished by contact with the Greco-Roman world.

Thus the counter arguments against the Cynic hypothesis have been reiterations of the traditional view about the "Jewishness" of Galilee in the time of Jesus and the lack of specific evidence for "known Cynics" being there in the first century. But the real reasons are clearly the lack of fit between a Cynic-like Jesus and the Jesus portrayed in the gospels, as well as the unlikelihood that a Cynic philosopher could have started the Christian religion. That is why few have bothered to take the Cynic hypothesis seriously, and none has acknowledged or tried to explain the obvious correspondence between Cynic discourse and the tenor of the Cynic-like sayings of Jesus. "How could a Cynic philosopher have started the Christian religion?" is the question that has stopped the debate.

John Kloppenborg-Verbin found this troubling and set out to investigate the reasons for this scholarly behavior. His study turned into a thorough review of this "debate" about "the Cynic hypothesis" and is published in his recent book, *Excavating Q* (2000, Chapter 9). His conclusions are (1) that the reasons for wanting to dispense with the idea are clearly and simply theological and apologetic, not academic; (2) that the evidence, research, and reasons for the hypothesis have not been engaged or called into question by its critics; and (3) that the hypothesis and its significance for Christian origins deserves thorough study and investigation by New Testament scholars. This assessment of the furor about the Cynic hypothesis is a statement of some importance about the way in which New Testament scholarship has gone about its business. That it appears as a chapter in a book about "the Q hypothesis" is even more telling. That is because Kloppenborg-Verbin argues convincingly and at length that those who say they "don't believe in Q" *because it is a hypothesis* are behaving strangely as scholars. My own assessment of the situation he describes is that such scholars have not worked through the texts and arguments for the document Q in order to show the weakness of the hypothesis and propose alternative theories to explain the data some other way. They would like to dispense with "the Q hypothesis" on the basis that it is an hypothesis, as if their own views are not based on hypotheses, as if all of our knowledge won through thinking, scholarly investigation and scientific experiments has not been won by constructing hypotheses, and as if a hypothesis does not have to be taken seriously because it is "just" a hypothesis. Kloppenborg-Verbin argues that the real reasons for not wanting to consider the Q document have to do with the desire to protect the traditional gospel view of Christian origins, and I would say the same about those who do not want to consider the Cynic hypothesis.

But what about the argument that a Cynic philosopher could not have started the Christian religion? This question assumes that the Christian religion started with the historical Jesus, and that the Cynic hypothesis must be the result of a quest for the historical Jesus who started the Christian religion. Neither of these assumptions is correct. The "Case for a Cynic-like Jesus" does not establish that a Cynic philosopher named Jesus must be thought of as the one who started the Christian religion. Its conclusions can be summarized otherwise by saying (1) that the earliest layers of the "teachings of Jesus" have close parallels to the sayings of Cynics which were popular at the time, (2) that the group responsible for these teachings imagined Jesus in ways similar to that of a Cynic teacher, (3) that the Jesus they remembered may be credited with starting a school tradition, but (4) that this is the closest we will ever get to the historical Jesus, and (5) there is no indication of a grand design to start a new religion, either on the part of the teacher as remembered or on the part of the school that remembered him reflected in the earliest layers of his teachings.

This is very different from arguing for a certain profile for the historical Jesus thought of as the one who inaugurated Christianity. It is different in two very important ways. The first has to do with the data base upon which the figure of Jesus is constructed. The second has to do with the way in which we can account for the tenor and content of that data base. In the first chapter I made it clear that those involved in the quest of the historical Jesus have had serious problems with their textual data, and that the "sayings" and "teachings" of Jesus used as data by these scholars were brought together from disparate textual locations for the sole purpose of reconstructing the historical Jesus. By contrast, the data base for the earliest layers of the teachings of Jesus in Q1 and Mark is not composed of sayings that were brought together for the purpose of profiling the historical Jesus. This data is the result of scholarly studies that have sought clarity about the earliest *textual* traditions of the early Christians. These studies have been pursued in the interest of solving intertextual problems such as the "synoptic problem," the Paul and gospels question, the Thomas-Q relations, and so forth. It is true that interest in the earliest texts and layers of texts has been driven in general by the quest for Christian origins, and that the impulse that started Christianity has usually been imagined to have had its origin in the specialness of the historical Jesus. But the critical work involved in solving the intertextual relations, the work that finally resulted in the reconstruction of Q and its earliest layers, required scholarly criteria that had nothing to do with questions about or interests in the historical Jesus. That the earliest textual layers of the traditions of Jesus's teachings turned out to have a correspondence with Cynic parallels was a surprise, not an expectation. And so, since the scholarly efforts and arguments for the construction of the data base were focused on text-critical issues, and since the tenor of the sayings is so clearly consistent and recognizable throughout the earliest layers, the proper approach to this material should be a concerted effort to account for it.

My own approach has been to account for this phenomenon in the same way I have tried to account for other tenors of discourse and views of Jesus in the early chapters of Christian beginnings, namely as mythmaking on the part of a Jesus movement in the process of taking itself seriously. It is true that I have emphasized the difference between the earlier more human and the later more mythic views of Jesus in all my work, and that has suggested to my colleagues that I was much interested in the quest for the historical Jesus who started the Christian religion. But it has always been the other way around. Marking the difference between the earlier and later views of Jesus has been a strategy to set up a contrast and foil for noting the mythic features of the later depictions and exploring the reasons for them. It has never occurred to me that the extraordinary and incomparable features attributed to Jesus on the part of early Christians were not mythic. And it has never occurred to me that the mythic features were attribtued to Jesus because something about his person demanded it. Thus it has been the mythmaking of the early Christians for other reasons that has interested me. If it can be shown that the mythic features attributed to Jesus were generated by social interests, and that they were not mystifications to be explained only by assuming that they had been generated by the historical Jesus, the investigation of Christian beginnings becomes a very interesting and thoroughly understandable pursuit of interest to historians of religion.

I do find it interesting to discover that the earliest layers of the Jesus traditions cast him as a teacher of sayings with Cynic-like tenor and content. That does allow one to think of Jesus in terms that are plausible, given the times, and fitting, given the fact that the Jesus movements all seemed to have understood themselves as "schools," and that they all cast Jesus as a kind of teacher. But the earliest layers of the teachings are not at first documentation *for* the historical Jesus. They are documentation for the teachings of the Jesus schools, groups that thought of their Cynic-like discourse as "the teachings of Jesus." Jesus may well be credited with linking a Jewish social notion with a Greek popular ethic and talking about their combination as "the kingdom of God." But others, his "students," were obviously involved in clarifying concepts and applying them to matters of practice. Thus they imagined Jesus as the founder of their "school." That fits what we know both about the cultivation of school traditions in the Greco-Roman world and about the way in which schools of thought are cultivated and embellished in general. An example would be the burgeoning bodies of knowledge about non-violent resistance in our time and all of the groups and schools that offer instruction in it. If one were to ask whose "teaching" it is, a reference to the founder-teacher is obvious. These schools would say that they were working with "the teachings of Ghandi and/or Martin Luther King." So it must have been with the people of Q in the school of Jesus.

CHAPTER THREE

On Redescribing Christian Origins

The Gospel of Christian Origins

For almost two thousand years, the Christian imagination of Christian origins has echoed the gospel stories contained in the New Testament. That is not surprising. The gospel accounts erased the pre-gospel histories. Their inclusion within the church's New Testament consigned other accounts to oblivion. And during the long reach of Christian history, from the formation of the New Testament in the fourth century to the Enlightenment in the eighteenth, there was no other story except satires of cabbages and kings. (I refer to the *Tol'dot Jeshu*, a Jewish satire on the gospel in which the Messiah is killed by being hung on a cabbage stalk. See J. Z. Smith, *Map Is Not Territory*, 230–231, note 74).

According to Christian imagination, Christianity began when Jesus entered the world, performed miracles, called disciples, taught them about the kingdom of God, challenged the Jewish establishment, was crucified as the Christ and Son of God, appeared after his resurrection, overwhelmed his disciples with his holy spirit, established the first church in Jerusalem, and sent the apostles out on a mission to tell the world what they had seen and heard. Telling what they had seen was enough to convince the Jews and convert the gentiles into thinking that God had planned the whole thing in order to start a new religion. The new religion was about sin and redemption. What it took to start the new religion was all there as a kind of divine implantation in the life of Jesus, needing only to germinate and develop as early Christians heard about it, believed it, and came to understand its import. We might call this scenario the big bang concept of Christian origins.

However, since the Enlightenment, the effort to understand Christian origins has been pursued by scholars as a matter of historical and literary criticism, and the New Testament account has slowly been dismantled. The New Testament is no longer seen by critical scholars as a coherent set of apostolic texts that document a single set of dramatic events and their monolinear history of subsequent influence and theological development. Instead of one gospel story, there are four different accounts within the New Testament and several other gospels that were not included. Instead of one picture of the historical Jesus that all early Christians must have had in mind, scholars have identified many competing views. We know now that there were many groups from the beginning, creating disparate traditions, responding to other groups differently, and developing various rituals and patterns of social congregation. Plural theologies and conflicting ideologies, as well as competing authorities and leaders, now describe the intellectual scene. So factors other than the marvels portrayed in the gospel account must have been at work.

And yet, the older picture of Christian origins according to the gospel story, largely Lukan, is still the way contemporary Christians and scholars think about Christian beginnings. It is as if the emergence of Christianity cannot be accounted for any other way. It is as if the accumulation of critical information within the discipline of New Testament studies cannot compete with the gospel's mystique. This is odd, for without a more appropriate picture of the way Christianity began, the data pursued by critical inquiry have no frame of reference to give them any significance. The results of the critical study of the New Testament seem to be floating free in the archives of a guild that has no log or registry to keep track of the knowledge it produces. It is as if everyone secretly hopes that the core of the gospel's account will eventually be shown to be true. Thus the scholarly production of the guild has become a brew devoid of recipe. Are New Testament scholars waiting for some magic to make the mix a potion, redeem the gospel account, and make all of their labor finally seem worthwhile?

My own view is that the time has come to account for Christian origins some other way, and that a redescription of Christian beginnings would ultimately have to account for the emergence of the gospels themselves. It could do that by turning them into interesting products of early Christian thinking instead of letting them determine the parameters within which all of our data must find a place to rest. With that in mind, I would like to take stock of the current state of New Testament studies and then present a proposal for a redescription of Christian origins.

Problems with the Gospel Paradigm

I can begin by making a list of items in need of explanation. Some of these items are well known gaps or holes *(aporiai)* in our systems of explanation. Others are clichés that have served explanatory functions, but are in reality unexamined assumptions in need themselves of explanation. Others are easily recognized as unresolved issues still under debate. Taken as a whole, the list suggests that, as representatives of a discipline, New Testament scholars are sure of less than they pretend to know. For the sake of brevity, I shall not add comments to any item. I will list them as topics in need of explanation, hoping that, in the majority of cases, the reasons for their inclusion in the list will be obvious:

The import of the teachings of Jesus in Q and the Gospel of Thomas.
The notion that Jesus was a reformer of Judaism.
Messianic expectations as definitive of the Jewish mentality at the time.
The presence of the Pharisees in Galilee during the time of Jesus.
The disciples as a select group.
The disciples as trained by Jesus for leadership in a kingdom program.
The meaning and conception of the language of the kingdom of God.
The reason for the attraction of the Jesus movements.
The historical data and the reasons for the crucifixion of Jesus.
The shift from Jesus schools to the congregations of Jesus *christos*.
The attraction of the Jesus *christos* groups for both Jews and gentiles.
The original impulse for using the term *christos*.
The occasion for and the logic of the *christos* myth (or *kerygma*).
Whether all early Christians met for common meals.
The significance of common meals for social formation and mythmaking.
The rationales and practices of baptisms.
The reasons for and modes of reference to the Jewish Scriptures.
The attraction of the concept "Israel."
The formation of the passion narrative(s).

The notion of a last supper.
Easter as a datable datum.
The notion of a first "church" in Jerusalem.
The reasons for and the locations of the Jew-gentile debate.
Accounting for the emergence and history of Jewish Christianity.
The notion of apostle.
The notion of mission.
The influence of popular Greek philosophy and ethics.
The intention to form an alternative society.
The concept of the church.
The notions of and fixations on persecution and martyrdom.

This is a list of *aporiai* and issues that the gospel paradigm presents but cannot explain. It means that the gospel paradigm is inadequate as a description of Christian origins. It also registers a kind of indictment of the guild, for the gospel story is still used to imagine Christian beginnings even by New Testament scholars. It is as if a ring of fire protects it, since no other explanation will do. This can be illustrated in the way scholars often acquiesce to the gospel's mystique even at the end of the most detailed, penetrating, and critical investigations of this or that feature of a New Testament text.

To take one example, the history of investigation into the miracle stories in the gospels has taught us much about the notion of the miraculous in the Greco-Roman age, its institutions, professions, practices, and genres of report. But it has not led to a critique of the gospel or a redescription of Christian origins. John Locke did not believe in miracles, but in the case of the miracles of Jesus he said one must accept them because they were so exceptional. D. F. Strauss thought gullible Galileans made up the miracle stories, mesmerized as they were by the superior person of Jesus. He did not say how they knew that Jesus was superior, what that may have meant, or why it called for miracle stories. The recent scholarship of Gerd Theissen, Morton Smith (1978), Paul Achtemeier, Anne Wire, Howard Kee, and others has emphasized the Greco-Roman parallels as if to say that, since the cultures of context had no trouble with miracles, neither should we. But each scholar has then found a way to note the differences between the pagan genres and the miracles of Jesus, as if to say that "*Something* extra special must have happened in the case of Jesus's miracles," meaning, "Let's not detract from the specialness of Jesus or explain the gospels away."

The current, hotly debated list of topics under investigation by New Testament scholars can all be understood as items that became issues because their study threatened the gospel paradigm. This is true of the quest for the historical Jesus, the debate about the historicity of the temple-cleansing pericope, renewed attempts to explain the crucifixion and argue for the historicity of the passion narrative, the furor over wisdom and apocalyptic, the consternation over Q, the dismissal of the two-source hypothesis, the redating of Matthew, and underscoring the importance of Paul's theology and religious experience as primary data for the way Christianity began. The juices are flowing because the New Testament paradigm of Christian origins requires a certain answer to each of these questions, and struggling with each of these questions has led some scholars and historians to conclusions that do not agree with the traditional picture.

The "Catch-22"

Allowing the gospel paradigm to define Christian origins is quite understandable. It is the only scenario that everyone automatically shares, thus providing a narrative frame of reference for scholarly research and discourse. It serves as a kind of map within which to place various, detailed labors. It also protects a set of assumptions about the way Christianity began, forming as it does the basis for what has been imagined as an otherwise inexplicable emergence of a brand new religion of unique conviction and singular faith. Something overwhelming must have possessed those early Christians, so the thinking has been, or they would not have converted to the new religion with its extraordinary claims. It is the gospel story that feeds that suspicion of an overwhelming set of appearances and miraculous events at the very beginning of the Christian time.

There are, however, three reasons for setting the gospel account aside. One is that the gospel paradigm creates a scholarly catch-22. Another is that the attempt to protect the gospel account sacrifices academic explanation to a hermeneutical desire for contemporary theological relevance. And a third is that doing so fosters a theory of religion that only Christianity can illustrate.

The catch-22 is that, for Christian mentality, the New Testament is taken as proof for the conventional picture of Christian origins, and the conventional picture is taken as proof for the way in which the New Testament came to be written. Thus the story of New Testament scholarship has been one of heroic struggle to overcome the entanglements of mythic text and critical history in the quest for Christian origins. Only a concerted effort to pop that catch can escape its circular logic and make it possible to explain Christian origins some other way.

As for the problems stemming from hermeneutical desire, they are firmly anchored in the objectives of New Testament scholarship as formulated by seminarians and theologians: historical research leading to critical exegesis, and hermeneutical translation that can spark contemporary theological insight. The tension between the two is sometimes stretched to the point of snapping, for doing exegesis requires critical historiography that seeks to understand Christian origins in terms of the humanities, while formulating a hermeneutic leaves the mystery of Christian origins untouched and treats the New Testament as the source for contemporary Christian experience and knowledge of God. New Testament hermeneuts seek to "meet Jesus again for the first time" (Borg, 1994), hear afresh the "Word of God," or contact once more the original fire that brought and brings Christian faith into existence. Thus the hermeneutical enterprise continues to let the New Testament stand as the church's myth and ritual text, the oracle that gives Christianity its charter and makes its claims legitimate. It will not help the redescription project. Interpreting the New Testament as a quest for contemporary theological relevance is a sophisticated form of mythic thinking. Its pursuit is not appropriate within the academy. Scholars will not be able to redescribe Christian origins if their ultimate goal is a Christian hermeneutic instead of a contribution to humanistic learning.

There is, however, a much more serious obstacle to a redescription project than either the textual catch-22 or the persistence of mythic thinking in the hermeneutical enterprise. These are problems of which New Testament scholars are somewhat aware and about which they sometimes talk. The phenomenon I have in mind, on the other hand, is seldom mentioned and hardly ever discussed. It may even be that many scholars are not aware that it exists. I refer to the theory of religion implicit in New Testament studies and naively assumed as natural. New Testament studies are generally pursued without feeling the need for discussing theories of religion, much less articulating the assumptions about religion that are taken for granted by most New Testament scholars. These assumptions are obvious, however, to historians of religion who happen upon this discourse in the quest to see how religion is being understood across the spectrum of humanistic disciplines. The historian of religion would say that New Testament scholars work with a concept of religion that is thoroughly and distinctly Christian in its derivation and definition. That may come as no surprise. Since New Testament scholars deal with Christian texts in the interest of understanding Christian origins, and since the discipline does not demand expertise in the fields of comparative religions, cultural anthropology, and religious studies, it has not seemed necessary to venture beyond the history of Christianity to look for a general theory of religion. Familiarity with the Christian religion has taken the place of theoretical discussion, and Christianity has provided the categories that are used to name and explain early Christian phenomena.

The problem is that the understanding of religion implicit in this discipline is inadequate for the task of redescribing Christian origins. Interest in religion among New Testament scholars comes to focus on personal transformations, or what is sometimes called "personal religious experience." By this is meant some kind of contact with the divine, a contact that requires a breakthrough from both sides of a wall that inhibits clear vision, communication, and personal relations. The breakthrough from the divine side is imagined in terms of revelations, appearances, miracles, and dramatic events. These are exemplified most clearly in the appearance of Jesus whose "unique" life and "ministry" are understood to have occasioned a new situation and released the powers that make it possible for others also to have contact with God. From the human side, the breakthroughs happen in terms of visions, conversions, and personal transformations that shatter older patterns of self-understanding and transfer persons into a new world order or relationship with the divine. Everything else in the myth-ritual package of Christianity, such as worldview, concept of God, history, human problematic, "Christ event," and notions of salvation, are merely reflectors hung on the walls of the Christian sanctuary for the purpose of intensifying the focus of divine light upon the individual positioned at its center. With such a fixation on personal religious experience and dramatic moments of divine transformation, is it any wonder that New Testament scholars have had trouble explaining the mythic data of the divinity of Jesus, miracles, resurrection, cultic presence, reports of ecstatic visions, and apocalyptic persuasions?

This ring of fire around which scholars dance has always occasioned caution lest they get too close to these mysteries and find themselves tempted to explain them. The history of the discipline is strewn with intellectual giants who, like Bultmann, set out to dismantle the encrusted mythologies, and arrived at some suspected core of the crucifixion *kerygma* (proclamation) or the *Dass* (sheer facticity) of incarnation, only to back off and leave the mystery untouched and unexplained. The rule seems to be that, "Neither the historian nor the theologian should try to answer these questions," as Koester put it. The questions he had in mind were such as ". . . whether Jesus expected a visible demonstration of God's rule in the near future as a result of his path to the cross?" (1982, p.84). The critical thinker is stunned and stymied when confronted with such scholarly hesitations in the face of the gospel's mystique. Taking up such questions directly, in the attempt to make some response, leads nowhere. That is because questions such as these are phrased in existentialist, psychological, and mythic terms which leave the gospel's aura of mystique in place. If one is drawn into this discourse on its own terms, one cannot avoid joining its dance around the gospel's ring of fire.

When chided by historians of religion for hesitations such as these, the caveat has sometimes been that New Testament scholars have *not* been unsophisticated in their attempt to find neutral concepts from the history of religions to explain early Christian phenomena. It is true that Eliade's phenomenology of religion has been particularly influential in providing categories for naming and comparing Christian phenomena with things held to be religious in general. The problem in this case, however, is that Eliade's phenomenology is hardly neutral with respect to Christianity. Christianity was, in fact, the religion that provided Eliade with the religious system he assumed and proposed as universal. Creating designations for religious phenomena in general that were actually (though surreptitiously) understood on the Christian model turned out to be a very seductive proposition. Many scholars played that game for a while, setting up this or that comparison of Christianity with other religions, only to find that a Christian exemplum invariably exemplified the essence of a category more clearly than any example from another culture.

Thus, both Bultmann's existentialist interpretation and Eliade's theory of religion have proven inadequate for redescribing Christian origins. One privileges the uniqueness of Jesus; the other assumes the superiority of the Christian religion. Neither has provided a model for the task of critical and balanced comparison of early Christianities with the religions of late antiquity. The flush of euphoria and the sense of understanding created by these exercises are now passé, to be sure, but New Testament scholars are still locked into comparative methods that always result in a demonstration of early Christianity's uniqueness and superiority. Such comparative studies are not only boring, they actually inhibit asking the next, and most fundamental question. The question should be: superior in respect to what, or merely different in respect to which criterion? There is always a criterion at work in the making of comparisons, though the standard used may well be implicit, taken for granted, or even unconscious. It is the failure to state and discuss the criteria implicit in comparative exercises that short circuits learning and leads to compromising conclusions that do not penetrate the gospel's mystique.

Entertaining Another Theory

To account for the emergence of Christianity, including the formation of groups and congregations, the development of their various practices and rituals, the production of their mythologies, and the writing of their literature requires a radical shift in thinking and theory. That is because the theory of religion implicit in the field cannot even ask about, much less account for the motivations involved in the investments early Christians made in their new associations. To account for the data that now confronts the New Testament scholar, a theory of religion is needed that can explain

Christian origins as a thoughtful, collective human construction, instead of the result of human response to an overwhelming activity on the part of a god. Only a theory that gives the people their due, a theory firmly anchored in a social and cultural anthropology, capable of sustaining a conversation with the humanities, can do that.

There are some common features to the many theories of religion now being formulated and tested in the humanities. I would like to suggest five such features that, taken as a set, provide a perspective on religion that can be used as a kind of lens or working hypothesis for getting started on a collaborative redescription project.

(1) Religion is a social construct. The notion of personal religious experience is inadequate as a point of departure for defining religion or developing a theory of religion. That individuals have religious experiences is not in doubt. But individuals in any culture experience religion in many different ways. The more interesting phenomena are the myths, rituals, symbols, beliefs and patterns of thinking that are *shared* by a people. These cultural constructs can be experienced and manipulated in a variety of ways by individuals, but it is their self-evident status as common cultural coin that marks them as the religion of a people. Persons do not see visions of the Virgin Mary in cultures where Catholic Christianity has not penetrated. In the case of Christian origins, we need to ask about the people who joined the various movements, entertained Christian myths, and practiced Christian rituals. We need to ask about the reasons for and the processes whereby their myths and rituals were first constructed and agreed upon, and how they came to be taken for granted. It is the social factor, the possibilities and rewards for coming to these agreements as groups in the context of a social history rife with other peoples, groups, and religions, that we need to understand.

(2) Social formation defines the human enterprise. Constructing societies large and small is what people do. It is a fragile, collective craft requiring enormous amounts of negotiation, experimentation, living together, and talking. And it invariably results in very complex arrangements of relationships, agreements reached on better and less better ways to do things, and practices established to pass on the knowledge and skills accumulated in the process. Social formation is hard work, creates as many tensions as rewards, and is overkill if

thought of simply as a strategy for survival. But despite the risks and repeated disasters, watching each other and talking about each other is what we humans find most interesting. If so, a social anthropology will be required to counter the endemic personalisms that pervade Christian mentality, and ask about the reasons for and the processes whereby early Christian myths and rituals were first conceived and agreed upon. What if the Jesus schools and the *christos* groups were attractive as intentional experiments in social formation and myth-making?

(3) Myths are more than fascinating fantasies, fuzzy memories, misguided science, or collective deceits. Myths acknowledge the collective gifts and constraints of the past and create a space for thinking critically about the present state of a group's life together. Myths are good for creating marvelous narrative worlds in which to stretch the imagination and work out theoretical equations. They are also good for defining a group's place and identity in relation to a larger world. This view of myth means that early Christians may not have entertained fantastic mythologies because they were overwhelmed by encounters with a god or a son of God, but because they wanted to comprehend and justify their investments in social formations for which only a god could render an account. That is what myths can do. So the questions to ask of these early Christians have to do with what social, intellectual benefits they got from the way they dared to imagine their pasts and their worlds the way they did.

(4) Rituals are more than divine placations or magical attempts to channel the powers of the gods. Rituals are the way humans concentrate attention on some activity or event of some significance to a group, and observe its performance apart from normal practice. Much can happen at a ritual, for rituals are social occasions, require roles, invite attendance, display skills, confirm loyalties, trigger commitments, evoke thoughtfulness, and reconstitute the structure of a group. In the case of Christian origins, then, it will be important to know what activities were chosen for ritual performance, why they were chosen, how they were performed, and what such observance may have achieved for the group. I can't resist the temptation to remark that, as far as I can tell, the supper texts in the New Testament were not taken as scripts for "reenactment" until the third century. If

so, scholars of Christian origins have a wonderfully elongated process of ritualization to describe and an interesting quest for theory to explain it.

(5) Mythmaking and social formation go together. In a stable situation, where pressure to change a way of life is not serious, a people's myths and social structure may not need constant tinkering. But when circumstances change and the social fabric tears, and especially in the case of a clash of cultures, the pace quickens, for the older plots will need revision and the social structure will need repair. Experimentation and *bricolage* mark the ways in which myths get rearranged and groups reform. Except for the case of an obvious pathology, even the most daring social experiments and the most fantastic mythic constructs turn out to be thoughtful and constructive attempts to regain sanity in a social situation that threatens human well-being. In the case of the early Christians, this proposition means that the making of their myths and the processes of forming social groups should be looked at together as constructive and thoughtful human activities. And whenever there is a chance to catch sight of both mythmaking and social formation happening at the same time in the same place, the relationship of the one to the other should be explored.

Toying with an Appropriate Method

I want now to propose a method for a project in redescribing Christian origins taken from the work of Jonathan Z. Smith. As an historian of religion, he works with texts from late antiquity and is thoroughly acquainted with New Testament studies. His value for a redescription project is that he always does his work as a contribution to the formulation of theory in the study of religion. It is the way in which he works that I want to propose as a model for the project I have in mind. His method can be described as the performance of four operations, though not necessarily in separate, sequential stages. The four operations are: description, comparison, redescription, and the rectification of categories.

(1) After identifying a text, topic, myth, ritual, genre, practice, or social-historical item as interesting and worthy of additional attention, as full a *description* as possible is in order. That involves paying

close attention to the forms of its documentation, social-historical incidence, cultural context, and the particular situation to which the item might be considered a response. Careful description is necessary to make sure the details have been noticed, and that traditional designations and meanings have not been assumed as definitive. Thick description is necessary in order to locate an exemplum in the texture of its social, historical, and cultural environments, the context that gives it significance. To emphasize the need for description keeps calling the scholar back to the arena of social and empirical reality, and makes sure that the example under review is treated as a human construct.

(2) The next step is to look for an example of a similar construct in some other cultural context. This second instance of a construct will be used for making a *comparison*. Comparison is fundamental to the cognitive processes whereby we notice, classify, define, and think about things. We cannot do much with an absolutely unique phenomenon, one that is incomparable, one for which we know of nothing similar in any respect whatsoever. And we do not find perfectly identical copies of a thing worthy of further observation. Comparison is always triggered by interest in something that is sort of like, but not identical with, something we already know about or at least have previously noticed. Since critical thinking always takes place in the process of comparing one thing with another, those engaged in a redescription of Christian origins will need more than a single or singular instance to study.

In setting up a comparison for the purpose of humanistic learning one must constantly keep an eye on the features that commend themselves as differences as well as those that appear to be similarities. These features need to be described and ranked in light of questions about the significance of each example in its larger social and cultural setting. Done well one shall have learned much about each example of a phenomenon and something about the situational factors that may have accounted for the distinctive variants of each. It may even be possible to detail the cluster of features both examples have in common that makes them instances of a general phenomenon. In Smith's essays, the frequent practice has been to select examples from two widely separate histories and cultures. That is because Smith's project has been to review those examples that have influenced the construction of theories of religion, examples that have in fact been taken from many disparate cultures, but also because his own approach to theory has demanded cross-cultural comparison.

Luckily, in the case of Christian beginnings, the cross-cultural component in Smith's project of comparison can be met without having to range so far afield. The Greco-Roman age offers more than enough data for comparison. Comparison with other examples from the Greco-Roman age is tricky business, to be sure, for proximity has invariably raised questions about influence and derivation in the history of New Testament studies, and the track record in dealing with this problem is not good. "Influence" and "derivation" are specters that have always derailed closer analyses and cut short the investigation of analogies too close for comfort. But having comparables close at hand can also be very helpful, for early Christian texts seldom provide enough data for full descriptions, and a good example of a similar phenomenon from an adjacent people can frequently suggest ways to make use of otherwise inexplicable features of an incomplete reference or report. Early Christians had to breathe the same cultural air as everyone else, even though their responses to particular social-historical situations may have taken quite distinctive turns. And besides, a concerted attempt to understand Christian origins as one among other responses to the Greco-Roman age is strategic because, if done right, others will have to take note. Using comparisons from the cultures of context is exactly what the discipline has said it was doing all along. The problem has been with the *way* in which comparisons have been set up and pursued, as Smith has shown in *Drudgery Divine*.

(3) Invariably, the process of comparison will give rise to a *redescription* of the objects under investigation. That is because the comparative enterprise, having to take note of situations, human interests, the investments of a people in a project, and the circumstances, skills, and effects of its production or cultivation, will produce an ever more complex and interesting set of details. It may be that something will have been learned about factors that make the two situations similar, something about the difference another context makes, something about the reasons for a people's interest in or fascination with a particular notion, role, or activity, and so forth. These insights will change the way in which the examples under

investigation are understood and thus require redescription. A redescription will register what has been learned in the study. My impression is that, although New Testament scholars have learned to be very thorough in the description of this or that feature of a text, it has seldom been thought necessary to describe in detail, much less redescribe, any piece of the social and cultural picture puzzle that needs to be assembled. Take the question of meeting for meals, for instance. What needs to be asked is how and why congregating that way would have happened, whether all Jesus people and Christians did it, and what it might have contributed to early Christian social formation and mythmaking. Few have thought it necessary to ask questions so seemingly banal. Studies of the supper texts have always been undertaken with only one objective—to anchor the origins of the Mass or Eucharist in the life of Jesus at the point of his passion. This history of scholarship has to be set aside. It has taught us very little about the importance that meals, congregating, and ritualizations had for early Christians and their mythmaking projects. Even after generations of studies on the origins of the "Lord's Supper," we still have only a mystery on our hands.

(4) At the end of such a comparative study it might be possible to rename the phenomenon of which the case studies are examples. This, at least, is what one should strive for. Smith's term for this operation is the *rectification of categories*. By that he means that the terms we use to name and describe things are important, and that the traditional terms we use are not innocent with respect to parochial connotations. It is frequently the case that a term can be found that fits the new descriptions better than older designations. I still remember a conversation with Jonathan Smith about ritual theory in which I used the term "reenactment" to describe what I thought Christians imagined they were doing when they performed the Mass or Eucharist. Smith demurred because he knew of no other instance in which ritual was best described as reenactment, so I asked him to come up with another term. When he said, "How about replication?" my heart leaped. I had been reading Victor Turner's description of Ndembu circumcision and "replication" fit the process perfectly. I mentally scurried through other rituals I had read about and found myself giddy with the difference changing a category made in the significance of a ritual's function. Now what if Christian ritual fell

somewhere between replication, with its focus upon the energies, skills, and thinking involved in a ritual's performance, and the peculiarly Christian combination of myth and ritual that reenactment connotes? Wouldn't that come close to marking one of its distinctive features without having to set it apart from all other rituals as unique and incomparable?

In a sense, all of Smith's work can be understood as a rectification of categories common to the history of religions. And the point? The point is nothing less than the construction of a theory of religion. A new designation for a recognizable phenomenon can become a building block for constructing a descriptive system. And the descriptions of phenomena in such a studied system can actually become mid-range axioms that might eventually be used to build a cultural (and in Smith's case, intellectualist) theory of religion. Note that, because the new designations are won by comparing examples cross-culturally, they have already been raised to a level of generalization without losing their descriptive power. That is the genius of Smith's program. It cannot spin out of control because its categories retain their descriptive power even while being raised to a level of cross-cultural generalization. It need not pretend universal validity, because the factors of difference and variation are built into the equation. Smith's categories for thinking about religious phenomena are neither culture specific designations, nor abstractions with universal claim (Mack, 1992). If New Testament scholars were to take Smith seriously, there would be a lot of interesting work to do, for almost every term commonly used to designate early Christian phenomena is ripe for redescription.

Thinking about Such a Project

Such a project does call for a concerted effort and a collaborative approach. There are, however, signs that the chances of starting such a project are excellent. The current furor about the historical Jesus and the historicity of the gospels, both in the guild and in the media, will run its course without resolution. In the meantime there is work to be done that can be done. Solid work is actually being done already on many other fronts that eventually might be brought together in the writing of a different history. Within the field of New Testament studies one might mention the following: the importance of extra-canonical texts is now taken for granted. There is agreement about the importance of finding and fleshing out a text's social location. The social history of Galilee and Palestine is now a matter of great interest. That there were many different ways to be "Jewish" and "Christian" is recognized by all. There is an effort to understand gnostic Christians as integral to the early history of Christianity. And, looking ahead, there are signs that much more can be learned about early Christian attitudes and practices, such as the attitudes of early Christians toward the Roman empire, the burial practices of early Christians and their relation to ancient cults of the dead, and the roles of bishops in the dispensation of social welfare. And what of work being done outside the guild on the archeology of Galilee and Palestine; the social history of the Levant; the emergence of the synagogue; the clash of cultures during the hellenistic age; the hellenistic institutions of education and learning; the arts and applications of rhetorical education; the philosophical discussions of kings, sovereignty, and law; the economic history of the Roman empire; the importance of associations as social institutions; the social role of women in Greco-Roman society; the mystery cults; and the entrepreneurs of divination and healing? What an exciting chapter of human history. It is chock-full of social experimentation, strategies for the preservation as well as the revision of cultural traditions, and bursts of creative intellectual energy trying to make sense of that complex, multicultural scene. Some features of that intermingling of cultures are bound to bear directly upon the quest to better understand Christian origins.

What has not appeared within the discipline of New Testament studies is a concerted effort to rephrase the questions one should ask of that complex social and ideological history that has come into view. A new map is needed, as well as a new plot, one that does not start with Paul and Mark and stop with Luke's Acts of the Apostles. A larger frame of reference has to be imagined within which connections can be made among the many studies that now languish as isolated findings because they do not fit the Lukan scheme. A collaborative effort seems to be called for in order to create and support a discourse that consciously keeps the goal of redescription in view, one that seeks a relatively consistent level of humanistic explanation for the emergence of Christianity.

I would like to share a list of studies that came to mind as I pondered such a proposal. Since the list grew in a hurried and helter-skelter fashion, and since it consists of ad hoc items recalled from several years of reading, I surely run the risk of failing to include other, similarly important works. I am willing to run the risk, however, in order to make a point. The point is that excellent studies have been produced by New Testament scholars that cannot be made to fit the gospel paradigm of Christian origins. Thus the list illustrates good work that gets lost, or worse, dismissed, because there is no place to register it as important, to regard it as a building block to be used in the construction of another history of Christian beginnings. I wanted to mention studies that, in my judgment, should and could make a difference for an understanding of Christian origins as the work of early Christians. Some are studies whose importance is mainly a contribution to the dismantling of the traditional Christian imagination. Some are by scholars who have tried to align their findings with the standard gospel paradigm and may *not* have wished to contribute to a markedly different vision of Christian origins. But all contain significant findings, in my opinion, with potential for contributing to a redescription project. And all therefore deserve more discussion of the "so what?" variety than they have received. As with the *aporiai*, I do not have the leisure to comment on any of these studies. I hope, nevertheless, that some of the reasons for my judgments will be apparent.

> Paul Achtemeier on the mythic pattern implicit in the chains of miracle stories.
> John Alsup on the post-resurrection appearance stories as *literary* performance.
> William Arnal on scribal deracination in Galilee and in Q.
> David Aune on the imbalance of the term *Christ* in Paul versus the synoptics.
> Daniel Boyarin on the intertextuality of the Mishnah.
> Daniel Boyarin on Paul as a radical Jew.
> Willi Braun on the rhetoric and social practice of feasting.
> Peter Brown on the holy man as entrepreneur in late antiquity.

Rudolf Bultmann on the wisdom myth background to the logos hymn.

Ron Cameron on the rationale for the earliest material about John and Jesus in Q.

Ron Cameron on Eusebius and the canonical (Lukan) myth of origins.

Elizabeth Castelli on *mimesis* as a discourse of power in Paul.

James Charlesworth on the lack of evidence for the notion of "the" messiah.

Adela Yarbro Collins on the myth of "persecution" in the Apocalypse of John.

Hans Conzelmann on Greek as the original language of the *kerygma*.

Kathleen Corley on the public role of women in Roman society and the synoptics.

Dom Crossan on the parables of Jesus in the Gospel of Thomas.

David Efroymson on the reason for the *adversus Iudaios* literature.

Henry Fischel on the *chreiai* in the early Hillel tradition.

Robert Fowler on the non-eucharistic function of the feeding stories in Mark.

Lester Grabbe on the intellectual vitality of Judaism from Cyrus to Hadrian.

Robert Gregg on the mixed demography of the Greco-Roman Decapolis.

K. C. Hanson on the "beatitudes" as non-eschatological attributions of honor.

K. C. Hanson on kinship in the Mediterranean and the Herodians.

Martin Hengel on the post-Alexandrian hellenization of Palestine.

Richard Horsley's critique of the scholarly category of "the zealots."

Luke Timothy Johnson on *pistis* as "faith*fulness*" in Paul.

Steven Johnson on two ideologies of baptism in early Christian texts.

Werner Kelber on the lack of evidence for Jesus naming twelve disciples.

Werner Kelber et al. on the passion narratives as Markan.

Karen King on gnostic ideology as social critique.

John Kloppenborg on the compositional history of Q.

John Kloppenborg on the Q hypothesis.

Lee Klosinski on meals and social formation in Mark.

Helmut Koester on the importance of the Gospel of Thomas for Christian origins.

Werner Kramer on the earliest use of the term *christos* — in the *christos* myth.

Jack Lightstone on scribalism and the development of the synagogue.

Bruce Malina on "religion" as integral to the social fabric in antiquity.

Luther Martin on "secrecy" in hellenistic associations and mystery cults.

Luther Martin on the "syncretism" of hellenistic religions.

Willi Marxsen on the Lord's supper as christo*logical* problem.

Christopher Matthews on the term *apostle* in early Christian usage.

Wayne Meeks on early Christian urbanity.

Merrill Miller on how Jesus became Christ.

Merrill Miller on the "pillars" in Jerusalem as a conundrum, not a datum.

Jacob Neusner on the Pharisees and the logic of the Jewish purity systems.

George Nickelsburg on the "wisdom tale" and the passion narrative.

Kenneth Pomykala on the lack of evidence for a "Son of David tradition."

John Priest on the lack of evidence for the notion of a "messianic banquet."

Jonathan Reed on the archeology of Galilee and hellenistic culture.

Vernon Robbins on the hellenistic rhetoric of the pronouncement stories.

David Seeley on the Greek background for the "noble death" in Paul.

David Seeley on the influence of the ruler cult on early "christologies."

Dennis Smith on the association pattern for communal meals in Corinth.

Jonathan Z. Smith on the "apocalyptic situation."

Jonathan Z. Smith on early Christian baptisms.

Jonathan Z. Smith on the term *mysterion* in scholarship and in antiquity.

Morton Smith on Palestinian parties and politics that shaped the Old Testament.

Stanley Stowers on the rhetoric of Romans and the hellenistic ideal of self-control.

Stanley Stowers on the politics of sacrifice in ancient Greece.

Shemaryahu Talmon on diversification in post-exilic Judaism.

Hal Taussig on the ritualization of meals in early Christianity.

Joan Taylor on the lack of sacred Christian sites before Constantine.

Sam Williams on the Greek background for Jesus's death as "saving event."

Stephen Wilson on Jewish-Christian relations from 70 C.E. to 170 C.E.

Vincent Wimbush on asceticism as a strategy for cultural critique.

Leif Vaage on the Cynic parallels to the teachings of Jesus.

How nice it would be if there were a forum where studies such as these would be taken seriously as contributions to a redescription of Christian origins. What if studies such as these were turned into building blocks for a redescription project? What if New Testament scholars found a way to wriggle free from the gospel's mystique and change the subject?

Changing the Subject

Taking the question of the disciples as an example, imagine scholars trying to make sense of the New Testament texts without letting either the orthodox mythology about Jesus and his disciples, or a piety focused on Christian life as one of "discipleship," set the agenda. It could start with the recognition that neither of these views can be supported by the textual evidence, and that reference to disciples in the early Jesus materials might be used to great advantage for a redescription project if only the questions changed. What then? Why then it would suddenly be very important that the earliest views in Q, Paul, Mark, the miracles stories, the pronouncement stories, and the Gospel of Thomas did *not* agree, could not be *made* to agree. What then? Why then one would have to ask about disciples in the cultures of context, about teachers and their disciples, about schools and their teachings, about disciples and their ways with the teachings of their teachers, about mutual recognition among kindred schools, about belonging to a school, and so on. This is interesting material and very important as analogy and foil for going back to the New Testament texts. Maybe the problems scholars have always debated about these texts are not really problems at all. Maybe the differences among the early texts are just what one might expect of kindred movements in competition who thought of themselves on the model of schools. Maybe the strange ways in which "the" disciples get named and storied in various textual traditions are more to the point than the question of why, if Jesus named and commissioned them, the earliest texts do not agree. One could actually use the role and image of the "student" in the Greco-Roman world to trace a vigorous and complex history of social formation and ideological position-taking in the early Jesus movements, then use it as a point of departure for understanding the emergence and significance of the plethora of later myths about "the" disciples *as* "apostles." Paul could be positioned. And Luke's portrayals of Peter and Paul might finally make sense as mythmaking instead of historiography. What is important to note is that discipleship is not the only category that could easily be redescribed and rectified. All of the *aporiai* mentioned earlier could be handled the same way. And, since all such studies would be interlocking, it would not take long before a plausible picture of Christian origins surfaced for theoretical contemplation.

The work of redescription could be very rewarding, making significant contributions both to the discipline of New Testament studies and to the study of religion in general. The Greco-Roman period is rich in interesting phenomena, and early Christian literature is full of puzzle-like material. To redescribe Christian origins as a history of human inventiveness would make of it a much more interesting story than any scenario painted by the gospels and Christian theologians. It could happen as well, for once, that the work of New Testament scholars might come to be seen as significant and helpful for scholars in other areas of the humanities. Historians of religion, for instance, might finally be able to take Christian beginnings as an example of the emergence of a new religion and learn some things about mythmaking. That is because the gospel myth of Christian origins will have been accounted for in the course of redescribing the human investments and inventiveness of two or three hundred years of early Christian mythmaking and social formation. A forum for redescribing Christian origins might even make a contribution to cultural critique in our own time by analyzing the charter documents of the Christian imagination.

PART TWO

Constructing a Social Theory

CHAPTER FOUR

Explaining Religion: A Theory of Social Interests

Introduction

I want to develop a theory of religion that can explain Christian origins without recourse to miracles and divine interventions. The currently popular definition of religion, the notion namely that religion refers to systems of belief and patterns of ritual that enable individuals to experience contact with a transcendent order of spiritual reality, cannot do that. But a social theory of religion can explain Christian origins, including the mythmaking activities and ritual practices that emerged, if only the social and intellectual investments of these people can be seen as variants of social interests common for all human social formations. To entertain such a theory will require a rather sharp shift in focus, for according to the popular view religion is not a human creation resulting from social activity and social interests as are the other structures that define the human enterprise. Religion is thought of as an independent and special form of human interest and activity, one that is concerned with a world of the gods and anchored in the individual's desire for contact with the divine. Social theory, on the other hand, offers explanations that do not require belief in the gods, do not start with accounts of personal religious experiences, or assume an order of spiritual reality that transcends the natural and social worlds. Social theory draws upon the archives of ethnography and the disciplines of anthropology, and regards religion as a human creation on a par with the other systems of signs and patterns of practices that humans have invented to structure their societies.

The social theory I have in mind works with three concepts. The first is the concept of *social interests*. I can develop this concept by making some observations about the systems of signs and patterns of practices that structure all human societies. The second concept will be that of *religion as a social structure*. This concept should not be difficult to imagine, for the public display of religious practices are all social occasions, and both social and religious studies have taught us that religions are affected by and do affect social and cultural configurations. The third concept will be a bit more difficult to describe, but is critical for the theory. It is the concept of *religion as social interest*, by which I mean to suggest that religion is generated by social interests, and that it functions to maintain and manipulate social interest just as the other systems of signs and patterns of practices that structure human societies. My plan is to develop the outlines of such a theory in this chapter. In the next chapter I shall use this theory to offer an explanation of Christian origins.

A Theory of Social Interests

In our time, the pursuit of knowledge about other lands and peoples has produced a rich reservoir of ethnographic data. This accumulation is so vast that even those dedicated to the collection and assimilation of descriptive reports, such as the Smithsonian or the National Geographic, have not been able to contain it all. It is a marvelous, multicolored collage of peoples living in so many varieties of social arrangement that our fascination with other cultures has often turned to consternation as scholars have tried to comprehend them. At first, noting their differences from us, and thinking that they lacked concepts such as history and the capacity for critical thinking, we called many of these peoples "primitives," "tribal," "aboriginal," as if they represented stages of human evolution long since left behind by the developmental histories of the world's great civilizations. Slowly, however, a series of breakthrough studies forced us to change our minds. We finally had to admit that all human societies were wondrously complex systems of social logic, created and maintained by amazing investments of thoughfulness and intellectual labor. A short list of these discoveries would include:

The social significance of "rites of passage," Arnold van Gennep, 1908.
The social implications of "totemism," Émile Durkheim, 1912.

The concepts of "gift" and "obligation" in archaic systems of exchange, Marcel Mauss, 1924.

The structural relation of a language to a culture, Franz Boas, 1940.

The intelligence required for calculations typical of basic technologies, Brownislav Malinowski, 1948.

The logic of tripartite social structures and their myths, Georges Dumézil, 1948.

The logic of kinship systems and social structures, Claude Lévi-Strauss, 1949.

The logic of dual systems of classification in social organization, thought, and mythology, Claude Lévi-Strauss, 1962.

The relation of ritual to processes of social formation, Victor Turner, 1967.

Performance and display as ingredients in urban genesis, Paul Wheatley, 1971.

The social importance of a shared imaginary world *(habitus)* and the function of the gap between it and actual social patterns of practices, Pierre Bourdieu, 1972.

The importance of a people's attitude toward land, language, and blood kinship for social behavior and the construction of cultural symbols, Clifford Geertz, 1973.

The importance of geographic and astronomical calculation for social organization and village orientation, Åke Hultkranz, 1979.

The intellectual ingredient in the formation of myths and the performance of rituals and its significance for social structuration, Jonathan Z. Smith, 1987.

In the course of studies such as these a number of systems of signs and patterns of practices have been discovered and analyzed. Cultural anthropologists now take these systems for granted as the means by which societies are structured. The list includes language, kinship systems, classification systems (frequently pairing natural and human objects in two systems of differences), territorial mapping, distinguishing social identities, technologies and production, social organization and the assignment of roles, calendrical systems, and rules for behavior, rectification, etiquette, and tuition. Several things can be said about these systems. They make it possible to live together in social units. None functions without the others. Together they form the complex system of interrelated devices that structure human societies. All are human creations, though none can be attributed to a single mind or moment of creation. None are thinkable without an enormous, collective investment of intellectual labor. All function as "grammars," i.e. they provide the underlying logic and rules for competence, but without demanding a conscious mastery of the rules as rules. And none are necessary for basic biological survival. This means that the energy driving the creation and maintenance of human societies cannot be accounted for as a necessary response to "needs" of any kind, or in terms of psychological motivations. Customary references to "calorie quotients," "biological needs," "acquisitive instincts," "fear," "aggression," and "species protection," are not enough to account for the intricate systems of signs that structure human societies or the processes of socialization and tuition required to master them.

The overall result of these and other studies has been a radical reconception of the human enterprise of social construction. It is now possible to imagine the interplay of complex systems of signs, codes, and practices that make possible the formation and maintenance of a human society. Many of these systems have been analyzed in detail, their logics worked out, and their significance for social organization and practice noted. The intellectual labor involved in the construction and maintenance of these systems is truly impressive, as are the inordinate amounts of curiosity, experimentation, and delight that have been invested in the fragile craft of living together in social units. At first it seemed that these systems of signs had purely practical purposes such as producing children, procuring food, assigning tasks, keeping track of time, foraging, and reporting. But then we noticed that such purposes are not merely practical. They already partake of interest in doing tasks together and making the performance of them interesting. There is a kind of reflexivity built into the application of these cognitive systems by which a raft of recognizably impractical human interests becomes all but inescapable. Language, for instance, is for more than communication about practical matters. It is for talking, putting constructions on events, making and sharing observations, embellishing reports, delighting in innuendo, creating metaphor, attempting persuasion, and joking. Kinship systems do more than guarantee healthy children. They govern identity, assign social place, acknowledge generational process, and define connections to those who have gone before. The distribution of labors is for more than getting the job done. Because of these social role assignments, people have to circulate, be with different folks at different times, and thus have the opportunity to tell stories on one another, and learn to laugh, complain, show off, or comply. The codes of honor and shame rank individual performance. The hierarchies assign responsibilities. A calendar is not only for marking time and identifying the appropriate seasons for basic activities. It makes such collective activities as planning, anticipation, and celebration seem natural. Let us say that these applications indicate social interest. Let us imagine that the human enterprise of social formation is elaborate and interesting because humans take interest in living together in social configurations. If so, I suggest we explore *social interest* as a concept.

Social interest carries a number of connotations. These are (1) interests in the social aspects of living together in social units, (2) shared by those who are living together, (3) presupposed of all agents in any human encounter or social activity, (4) functioning as a bond that defines the social as social, and so (5) taken for granted in every human transaction. Social interest should not be ontologized or psychologized. It should not be ontologized, for although social interest exists apart from any individual, it does not exist apart from a society. Social interest, like cultural "mentality," exists only among a people living together in social formations. It is a creation of the interests people have taken in the social, an interest that has been cultivated and honed in the long reaches of life together, i.e. a collective human creation.

Social interest cannot be described in terms derived from psychologies of the individual, for it functions at the level of shared expectations about the way a social unit works. Both personal interest and social interest are terms of motivation. But in the context of a psychology of the individual, motivation is thought of as personal. That is not possible in the case of collective motivations. We have no language for the ways in which a society "thinks," "agrees" upon patterns of practices, "feels" about this or that contingency, or "makes judgments" about better and less better ways to do things. Instead, one has to imagine myriads of moments of mutual recognition throughout a group and its history in order to grasp the way in which social interest pervades the intercourse customary with human social formations. Social interest is a real factor in the construction and maintenance of social formations. It is also the real result of the construction of social formations. It is always already taken for granted in any given social formation as a principle of mutual recognition, reflexive identity, behavioral constraint, and motivational allowance. It functions to undergird behavioral codes, tweak curiosity, push performance, allow for laughter, make possible the enjoyment of the incongruous, and suggest rewards for accomplishment. Social interest is not something that individuals have or produce by themselves. Social interest is a dynamic feature of life together. It is that which has impelled the long periods of collective activity we have to imagine in order to account for the complex structures of human societies.

Thus we humans take this feature of life together for granted. That is one reason why it has not been conceptualized, named, and described. For any given individual, social interest is both given and learned in the process of socialization. And as with the mastery of all the other systems of signs, a person does not need to learn a grammar before acquiring competence in a skillful manipulation of social interests. Social interest is so obviously a part of human motivation that it is hardly ever noticed. Social interest must be presupposed even in cases where "anti-social" attitudes and behavior are in evidence. If one stops for a moment, however, and asks about the senses of belonging, attraction, constraint, and alienation that underlie all social behavior, what I am calling social interest can readily be imagined. If asked whether I have a birthday coming up, I would say "Yes." If asked whether I would like to be with family and friends on my birthday, I would say "Of course." But if asked "Why?" I would probably say something like, "Surely you jest." We are not accustomed to questioning the obvious, but once pointed out, the obvious should not be difficult to recognize.

Religion as a Social Structure

Religious studies have rightly focused on myth and ritual as the primary phenomena of the social and cultural constructs we call *religion*. All of the other manifestations of religion, such as priests and practicioners, institutions of religion, formalized ceremonies, and modes of personal religious experience, can be understood as elaborations and manipulations of these primary phenomena. It is obvious as well that rituals are public occasions; that myths are shared stories; that religious institutions are social structures; and that religious images are often cultural symbols. It has become a matter of common acknowledgment that religious orientation and cultural identity tend to overlap, and that religious persuasions and ideologies have social effect. What we have often lacked is a description and theory of religion as a social structure. We have not yet learned how to locate religion among the other systems of signs and patterns of practices that structure society. And we have seldom asked how religion functions in relation to social formation.

There are many reasons for this state of affairs. One is that religion as a system of signs describes a world other than that of the social and empirical worlds as actually observed and experienced. Another is that the world projected by religious myth and ritual is imagined as the location of divine agents capable of influencing human life in ways not matched by a human capacity to influence the divine. Still another is that the modes by which that other world impinges upon the social order are frequently experienced at the level of imaginary, internalized moments, not at the level of publicly observable effect. And a fourth is that, in the history of the academic study of religions, religion has always been defined as a traffic with transcendence, not a social construct. Thus the factors of mystery, belief, and sacrificial ritual have always been thought definitive for religion. The only questions we have thought to ask have been about the nature of the gods inhabiting that other world, the revelations and experiences thought to be necessary in order to contact or understand them, and the enlightenment required to overcome mystification, superstition, and the thought that ritual exchanges with the divine were magical manipulations. "How could these primitives believe in such gods and perform such sacrifices?" were the underlying questions for the last two centuries of scholarly investigation.

However, despite working with an inadequate theory of religion (the notion that religion is the way humans experience transcendence), the social circumstances and effects of particular religious practices have often been noticed by scholars and thought to be important. You may have noticed that many of the breakthrough studies on social structures I mentioned earlier focused on religious practices. Van Gennep's study on the rites of passage showed the close relationship of rituals to critical moments in the rearrangement of a social configuration undergoing generational change. Émile Durkeim's studies of totemism came to the conclusion that the object of religious devotion, which he called "the Sacred," was in fact the imaginary location of forces peculiar to social existence. Victor Turner's study of the Ndembu circumcision ritual demonstrated the extent to which a ritual of initiation into the adult world became the occasion for an African society to rearrange its assignments of roles according to its system of honors and obligations for another period of time. And a remarkable essay by Jonathan Z. Smith on the origins and significance of animal sacrifice has demonstrated that this ritual was designed to enable critical reflection about a society's preoccupation with animal husbandry. No such ritual can be documented before the domestication of animals (1986).

It would also be possible to make a list of the themes typical for mythologies and note their similarity to the set of social interests already discussed. Both lists touch upon such themes as ancestors, genealogy, kinship, territory, discoveries and inventions, codes for behavior, honor and shame, achievement and failure, the assignment and function of social roles, precedent-setting events, the consequences of wrong behavior, rewards for doing things right, relations with other peoples, and so forth. It would not be difficult to show, for instance, that mythic events, calendrical calculations, and ritual celebrations are sometimes inextricably joined. The same could be worked out for the characterization of mythical heroes and kings intertwined with etiquette for real social roles. Patriarchal legends can be closely related to kinship genealogies; creation myths overlap with territorial mapping; and so forth. Thus there is a general consensus among cultural anthropologists that myths and rituals function to structure human societies just as the other systems of signs and patterns of practices. Ethnographers have found that it is impossible to describe a society without also describing its myths and rituals. What we have not had, however, is any way to account for the special effects of myths and rituals. Thus the questions we need to ask are (1) why religion at all, supposing that the other systems of signs function sufficiently to structure and maintain the practical workings of a society; (2) if religion adds to the practical working of a society, what does religion do that the other systems do not; and (3), how does religion function if it does have a special role in the structuring and maintenance of a society?

Religion as Social Interest

When compared with the other systems of signs and patterns of practices that structure human societies, systems of myth and ritual manifest three distinctive characteristics: (1) They focus attention upon figures and actions in orders of time and space at a distance from the everyday world of activity; (2) They exaggerate the descriptions of the figures and activities that inhabit those imaginary worlds in ways that mark them as different from their counterparts in the world of actual experience; and (3) They emphasize the attributes of intention and performance of the frequently powerful agents located in that imaginary world. In sum: imaginary world; fantastic features; powerful agents. We can turn these characteristics to theoretical advantage by noting that they stretch the imagination beyond the parameters of everyday experience, empirical observation, and access to confirmation. It is the relationship of this imaginary world to the everyday world of social experience that provides the answers we seek.

As for the way in which myths and rituals expand the horizons of the normal senses of time and space, several observations can be made. Myths are set in the past, sometimes in a "once upon a time," sometimes at or before the very beginning of the world. Rituals are actions that take place in the present time, but in spaces that are marked off from the everyday. This means that the horizon that controls the outward limits of credibility may be as vast as all of imaginable time and space.

The logic of these manipulations of the ordinary, everyday experience of time and space has been worked out by Jonathan Z. Smith. According to Smith, ritual takes an ordinary activity away from its ordinary place in the everyday and performs it in microadjustment in a marked-off space. Attention is drawn to the difference between a "perfect performance" of the activity and the customary, an invitation to critical reflection upon the everyday. Myth sets up a contrast between the "now" and the "then." Ordinary figures take on extraordinary features when transposed into the mythic past. Attention is drawn to the differences in such a way as to underscore the inaccessibility of precedent-setting agents and events as well as to invoke thoughtful reflection on the structures of the ordinary. By design, then, myth and ritual manipulate ordinary orientation to space and time in the interest of bringing critical thought to bear upon the ordinary. They do this by marking differences in perspective that invite comparison and create a space for critical reflection. In myths, the concentration of an unlikely combination of features in a single figure can bring thought to focus intensely on a particular, perhaps heretofore unexplored configuration of social forces. In the case of ritual, an action common to the everyday will be slowed down and unraveled into moments so minute that time stands still and the space becomes otherworldly. It thus appears that myths and rituals are designed to exercise the imagination by placing ordinary objects in extraordinary settings, and extraordinary figures in ordinary settings. They fill both the long reaches of the past and the vastness of space with figures and moments that, though distant and detached, are very much present to the imagination and bear some relation to real life. Let us say that the contrast between the empirical world and the imaginary world not only prompts reflection upon aspects of actual social situations which otherwise may not have been noticed, but also creates a certain fascination with the strange and interesting figures inhabiting that imaginary world. Pierre Bourdieu has helped us see the importance of this expanded world and has given it the name of *habitus*, that is, the imaginary world in which a people's collective agreements reside.

Why would a people want to do that? Well, what if the process of social formation creates and draws upon social interests and forces that cannot be explained by reference to any contemporary source or cause? What if a people recognize that for any given generation, the structures governing their lives together were already in place? What if belonging to human society is not merely a matter of voluntary association, but a coming into a world set by circumstances prior to anyone's doing? Why then, any attempt to give an account of oneself living within a social formation would require pressing beyond the borders of the observable and known. Such would be the case, for instance, when reflecting upon one's sense of belonging to a people; sharing a particular attitude toward the land; accepting, marking and honoring genealogical loyalties; cultivating the memory of forebears whose influence cannot be accounted for simply in terms of biological descent; bewondering the "cosmic" and natural arrangements of the world that determine the pace and direction of activities; experiencing the constraints of another's views in the way in which judgments, construals, and "memories" redound; looking for reasons for ranking and the assignment of tasks; noticing the shared world of the imagination in which reports, plans, questions, curiosities, jokes, and intellectual achievements are located and managed; and wondering about the effects of gift-giving and obligations. Myths and rituals are the ways humans have of acknowledging the complexity of the social by locating social determinations outside the world of the everyday even while configuring them in such a way as to cast their reflection back upon the everyday.

Now then, an odd thing happens when the interests derived from the other systems that structure human societies are transposed into the worlds of myth and ritual. We have noted that the themes typical for mythologies correspond to these social interests. Kinship, classification, calendrical orders, territory, production, and so forth, are all there. The remarkable thing about these themes in mythic mode, however, is that their transposition into the once-upon-a-time of myth triggers a transformation of the theme. Interest in kinship as a system shifts to interest in genealogy and descent. Mapping one's territory is often transfigured as an account of creation. Technologies of production are imagined as discoveries, inventions, or first time stories. Tuition takes the form of example stories set in a fantastic past. And the alreadiness of social arrangements is accounted for in terms of origin stories in which precedence is established by patriarchs, powers, and authorities not accessible for questioning. Thus the imaginary world does not reflect the faces one actually sees in the real social world, nor is the imaginary world as lovely, sensual, detailed, and inviting as the natural environment of a group and its polished artifacts. The mythic world is much too large for normal comprehension on the one hand, and much too grotesque to serve as a mirror on the other. Can these fantastic features be explained?

93

The fantastic configurations of the world of myth are a result of compressing many social forces and features into imaginary figures and moments of agency. The mythic world allows for recognizable features of the social world to be exaggerated, concentrated in odd configurations, parcelled out and distributed among several agents, set in situations of conflict, and observed in moments of narrative transformation. I have already noted that the complex systems of signs and patterns of practices that structure human societies cannot be the creation of individual agents. But attribution of agency is a primary mode of accounting for things that appear and happen, and agency is the only way we know to attribute purpose to an event. If a people wants to think of their social structures as having purpose and design, mythic moments and agents will have to be imagined. And they will often have to be imagined as persons even while establishing social circumstances of which no real person is or could have been capable. It should not be surprising, then, that the agents who populate this expansive world of the imagination look strange. That is because they are imagined as agents of and representative figures for social roles and forces that structure a society as a whole. Think of starting with the human figure of an ancestor to account for some of the social arrangements already in place when any given generation comes along, compressing more and more stories of an-cestral memorial onto the single configuration of the representative ancestor, then adding some first time, precedent-setting, establish-ment episodes, and what do you end up with? You end up with bigger-than-life ancestors, superhuman heroes, and gods. It is the same with accounting for any of the social arrangements for which no single individual can be named or imagined as the responsible creator, or cause. What kind of an agent might be imagined as the culture bringer, law giver, arrangement setter, terrain creator, or "person" responsible for all of the little cracks in the natural-social system where mistakes, failures, jokes, tricks, and serendipities hap-pen? Just to ask the question lets the familiar mythic figures appear.

Thus the mythic world cannot be a perfect reflection of the social world. Neither is the mythic world the picture of an ideal society with which the social order is to be constantly compared. The imag-inary world of a people is a motley conglomerate of disparate images that vary in intensity and clarity of profile. The mythic world does not inhibit the energies required to manage social relations and practices in a dynamic social formation, though it may set limits for acceptable conceptual and behavioral experimentation. In a situation of social and cultural stability, the gap between the social world and the mythic panoply may be thought of as creating a space for play, experimentation, thoughtful meditation, as well as a bit of cheating, winking, and/or calling one another to task. But creating a space and backdrop for the theater of human activity is not the only way a mythic canopy functions. It may also be treated like a collage in which the arrangement of its figures is susceptible to reconfiguration. In a situation of social and cultural change, the mythic world can become a battlefield for ideological advantage. That is because the symbols within the mythic world can be manipulated. They can be highlighted in order to argue for traditional ways and values, or reconceived and rearranged in the interest of calling for social change.

This means that myths and rituals should not be thought of as practices that cultivate "religious" interests in contrast to social interests and practical interests. Myths and rituals are the ways in which the expanded *habitus* of human societies is acknowledged, memorialized, manipulated, and contested. Religion thus explained is not only part and parcel of the systems that structure human societies, its distinctive functions appear to be essential extensions of the other systems of signs and patterns of practices. This means that myths and rituals are not only generated by social interests, they are the ways in which social interests continue to be shaped, criticized, thought about, and argued in the ongoing maintenance of a society.

I would like to conclude with a description of a ritual in antiquity, one that involved the manipulation of myth and that functioned in the interest of insuring the generational continuity of patriarchal estates. The pattern of the ritual varies somewhat as we find it in different times and cultures, but seems to have been a widespread practice among peoples living in the ancient Near East, the Levant, and around the Mediterranean. The evidence from Greece is the richest, and documents the practice from the Minoan and classical to the hellenistic periods. But the Ras Shamra tablets from Ugarit, as well as later texts in Hebrew and Aramaic, tell us that the ritual was performed in North Semitic and Israelite cultures from at least the middle of the second millennium B.C.E. until the Roman period.

Scholars of the Greek history and culture have called the ritual a sacrifice or a hero cult. However, these terms carry connotations from older scholarly discourse that focused on only certain aspects of the ritual thought to be important for comparison to early Christian practices. We have since learned to be more careful about the terms *sacrifice* and *cult* when applied to Greek ritual. The term *sacrifice*, for instance, *thusia* in Greek, was used by the Greeks to refer to any and all occasions of special celebration and memorial for which a banquet was held that included a meat dish otherwise not a part of the regular daily diet. Scholars of late antiquity in the Near East refer to the *marzeah*, using the name given to the ritual at Ugarit. And because the *marzeah* was closely related to funerary rites, Old Testament scholars have sometimes used the term *cult of the dead*, a term that had negative connotation in the world of biblical scholarship until recently. It used to be thought and said that no such "cult" existed in Israel. We know better now.

In Greece, the ritual was performed at the tomb of the local *hero*, the term used for an early or founding ancestor of the district's leading family. As we know from the huge reservoir of stories, songs, and written descriptions of heroes in Greek antiquity, their social and cultural roles were taken so for granted that the imaginative embellishment of their escapades produced genres of literature for celebration, entertainment, pedagogy, and even allegorical and philosophical treatises. The ritual consisted of a meal for which an animal was sacrificed and to which the people who lived in the district were invited. Oblations were made at the tomb, frequently covered by a round, flat stone with a crevice to receive the wine. This physical gesture of refreshment was the way in which the Greeks acknowledged their sense of indebtedness and connectedness to the ancestral tradition for whom the hero was the prime representative. As the animal was prepared for roasting, certain parts were thrown into the fire as a gesture to the gods. But the rest of the meat, meal, and wine was then consumed by the people as a banquet. Judging from the general descriptions of Greek sacrifices and banquets, it was a grand occasion for stories, song, socializing, and drinking.

The people took part and were served according to rank reflecting the hierarchies throughout the district. The father of the leading family provided for the sacrifice from the resources of the estate. As the Greeks put it, he was the one who "sacrificed" or "gave" the sacrifice, although the dirty work of building the fire, killing and roasting the animal, and preparing the meal surely must have been done by the servants. And the custom was that the father would ask one of his sons to sacrifice with him. It is this aspect of the sacrifice that Stanley Stowers at Brown University thought curious and worth investigating. What he found is a very important clue to the social functions attached to the ritual. The father's invitation to his son "to sacrifice with him" was the way in which the head of the estate announced his choice of an heir apparent. It was his will and testament, so to speak, and functioned as a legal contract. In cases where siblings may have contested the right of that son to inherit the estate and manage the family's financial affairs, the son needed only to have a witness that he had in fact "sacrificed with his father." Thus the ritual was the occasion for linking the past with the future by insuring generational continuity at the top of the district's hierarchies. It also reconstituted the social structure of the district as a whole, centered as it was on the memorial of the district's hero with an invitation to all the gods to be present.

Evidence for the *marzeah* in the Levant is not as rich, clear, and descriptive. I have consulted Loren Fisher who directed the Ugaritic and Hebrew Parallels Project at Claremont and who graciously let me see his new translation of Genesis in manuscript. In the introduction to this translation, Fisher describes the ritual and refers to the relevant texts. There are texts that mention the "men of the *marzeah*," their banquets, and their leader. Other texts describe a *marzeah* as the ritual banquet for a funeral. In the so-called *rephaim* texts from Ugarit, the gods are depicted banqueting at a *marzeah*. Still other texts suggest features of the funeral ritual that involved calling upon the ancestors to be present for the banquet. It is these features I find interesting, for they tell us that the transition from the world of the living to the world of the dead created a shift in representation that resulted in imagery we usually associate with the gods. On the occasion of the death of the patriarch of a district, tribe, or petty kingdom, the sons and other leading men would gather for a *marzeah*. The spirits of the ancestors would be called to be present, and the name of the patriarch, now deceased, would also be called in order to give their blessing to those still alive. The blessing was for the general well-being of the people, but especially for the sons of the patriarch, that they would in turn have sons and so assure yet another generation.

It is the conception of the spirits of the dead that intrigues me. The patriarchs were called by using their personal names, as for instance in the description of the call and the blessing in Genesis 48: 15–16, as Fisher's translation clearly shows. Just as Jacob calls upon the God of Abraham and Isaac, his ancestors, to bless Joseph and his sons, so he instructs Joseph to call his name along with the names of Abraham and Isaac in order to receive the blessing that will insure generational continuity and make of them a great people. But the spirits of the dead as a collective were also called by using a plural designation, sometimes *rephaim*, sometimes *elohim*. *Elohim* is the term used most frequently in the Hebrew scriptures to refer to what we have understood and translated as "God." And it is this term that occurs in the blessings of Jacob and Joseph, just referred to. Although it is a plural form, it usually occurs in grammatical constructions that assume a single entity. There are, however, exceptions, highlighted in Fisher's translation. While I know of no one who has made the argument that the concept of the *elohim* as a single divine agent in the Hebrew scriptures must be related to the concept of *elohim* as partriarchal spirits, the *marzeah* ritual would surely help us understand how that could have happened. We know that *elohim* was the generic term for the spirits of the ancestors as a collective. We know that the patriarchs of particular tribes and families were remembered by name even though they were also included among the unnamed *rephaim* and *elohim* as the collective for ancestral spirits. And as for the concept of these named patriarchs, we know that the singular figure was storied as an individual, but understood as a collective. Each became a condensed symbol of a people as a whole. Sometimes this mental shift from an individual to a corporate characterization was acknowledged, as in the case of stories about Jacob who was given the name of Israel, a generic designation, in a blessing by the *elohim* or "God" (Genesis 35:10). It could also happen that a generic designation of a people came to be treated as a name and storied as a single person. Such was the case with "Adam," for instance, a term which simply means "the human," or "humankind." This mode of abstraction, representing a social entity in a single figure, was a typical and very important intellectual pattern of thought in the ancient Near East. And if this is so, it does appear that the concept of God in what we have come to call the Judeo-Christian tradition may well have roots in ancient Near Eastern myths and rituals in which partriarchs and kings joined the company of the unnamed dead. If so, the *marzeah* would best explain the process and best be explained by a theory of religion as social interest. What we have called "the gods" would be the mythic form of attributing agency to a people's ancestry. What we have called the concept of god in the singular could then be accounted for as the personified form of the collective abstraction.

CHAPTER FIVE

Explaining Christian Mythmaking: A Theory of Social Logic

To consider a social theory of religion, though challenging, is much simpler than applying it to the data available for explaining Christian beginnings. Reasons for setting aside the traditional imagination of Christian beginnings are not difficult to grasp, but a redescription of Christian origins based on theories of social interest requires asking a set of questions for which there is little guidance. A radical reconception of early Christian social formations is required in order to analyze the social logics of their myths. However, now that the quest for the historical Jesus will not suffice to explain Christian origins, and now that the developmental notion associated with the Lukan outline is no longer tenable, the scholar has no option but to proceed. Not to proceed leaves the old mystique in charge of explanations.

The point has already been made about the social and ideological diversity of early Christian groups reflected in the texts of the New Testament. A brief overview of this material will help focus attention upon the issues of difference that determined the diversity. It will then be possible to ask about features of social formation and mythmaking that some of these groups may have had in common, analyze the social logics of their various myths, and draw some conclusions about the social interests that appear to have driven their social experiments.

The Many Different Texts

There is a sizable collection of textual material from the early Jesus movements, such as Q, the Gospel of Thomas, the pre-Markan miracle chains, the pre-Markan pronouncement stories, and other less obvious bits of evidence. The remarkable thing about this material, as we have seen, is that there is no mention of Jesus as a messiah or (the) *christos*, no critique of Second Temple Judaism, no reference to a crucifixion, and no hint of a resurrection. That makes it very difficult to link the evidence from the early Jesus movements with what other New Testament texts say about the death of Jesus *christos* or Jesus the crucified Christ.

When one takes a closer look at these Jesus materials, it becomes clear that there is very little agreement about who Jesus was, what he taught, and what the priorities were for those who joined his school. Some thought that debating the Pharisees was the biggest challenge; others were not at all worried about that. Some thought that a change of life-style was the litmus test for those who wanted to belong to the Jesus school; others sniffed at such ideas. They thought that the teachings should lead to meditation and insight about one's true nature as a child of the universe. Social formations of various kinds are in evidence. At first it appears that loosely knit groupings met in ad hoc ways to talk about the "teachings" of Jesus. And as for the matter of Jesus having had students who surely must have known what it was he intended, there is no evidence of any such group. This means that the notion of a select group of students is the result of mythmaking at some later time when different schools of thought in the Jesus movement wanted to trace their teachings to special students of Jesus. Thus the first lists of these special disciples, usually numbering seven or twelve, show that there was no agreement on their names or what it was they had learned from Jesus. And the Thomas people used the very idea of Jesus's special disciples to poke fun at them for getting the teachings wrong.

Turning to the letters of Paul, what we find is a message about Jesus *christos* who was killed and raised from the dead. The transformation of Jesus *christos* into the Lord of the cosmos is what Paul considered the main point of the message, and he wanted his congregations to cultivate continuing contact with the powers unleashed by Jesus's resurrection. There are only a few teachings of Jesus left in Paul's notebooks, and no memories of the historical Jesus that make any difference for the way in which Paul imagined the transforming event. One might think that such a focus on such a miraculous moment would be overwhelming and thus cancel out mundane considerations, but no. Issues of ethnic extraction, seating arrangements at the table, obligations, honor and shame, and who gets to say what Christians should do, are frequently in evidence. So the letters of Paul not only put us in touch with a radically different kind of Jesus legacy, they also reveal a most contentious debate among and within these groups about their identity and purpose. The contrast between the Jesus *christos* congregations and the early Jesus schools is therefore quite striking. The early Jesus schools knew nothing of a mission to the gentiles or of Jesus's grand plan to start a new, worldwide religion. For the first forty years, ideas such as these are found only in the letters of Paul.

The story of diversity among the earliest groups of Jesus people and Jesus *christos* groups continues with studies in the narrative gospels. Mark is the one who came up with the idea of writing a narrative of Jesus's public appearance and crucifixion. He was the one who worked out a way to merge the traditions of the Jesus schools with the myths of Jesus *christos*. Only in Mark does the term *Christ* (for "the messiah") begin to appear as a title and designation for Jesus-the-teacher destined to be crucified. And it was Mark who portrayed the disciples as those who learned why Jesus appeared by following along until the crucifixion. In the story, they will also be told of the resurrection, but that is where Mark drew the line. He could use the logic of martyrdom taken from Paul's *kerygma* in order to imagine the rejection and vindication of the Jesus of his story. He could also tell that story in such a way that the Jesus movement to which he belonged and its concept of the kingdom of God could be seen as vindicated as well. That was a helpful notion for his little band who had become confused about their future in the aftermath of the Roman-Jewish war. But cultivating the continuing presence of Jesus's spirit was going too far. He was not at all interested in turning his Jewish Jesus group into a hellenistic cult of Jesus *christos* on the Pauline model. So he could not end his story of martyrdom with any hint of an ascension to lordship, or appearances of the resurrected one, or instructions in how to worship or imitate the newly apotheosized Jesus. Instead, he ended his story with an emphasis on Jesus's departure from this world only to appear again at some future apocalyptic transformation of the world when he and God's kingdom would be revealed in glory. Mark's story only makes sense as fiction, of course. It was written in the shadow of the Roman-Jewish war of the 70s to suggest that the destruction of the temple during this war was an act ordained by God as punishment for the Jews who killed Jesus forty years earlier. Paul would have been shocked. A narrative of the crucifixion in which the Jews killed "the messiah" would have ruined the whole point of the *christos* myth.

Matthew and Luke wrote from a later time when the raw wounds of the war had healed and other Christian groups had taken a fancy to Mark's story of Jesus's crucifixion. Their distance from both the time of Jesus and the destruction of the temple apparently made it possible to overlook the factual implausibilies and the logical inconsistencies of the story. Both Matthew and Luke used Mark's story as the narrative frame for their own biographies of Jesus, but each softened its dramatic and apocalyptic tones in order to imagine the teachings of Jesus to call for the kind of group to which they now belonged. Matthew wrote for a Jesus school that had learned to think of its teachings as a profound interpretation of the Mosaic torah. Luke wrote for a network of gentile Christian congregations that had learned to think of themselves as leaven for the moral good of the Roman empire. As for the John tradition, the story of Jesus who knew himself to be the son of God from the very creation of the world, inviting "the Jews" to be "born again," is truly distinctive and cannot be made to agree with the Lukan scheme in any respect. Only Luke makes it look as if there was a straightline development of a simple message and a single institution that continued an Israel epic history and travelled from Jerusalem to Rome in the span of twenty years.

The Social Experimentation

At first it seems that what we find in place of the Lukan picture is a chaos. It turns out not to be a chaos, but compared with the Lukan view, it is certainly a lively scene of divergent and extravagant claims. It contains fantastic imagery, raging ideological contestation, social rifts as well as the creation of new social bondings, personal risks, and many failed attempts at social control. If the focus falls on the polemics, catcalls and innuendos, the scene does take on a decidedly vociferous tenor. But when one catches sight of the aspirations driving this outpouring of energy, the picture takes on another cast. It is more boisterous and wild than chaotic and dark. The descriptive term that comes most quickly to mind, once the focus is on the social formations that generated these texts, is *experimentation*. What we have is clearly evidence of social experimentation. These were people involved not only in thinking new thoughts about living together in a world in which age-old patterns of life were no longer working, they were actually creating new and different social formations. The question is whether something like social experimentation can be regarded as an important feature in common among all of these different groups and their views. The answer seems to be yes. And it looks like a good place to start painting a new picture of Christian beginnings.

That social interests were driving these experiments begins to make sense when we shift to a wide-angle lens and catch sight of the larger world in which these Christians found themselves. It was the close of the hellenistic age in which a cultural and military conquest brought an end to the viability of the ancient Near Eastern temple-state. The *pax romana* in Palestine was just in the process of destroying the last attempt to keep that ancient model alive. The imperial forces of the Greco-Roman age did little to nurture human well-being in the lands and provinces of the Eastern Mediterranean. And throughout the so-called *oikoumene*, the Greek term for "global civilization," transplanted peoples and conflicting cultures were thrown together without the benefit of any new, overarching multicultural model for the single "house" *(oikos)* in which everyone knew they were living. The Roman armies kept the roads open and the procurators at their posts, but did nothing to make possible putting the fragments of broken social structures and cultural traditions back together. The processes of cultural ferment and social change quickened during the first centuries B.C.E.-C.E. Issues of social identity were pressed to the point where critical and creative energies were released among all peoples throughout the Levant.

Thus the times were ripe for social experimentation, and early Christians were not the only ones behaving in this way. Many other social experiments were taking place during the time that did not need Jesus for justification. It was a time for new configurations of the older philosophical schools. Private clubs and associations, sometimes called *fellowships (koinoniai)*, sometimes *companies (thiasoi*, a "troop" or "party" of Bacchic revelers), emerged throughout the Eastern Mediterranean. Craftsmen working in a particular trade created voluntary associations called *collegia*. Displaced people of common ethnic heritage formed cultural centers in the diaspora. Jews and Samaritans formed synagogues. Egyptian priests replicated the public processions of Isis. And others, from Macedonia, Asia Minor, Syria, and Mesopotamia founded "mystery" cults to stay in contact with their old national gods and provincial heroes. The Greeks built new shrines and temples throughout the Mediterranean world on the one hand, and encouraged pilgrimage to the old sites of ritual and healing at Athens, Epidauros, Delphi, and Delos on the other. Gnostic enclaves and monastic communities also began to appear. So what does this tell us about the early Christians? It tells us that they must have been normal human beings responding to their times just as others were. This is a very important notion, for it takes away the aura of the exceptional and unique that the grand narrative of the gospel has always evoked, and makes it possible to imagine other ways to account for Christian beginnings.

If we stop for a moment and consider the importance of this observation about "responding to their times," a bit more can be said about the nature of these social experiments on the part of early Jesus people and Christians. Evidence of various attitudes toward the Romans, the Jews, the temple priests, Pharisees, Greeks, hellenistic cults, civic authorities, public behavior, customary codes of civility, courts, and popular ethics are evident everywhere in this literature. These attitudes are marked by social and cultural critique, indicating that judgments had been made about matters affecting patterns of social life. This means that the social experimentation characteristic of these Christian groups was not just responsive, as if to take advantage of a situation to promote one's own group or agenda. They were actually being *critical* and *reflexive* with respect to their social and cultural worlds. If so, it means that these Christians were alert, savvy, and concerned about the social and cultural state of affairs around them. It might even mean that their social projects were driven by the desire to repair, restore, or replace lost or broken social institutions, or even to create new alternative social arrangements in the face of an untenable world. They spent a great deal of time and intellectual effort marking themselves as distinctive when compared with a rather large congeries of other viable social options of the time. Can anything more be said about what these Christians were doing?

One bit of evidence can be seen in the way they named and talked about themselves. They said that they were a kingdom, a household, a family, children of God, an assembly *(ekklesia)*, a righteous nation, an Israel, a holy people, children of peace, disciples in the school of Jesus, the body of Christ, and so forth. Notice that all of these self-designations are collective. This means that social formation and collective identity were high on the list of motivations and preoccupations. If taken literally, the claims in every case were fictions and, in relation to other indications of the practices and constituencies of these social experiments, quite far-fetched. However, all of them were applications to social experiments of social models that were common to the cultures of context. They did not invent self-designations that were completely novel or unattached to standard metaphors for social units. This tells us two things about these people: they knew they were involved in social formation; and they knew that their social formations did not conform perfectly to any single traditional model. If the project outlined in Chapter 3 and the Annex can find a way to describe the social formation and practices of groups in relation both to the models available for association at the time as well as their self-designations and their mythic potentials, it may be possible to theorize the social interests and reasons involved in the formation of these groups. Early Christian mythmaking was neither pure "speculation" nor simply the elaboration of a "received tradition." In each case the social reasons for and the effect of imagining a mythic configuration need to be determined. Social effect means marking or making a difference in overt behavior, attitudes, social structures, social relations with other peoples, or shifts in the mental framework of a group's imaginary *habitus*.

A second observation can now be made about another common feature of these early Christian groups. They all treated the cultural traditions of both Jews and Greeks in much the same way, making claims upon certain aspects of each tradition while remaining critical of others. For instance, all of them sought some way to link themselves with one of the current versions of Israel's epic. Some did that by casting Jesus as the fulfillment of the divine promises and illustrious aspects of a history of Israel. Others did that by recasting the epic of Israel to agree with what they had come to say about Jesus and themselves. And still others did it by setting up a critical opposition between Jesus and current Jewish social institutions as a critique of those institutions and a justification of their own practices. It does appear that the preferred social models used for self-designations were weighted on the side of allusions to the people of God idealized in the various epics of Israel. Since these early Christian groups were unlikely candidates for carrying the epic traditions of Israel into the future, these attempts to claim epic precedence are remarkable. They wanted very much to think of themselves as belonging to "Israel," but they knew that in reality they did not have and could not produce the proper credentials. Thus their mythic claims would have to be extravagant.

In the case of Greek traditions, the current culture of license was regularly criticized even while the languages of logic, rhetoric, and philosophy were pressed into the service of imagining the kingdom of God as a cosmic and universal order of sovereignty and themselves as the *demos* (people), *ekklesia* (senate or council), and *soma* ("body") of citizens who rightfully belonged to it. This balancing act between approval and critique in respect to both of the important cultures of context means Christians were living in the cultural overlaps of the hellenistic period. This comes as no surprise, of course. But it does confirm and advance the theory with which we are working, and it does reveal that early Christians had sensibilities both Jewish and Greek. It also means that the Christian experiment was made possible by combining features of these two cultures in a novel configuration. Though it is much too simplistic to reduce those features of the two cultures to single, basic concepts, it might help to suggest that the Christian experiment dislodged the Jewish conception of the people of God from its national and ethnic roots, thought of individuals on the Greek model as agents capable of changing their minds and social identities, and rationalized both of these moves as essential ingredients of novel social experiments. Some scholars have thought that the genius of this merger of cultural mentalities might well define the attraction of the social visions that inspired Christian beginnings.

This combination of the two most important cultural mentalities of the time, reduced to the essential predicates of their fundamental anthropologies, can be detected in the earliest layers of the teachings of Jesus and traced through many of the subsequent mythologies produced by the Jesus movements. In the Cynic-like teachings of Q1, an address to the individual was combined with the collective concept of the kingdom of God. The novelty of this combination of concepts was attributed to Jesus as the founder-teacher of their school, but in the subsequent developments of this school tradition it becomes clear that the concept of the kingdom of God was not just the idea of a teacher around which a new school of philosophy had gathered. The concept was actually quite fuzzy and incapable of conceptual elaboration. It was the invitation to experiment with its applications that produced the Jesus schools. The Jesus schools were actually kingdom schools, and the kingdom schools were working on their self-definitions not only by elaborating a concept but by experimenting with appropriate life-styles and social formations. Thus they were busy marking their social borders as well as their ideological positions. They were taking steps to clarify and enhance what it meant for a person to belong to their group and share their vision of the kingdom of God. It was the same in all of the Jesus movements. Each elaborated the social vision differently, but these elaborations did not threaten the special combination of anthropologies and conceptual systems made possible by living in the overlap between the two major cultures of context.

The Social Logic of the *Christos* Myth

Many social factors and historical experiences affected the ways in which different movements cultivated the "teachings of Jesus," and this resulted in various resignifications of the teachings as well as changes in the ways in which Jesus was imagined and storied. Recasting Jesus's role was the only way to forge a link with the epic tradition of Israel, and drawing upon the intellectual resources of the hellenistic world was the only way to elaborate the "teachings," rationales, and supporting arguments and embellishments that had to accompany developing social formations. Those who elaborated the teachings into a program for the demonstration of a countercultural ethos, as in the Q tradition, thought of themselves on the model of a philosophical school and thus depicted Jesus as a teacher of penetrating wisdom. Jewish Jesus people, however, wanted to work on the contrast between the new teachings of Jesus and the traditional teachings of Moses so they compared him to Moses or one of the prophets. Movements with gnostic tendencies became interested in the challenge to the individual to reject the social constraints of traditional collective identities and think differently and deeply about their true identity as "sons of the living father" ("God," "Light," the "All"), as in the Thomas tradition. Thus they cast Jesus as the revealer of a hidden potential for pure self-knowledge untarnished by concern for contemporary etiquettes and taboos. Others painted him as a prophet, a divine man, a healer, an exorcist, or a messiah. That is mythmaking in the interest of justifying what each group had become or wanted to become. Mythmaking of this type works by manipulating the image of an agent or event of precedence to which no one in the present has access. A founder-figure of the past, even of the recent past, can be reimagined to provide links to yet older epic anchors for cultural and social legitimation. By imagining a match between what a group thought of themselves and what the original intention of such a founder-teacher had been, early Christian groups could think of themselves as having a proper, if novel place in the larger world. Because their views of Jesus were mythic, the fact that all these groups claimed to be followers of Jesus tells us little about the historical Jesus, but much about these groups.

A particularly interesting example of a Jesus myth that can provide information about the social formation that produced it, is the so-called *christos* myth that Paul cited in his letter to the Corinthians (1 Cor 15:3–5). This myth summarizes the events that Paul considered essential to his gospel, and it is the text that Bultmann regarded as the *kerygma* definitive for Christian faith from Paul's time until the present. I want now to make the point that the myth has a social logic and that it was formulated in the interest of that logic. I have worked this out in some detail in my book on the Gospel of Mark (1988, Chapter 4). If one cannot discern the social logic and reconstruct the social situation, the myth seems extravagant, exaggerated and dramatic. The usual explanation therefore has been to think of it as the response of early Christians to their experiences of the overwhelming events of an historical crucifixion and resurrection. But when you know that martyrologies of even more graphic depiction were being produced by Jews in Antioch to memorialize the brief but illustrious chapter of the Hasmoneans (or Maccabees) in Judea, the intention of the *christos* myth begins to be understandable. It must have had something to do with the way in which the logic of a martyrdom could have applied to the social situation of these early Christians. As a matter of fact, that is exactly what the logic does. The logic of a martyrdom is that the martyr "dies for" a cause. The martyr is honored for his integrity, and the cause is justified as that which is worthy of such devotion. Thus the point of the *christos* myth was that, if the God of Israel thought that what Jesus "died for" was right, approved of Jesus's "faithfulness unto death" as a martyr for that cause, and "vindicated" him by raising him from the dead and installing him as Lord, then the cause for which he died is also "vindicated." That could only mean that those who belonged to his kingdom, the cause for which Jesus died, must be acceptable in the eyes of the God of Israel.

It is important to see that the Greek notion of the noble death was mythologized by viewing Jesus's death *from God's point of view*. Paul was quite aware of this additional construction upon the logic of a martyrdom, for he mentions it expressly in his description of its effect in his letter to the Romans (Rom 3:21–26). It was Sam Williams who noticed the significance of this mythologization and traced its language and logic to the Greek concept of the noble death (1975). It is also important to notice that the terminology used to express both of the vindications involved in the logic of the myth was the language of "justification" or "righteousness" *(dikaio-sune)*. This language is basic to Lutheran theologies of personal conversion and redemption. According to Lutheran theology, that from which the individual needs to be redeemed is "sin" and "sinfulness," notions that were hardly possible until developed by post-Constantinian theological anthropologies. Thus the Lutheran interpretation of the *kerygma* misses completely the social logic of the myth. The reason that the social formation ("cause") for which Jesus died required vindication was that it had no claim upon the God of Israel and no credentials to pose as the "children" of this God, i.e. "Israel." Why? Because it was composed of both Jews and gentiles, the gentiles uncircumcised and the Jews toying with the teachings of a teacher (Jesus) that pulled them away from loyal participation in the diaspora synagogue. This means that the question to which the myth answered was "Jewish": How can this unlikely congregation of mixed constituency possibly think of itself as "Israel"? And the logic of the myth that answered that question was Greek (with a little help from hellenistic Jewish intellectuals who had already worked out ways to combine their story of the persecuted righteous with the Greek martryology). The logic is especially Greek in regard to the themes of "faithfulness unto death" (a "virtue" worthy of high "honor"), and "apotheosis" (post-mortem elevation to divine rank). Thus we have every right to peer through the window offered to us by this text and imagine the fireworks and energies that must have been the accompaniment to this moment of social formation and mythmaking. A Jewish question, a Greek answer, an unlikely congregation, an implausible claim, a stunning myth, and an extravagant social logic—all because of the attraction of a Jesus school that wanted to *be* what they had come to think the social vision of the kingdom of God required.

It would not be wrong to notice the similarities between this *christos* myth and the myths of the Maccabean martyrs. Perhaps the stimulus for daring to imagine such a foundation myth was not limited to questions the Jesus people had raised about themselves. What if this group of Jesus people were getting together around the edges of a diaspora synagogue, and Jews from the synagogue were asking them to "justify" their claims to be a legitimate form of "Jewishness" when their teachings and social constituency did not look like they were? The myth would say, in effect, "Look, the Maccabees were martyred for the torah, and God rewarded them. Jesus was martyred for the teachings about the kingdom, and God rewarded him." Thus the myth would have made it possible to answer questions from that direction as well.

It is very important to see that the *christos* myth (1 Cor 15:3–5) was not a statement about what happened to "the Messiah" as that concept has been imagined by subsequent Christians. The *christos*-martyr myth in 1 Cor 15:3–5 has been *called* the "Christ myth" because *christos* is the name Paul used for Jesus when he cited the myth. And also because, in the history of the Christian imagination

112

it has always been thought that Jesus *was* "the Messiah." It could only have been the recognition of Jesus as "the Messiah" that inaugurated the Christian faith, mission, and religion, or so the traditional account of Christian origins has imagined it. However, as mentioned earlier, there are many problems with both of these reasons for thinking that the *christos* myth was about the killing of "the Messiah." In the first place, the designation "Christ" is no longer appropriate. It is misleading in light of work on the term *christos* in Paul and the pre-Pauline movements that determined its use as a cognomen for Jesus. In the second place, the logic of such a conception as the killing of the Messiah and its redemptive effect is absurd as the long history of tedious rehearsals of failed attempts to make theological sense of it demonstrates. In the third place, the notion of the Jewish expectation of an eschatological appearance of "the Messiah" is a myth first formulated by Christians. Scholars have shown that the concept is "curiously" not present in the Jewish literature of the time, and that the texts usually pointed to by Christians as support for the idea have to be interpreted in other ways (Neusner, 1987; Charlesworth, 1992). In the fourth place, the term *christos* (or *messiah*) does not appear in the teachings material produced by the Jesus schools before Mark. In the fifth place, the use of the term by Paul is odd. As Merrill Miller has shown, Paul understood *christos* as a cognomen for Jesus (1999). He never used the term as a technical, titular, or predicate designation to define Jesus's special identity or role. There is no statement to the effect that Jesus *was* "the *messiah*" or "the *christos*," or that it was important to see or believe that he was.

Knowing that there was no concept of "the Messiah" upon which to draw, it is not surprising that the term was not used to imagine that Jesus "fulfilled" that role or expectation. But the term *messiah* was also never used as a name for anyone in any of the Jewish literature of the period. The term was used as an attributive adjective, as in "anointed priest," "anointed prophet," "anointed king," or "God's anointed one." The concept was that of the selection and approval of a person for a social task or role. The term did not define which role it would be. This means that the first use of the term *christos* (the Greek translation for *messiah*) for Jesus must have been attributive, as in "Jesus was anointed by God to . . . ," or "Jesus, God's choice to . . . ," or "the anointed Jesus," or "Jesus *christos*." It is easy to imagine how such a usage could have turned into a cog-nomen, especially after using it as an attributive. And what may the original intention of the attributive have been? What was it that God had "chosen" Jesus to do? It could easily have been any of the founder-teacher roles that early Jesus schools had already imagined for Jesus. And that could have been imagined as soon as it was important for one of them to claim legitimacy as a school of thought and as a people. The first thoughts need be little more than saying, "Why don't we think of Jesus as the teacher God chose for the new age." Note that the term *christos* does mean "anointed" in Greek, but that being "rubbed with oil, ointment, or salve," would not have been used by the Greeks to mark the selection of a person to office. Thus the meaning of *christos* in application to Jesus had to draw upon the connotations of the Semitic *messiah*. If so, another moment of social formation and mythmaking can be imagined for the use of the term before it was attached to a martyr myth as cognomen for Jesus. The claim would have been to think of Jesus, his teachings, and those who belonged to his school as having been "selected" or "chosen" by God for a special role or task. That is all "Jesus *christos*" would have implied, but that would have been more than enough to create smiles within the movement, and frowns without. For a Jesus group to claim epic anchorage in this intentionally generalized way would have been a startling thought and very difficult to counter. And if the Jesus group that started talking this way was composed of a Jewish-gentile mix, the attribution of *christos* to Jesus would be a "Jewish" *answer* to a "Jewish" question about the legitimacy of the group. That could easily have created consternation. After all, claims to ethnic privilege, recognition, and identity are very important matters. This claim would have to be negotiated. But since it was based upon a mythic reach of the imagination, the process of negotiation would have to be played out in the subsequent social histories of the various groups with interest in claiming that epic heritage.

Briefly, to complete this set of mythmaking moments with focus upon the term *christos*, it can now be underscored that Mark's fiction of Jesus as "the Christ" also created the concept of "the Messiah." He did that by merging Jesus traditions with the martyr myth of Jesus *christos* and by placing the narrative of the martyrdom in an apocalyptic view of history.

The Social Interests of the *Christos* Congregations

The Jesus myths produced by these early Christian groups can now be understood as imaginative moves in their quests to legitimate forms of social identity. This means that their mythmaking activity can be understood in terms of the myth theory presented in the previous chapter. That they were interested in justifying their new social formations by making claims, though fictive, upon traditional models of collective identity also can be understood in terms of the social theory of culture and religion discussed in that chapter. The questions that remain, however, have to do with the range of social interests that may have been involved in these early Christian social experiments. The theory of social interests draws upon two major archives of the humanities, ethnographies as analyzed by cultural anthropologists, and mythologies as studied by historians of religion. It was possible to convert the several systems of signs and patterns of behavior that structure human societies into what I am calling *social interests*. These systems are intellectual creations oriented toward the empirical and natural orders in the interest of living together, the human enterprise of constructing and maintaining society.

Myths and rituals are also driven by social interests even though they seem at first to draw attention to an imaginary world of time and place that transcends the natural and observable world. The theory is that the imaginary world of myth and ritual has much to do with the activity of social formation. It expands the horizons of space and time to gain perspective on the current state of affairs, accounts for the fact that the social structures are already in place when any given generation comes along, provides a medium for thinking critically about social forces that are not easily traced to any individual human agent, and offers the images and concepts for rethinking and rearranging older social patterns and cultural values.

Suppose we apply this theory to the early Christian experiments in social formation. It may at first seem inappropriate, in that early Christian communities were not productive societies in the usual sense of that term. There was not much mapping of a habitat; no interest in the classifiction of flora and fauna; kinship talk, but no system that could be used to make marriages legitimate and produce healthy Christian babies; and no attention to the technologies and apprenticeships that guarantee the production of basic goods. As a matter of fact, it would be difficult to imagine that these Christians were any earthly good.

But in fact, most of these social interests are very much in evidence in early Christian discourse. The problem is that this discourse was designed to mark their differences from other social configurations in the larger world. Thus their discourse was torn between extravagant mythic claims and defensive maneuvers against standard social practices that may have threatened their mythic claims. They had to acknowledge features of the real world they shared with others even while focusing on the imaginary world they were creating as their *habitus,* a world that was mythic. The mythic world was, in fact, the only place in which their own primary social interests could be located. Take the datum of kinship systems, for instance. There was much talk about kinship among these early Christians. But the kinship they imagined was a fiction. They were not really "brothers" and "sisters" in a "family" with a genealogy that stretched back to Abraham as Paul said (Galatians). There were far too many uncircumcised gentiles of diverse ethnic lineage to say they were the "children of Abraham." They were only to think of themselves that way, and they had to work very hard to convince themselves and others that it was possible to do so. Paul's effort in Galatians was to argue that, since Jesus, Jewish ethnicity as traditionally defined was no longer a necessary requirement for belonging to "Israel." This argumentation was a rhetorical disaster. Should they think of Jesus as the "seed of Abraham" as Paul said? But would not Jesus then be the "father" of the new family of God? Maybe adoption by God would be the more judicious metaphor. But then, what might Jesus have had to do with it? Was Jesus God's son because he was the "seed of Abraham"? Or was he the "seed of Abraham" because he was God's son? And God's position also had to be declared. Thus the embarrassing questions could hardly be avoided. His letter to the Romans shows that Paul's line of argument didn't survive even in his own eyes, and that he had to find other ways to support the family fictions. And yet, the attempt in Galatians is telling. It reveals the intellectual effort invested in the interest of justifying a social experiment by means of a mythic fiction about kinship.

It is the same with the social interests that generate the other structures of human societies: territory, classification, calendar, social roles, codes of behavior, and production. These interests, basic to human social formations, are all there, even if transposed into the register of mythology. Take territory for example. Interest in mapping the territory was translated into social geography. These Christians were very good at marking their social borders and locating all competitors somewhere on the other side of the line where accommodation and/or conflict was most manageable. The same was true of the other systems of signs that structure human societies. Regnant ideologies across the cultural landscape were classified according to their usefulness or danger. Calendars were forced to accommodate new patterns of practice. Social roles were created, debated, and institutionalized. Note that it was the mythical frame of reference, the expansion of the horizon to include epic history, divine purpose, and cosmic order, where the prototypes were found and the claims to being right were anchored. It was there that these early Christians found their ancestors, worked out their genealogies, lined up their heroes, discovered precedents for their founder, traced the ways of God, and located the powers that turned the cosmos into the "house" of God in which they could feel at home.

No wonder they had trouble knowing what to do about practices customary for people living in the real world. The issues that soon surfaced included what to do about burials (the customs for which were based on altogether different notions of ethnic identity), participation in civic festivals (all of which were also "pagan" rituals), sex with spouses who had not converted, eating meats from the marketplace (all of which had been "sacrificed" to "pagan" gods), Jewish purity codes (which sounded good but could sweep you into another sphere of influence), circumcision, banqueting, going to court, and honoring the emperor. The "house of God" that these Christians had constructed for their *habitus* was truly otherworldly. It did sustain social formations of a certain kind, however, those that we would now call "religious" communities. Debates rage as to whether the early Christian communities should be seen as the beginning of the western pattern of the separation of religious institutions from the state. But there is no debate about the fact that the early Christian experiments did create a split view of the world in which the structures of each half did not easily mesh and were hardly expected to do so. One was the world of the everyday, populated by peoples and governed by structures held to be much in need of repair or transformation. The other was the kingdom of God, an ideal order imaginable only via the genre of myth, and available only by entering into the Christian community. Christians lived in both worlds, but took their bearings from the mythic world. They created institutions and rituals to make it accessible, and formed religious communities to represent, apart from the real world of the everyday, social orders imagined as fitting for the kingdom of God in the heavens above. It is this cultivation of a purely mythic *habitus* that justifies the description of the early Christian social formations as "religious" communities. Once that is seen, however, the theory of social interests we have been exploring, both in application to social formations and to the institutions of religion, is fully applicable.

The Social Logic of the Apostolic Myth

By the end of the first century, most of the mythic options for Jesus had been explored, giving Christians a chance to relax from the exhausting labors of constructing new Jesus myths and *christos*/Christ myths fit for new mythic worlds. They took a breath, looked around, and viewed the social landscape they had created. It was not a particularly pretty sight. This group and that group had settled into practices and ways of thinking about themselves that did not mesh with one another. There were gnostics, ascetics, Jewish-Christians, spiritualists, mystery cults, Jesus schools, local cults of the dead, and overseers in major cities sending letters of instruction about beliefs and obedient behavior to congregations of the Christ throughout their districts. Some groups had worked out their ways of living in the world in conscious opposition to other groups. Contacts generated conflict. And the quest to guarantee the truth of a group's own views and traditions signalled the next round of mythmaking. Readers interested in a more detailed description of this chapter of Christian beginnings will find it in *Who Wrote the New Testament?* (Mack, 1995).

The solution that commended itself was to anchor a group's tradition in a special instruction from Jesus to a certain apostle. The apostle would be the guarantor of the truth of a group's teaching. And the best candidates would be the disciples of Jesus who had known Jesus "in the flesh," as Paul put it, and perhaps had received instructions after his resurrection. But several problems had to be resolved in order to imagine that. The first was that, since Paul, the notion of an apostle was not necessarily linked to the notion of a disciple of Jesus. And as for the notion of disciple, it was first used of anyone who joined one of the Jesus schools. The Jesus movements had gotten along quite well without appeal to special disciples who had known Jesus personally. Named disciples were not mentioned in the sayings gospel Q, for instance. In Paul's letters, Peter, James, and John were referred to as apostles and "pillars" of a group in Jerusalem, but without mention of their having been disciples. In the Gospel of Mark, these three *were* named as special disciples of Jesus, but they were cast as disciples who did not understand him. And in the Gospel of Thomas, Peter, James, John, and Matthew represent dumb disciples who always asked the wrong questions and thus were not the "true" disciples of Jesus. So there was work to be done.

We can trace the various moves that had to be made in order for the concept of disciples in the school of Jesus to become the disciples *of* Jesus, then apostles or hand picked representatives, and finally the guarantors of a particular tradition of instruction that was imagined to have started from Jesus. Descriptive features that played a role in the mythmaking process included: the notion of "the twelve" (or sometimes "the seven"), several lists of the twelve by name (no two of which fully agreed), stories of Jesus's appearances to them after his resurrection, and finally Luke's story of the twelve disciples reconstituted apostles after the death of Judas by casting lots, their reception of the Spirit on the day of Pentecost, and their commission to spread out and take the gospel to all the world.

Luke's story of the Acts of the Apostles, written early in the second century, can be seen as a major moment in the development of the apostolic myth. But it was not the only way to forge the link. And it was very political and self-serving, garnering all twelve apostles for Luke's own tradition. It purposefully overlooked the many other

Christianities that were vibrant and strong at the time. These would also be wanting to lay claim to a special transmission of truth from Jesus through one of his disciples/apostles. And the way to do that would be to have in hand some written record of their instructions, memoirs, letters, or sermons. Luke, for instance, had written a standard sermon to be imagined as the preaching common to all the apostles. What would the other groups do, with their differing gospels, sayings, stories, letters, and teachings? With the exception of the letters of Paul, most of the early literature had been composed and revised many times by anonymous scribes in the interest of a group's own tradition of memory and imagination. In keeping with ancient near eastern tradtions, no scribe dared take credit for stories and sayings that were crafted as if they already belonged to the common discourse. But each of these writings would now need a guarantor. Who would it be, and how could a group make sure it was true? Thus there were problems of major proportions that called for a new round of mythmaking. This round would not be about Jesus, but about the apostles, and it would last for much of the second century.

James was given credit for a little composition of ethical teachings on the border of Christian and Jewish sensibilities. The people who cultivated the sayings in the Gospel of Thomas *switched* guarantors for some reason, from James to Thomas, at some point in their history. The first narrative gospel, originally unsigned, was later attributed to a certain Mark who, though not an apostle himself, was thought to have known both Paul and Peter, and was imagined to have written his gospel by following Peter's memoirs. Peter also got credit for yet another gospel and two letters written later in his name. Pastoral epistles were also written as if from Paul. And the sayings gospel Q ended up in a narrative gospel that was later attributed to the apostle Matthew. Philip got a gnostic gospel. Andrew was featured in the Acts of Andrew. And so on. What about John?

The Gospel of John is an especially interesting case of attribution. That is because the composition of the gospel reveals a long period of cultivation and repeated revision in a self-conscious community that did not need any named disciple as the guarantor for the truth of the words of Jesus they had ringing in their ears, much less John whose name does not even occur in the story. Around the turn of the second century, however, this community ran into big trouble. In the gospel there are hints of a critical difference of opinion with other Jesus people who appear to have appealed to Thomas as their guarantor. And in the letters written by an elder in the community, and only later attributed to John, there is evidence of a painful parting of the ways between a faction that became gnostic and one that turned toward merger with the congregations of the Christ. It appears that both factions were partial to the gospel that had been produced in the course of their earlier history in common, and each took a copy with them when they went different ways. Later, some said that Cerinthus, an early second century gnostic teacher, had written the gospel, so its authorship and authority were up for grabs, it seems, and the gnostics may well have made the first move to claim it for themselves. We do not know for sure, but that may have put the pressure on for the more conservative Christian wing to come up with an apostolic attribution. But which of the twelve was appropriate? And with so many already taken, who of the twelve was left to garner?

At some point, a scribe in the Christian tradition devised a clever solution. A "beloved disciple" without a name, appropriately portrayed as a representative of the community's piety, was added to the story toward the end. It was this disciple who then figured prominently with Peter in the final appearance of the transformed Jesus when the last chapter (21) was added. At the end of this chapter, at the end of the gospel, the note says that, "This is the disciple who is testifying to these things and has written them." If the scribe had one of the twelve disciples in mind, something which may not have been intended, the riddle he created of the "true" identity of the "beloved disciple" was more than clever; it was foolproof. There were, however, some features of the account in Chapter 21 that made it possible later in the second century to propose an acceptable, if unprovable, answer. And the answer was that it must have been John. Other Christians apparently liked the suggestion, and the gospel was finally attributed to John the disciple, as were the letters from the elder, and even the unlikely apocalypse that had been signed by another John ("the Presbyter"of Patmos). And so John's gospel became a candidate for inclusion in a special collection of writings eventually to be known as the New Testament: 4 gospels, 1 Acts, 1 Revelation, and 21 letters, all with apostolic imprimatur.

The Social Logic of the Epic Bible

A third phase of mythmaking started around the middle of the second century. A new generation of bright young Christian scholars found themselves troubled by two embarrassing features of the gospel story, largely Lukan. One was that, as Marcion saw and Trypho said, "Christians pay homage to the God of Israel but do not keep his laws. How can that be?" The other was that the claim to be a brand new religion flew in the face of every intellectual sentiment among cultures and the schools of philosophy current in the Greco-Roman age. Novelty was not good news. Wisdom worth its salt had to be ancient, an important ingredient in how the gods laid their plans, the world came to be, and the first heroes and sages started the human venture on its way. Marcion, Valentinus, Justin Martyr, and all early Christian theologians struggled with these two embarrassing questions.

As if the Christian show was now on the road, and its circus tent had newly come to town, these third generation theologians felt that the whole world was watching. We can see them scurrying around, closing down some peep holes on the one side, opening up the barker's box on the other, redesigning the posters, rewriting the scripts, and in general wanting to please their hosts with their show without looking too foolish. It was a tough assignment. They had to walk a very tight rope, linking up with the grand traditions of Greek philosophy while heaping ridicule on the feasts and festivals of the Greek gods and religion. They had to explain to the Romans that they were law abiding citizens while giving allegiance to another king whose subjects did not need any law. And they had to say that their wisdom could be seen at work in the world from its creation at the beginning to its revolutions now, even though their wisdom did not agree with the wisdom others had discerned in the very same creation and history. Naturally, there were several ways to position the tent, work the flaps and call for the show.

Marcion decided not to back down. As any new ager might put it, he said, "What's wrong with novelty? History is the problem. Why coddle the old world with all its old laws and gods of wrath and violence? The Spirit of the gracious, unknown God has finally broken through the barriers built by all those jealous gods and their puppet kings. The Spirit of Christ has set us free from the old world, free from its laws, free from its greed, free from guilt. Come on in, watch the performance, catch the Spirit, and join the show."

That was a hard act to follow. Freedom, spirit, and the anticipation of a destiny up and out of the world made sensational billing. That was especially true, if all you had to do was have a religious experience. Valentinus and the Gnostics were also much intrigued by the thought of such a transcendent destiny. Their approach, however, was not to brush all the wisdom of the past aside, but to invite the pagan philosophers in, open the tent to the heavens above, and use the stars to set a new stage for fanciful speculations. They would ask the philsophers to work out the heavenly sets for imagining the cosmic dramas that must have been played to get from creation to Christianity. They obviously preferred noetic experience to spiritual ecstacy, and philosophical systems to events of transformation. And my oh my, the worlds within worlds they imagined in order to place the Christ at creation and still account for his recent appearance in human history.

Justin Martyr did not like either of these approaches. He closed the canopy to the heavens, shut out the stars of the gnostics' set, said boo to the spirit of Marcion's parochial sensations, lifted the flaps of the tent to the winds of the world around him, looked the problem of law in the eye, and set the stage for a replay of the epic history of Israel. He would lay the foundations for centrist Christianity by showing how to make it respectable. As for the question of the God of Israel, he said, look at the Jewish scriptures. God *had* to give the Jews the law and threaten them with destruction because they were incorrigible. The law was given as their dispensation; it was certainly not God's will for all time. Read the oracles, listen to the prophets, notice the warnings and judgments against them. God did not want to destroy their temple and expel them from the holy land at the hands of the Romans. But he had to. The Jews made him do it. They did not know him truly and they failed to keep his laws. They were intransigent. As one of their own prophets said, speaking in the voice of God himself, "Israel does not know me; my people have not understood me" (Isa 1:3). So that took care of the troubling question about the law. It was a strictly Jewish dispensation. Of course Christians did not have to keep it.

We meet here with the repulsive literature of the Christian fathers known as the genre *adversus Iudaios*. David Efroymson and other historians have explored this literature in detail. Efroymson's conclusion is very telling. I think he is right. The disgusting tirades against the Jews that permeate the sermons and tractates of the early church fathers were not the result of a simple anti-Semitism. They were driven by a single objective—to tear the Jewish scriptures away from Jewish hands and read them as Christian epic. Why? To counter the charge of novelty and imagine the Christian religion to be rooted in the story of God and his people from the very beginning of the world. To answer the charge of novelty was a bit more difficult than to answer the charge of lawlessness, but with a bit of ingenuity it could be managed, according to Justin. You had to read the Jewish scriptures a second time. This time it was not the story of Jewish disobedience that was important, it was the hidden meaning behind the text that one had to find. This hidden meaning was the real plan and eternal desire of God for an obedient people. The hints were there in the words of God and the story of his struggles with Israel. If one looked for the underlying *Logos* of the text (the revelation of God's thoughts, desire, mind, reason, speech, and plan for the world), one could see that the Christian revelation was God's intention from the very beginning. The Jews did not see it, but finally Christians did. So God must have had Christians in mind all along. A brand new revelation and religion? Not at all. "We Christians are the flowering of God's wisdom," these first theologians of the church said, "the wisdom that created the world and set the human story in motion. All you have to do to see it there, is to read the scriptures allegorically, as the story of God's eternal Logos and the divine quest for an obedient people. Read the scriptures on the surface as the negative history of Israel. Then read it again as the history of Christian promise."

And so the Jewish scriptures became the Christian epic. And the apostolic writings became the record of the new epic's ending. And together they became the Old and New Testaments of the Christian Bible. Ever after, the Bible would be the myth and ritual text for the Christian religion. This codification of the scriptures took place during the late second and through the third century. By the time of Eusebius and Constantine, the Christian Church with its bishops, priests, rituals, credo, and calendar became the religion of the Roman Empire. And so, the social interests represented by the staff, and those represented by the scepter finally converged in a single social formation, one that would allow the Christian myth to create a cosmic canopy and produce a grandly encompassing culture.

Conclusion

Can social interest theory account for Christian origins? The answer seems to be yes. I have not been able to see that any feature of the Lukan-Eusebian story, whether interventions of the divine, the mystique of a unique individual, or the help of a cosmic spirit in discerning the critical shift in a holy history, is neccessary. Instead, the story of an inventive, highly imaginative people comes into view. If we let the focus fall on them, Christian beginnings make sense as social experimentation concerned about the full range of social interests typical of the human enterprise. They do present us with a number of rather extravagant practices and persuasions. And what they produced turns out to be a rather odd array of social formations, none of which was able to integrate a full range of practical social interests in a single social formation, institution, or concept. But there are understandable reasons for both of these features, and Christians were not the only people creating subcultural associations in response to an extraordinary period of social and cultural change. That they managed this challenge should be seen as their achievement. They dared to cultivate a social vision of human community in the face of a world held together only by the armies and political interests of the Roman imperium.

PART THREE

Tracing the Logic and Legacy

CHAPTER SIX

Innocence, Power, and Purity in the Christian Imagination

I want to discuss the notion of power in the Christian imagination. Understanding power is a fundamental challenge not
only for the Christian's encounter with the world at the turn of the
twenty-first century, but for theories of religion and society and for
seeing the way in which power is construed in cultural symbols. My
approach is historical and my thesis is complex. One axiom is that
power and purity were fundamental notions in the social constructions of the ancient Near East, and that they formed a complemen-
tary pair of opposites. Another is that power and purity were
collapsed in the early Christian portrayals of Jesus. And a third is
that, in the process of early Christian mythmaking, the narrative
gospel construed the encounter of this Jesus of power and purity
with the social and political powers of his world under the rubric of
innocence and guilt. Thus the topic: "innocence, power and purity
in the Christian imagination."

The outline will unfold in seven sections as follows: (1) A social
theory of power and purity with application to Second-Temple Judaism; (2) Jewish reconfigurations of the temple-state as a social
model during the Greco-Roman age; (3) Conceptions of the *polis*
during the Greco-Roman age; (4) The early Christian notion of
the kingdom of God; (5) The myth of Jesus as king of the kingdom;
(6) Purity, power, and innocence in the Gospel of Mark; and
(7) Innocence and power in contemporary Christian and American
imagination.

A Social Theory of Power and Purity

Jonathan Z. Smith has an intriguing theory of religion and society, best laid out in his book, *To Take Place: Toward Theory in Ritual*

(1987). In it he draws upon a canon of intellectuals in the fields of ethnography, cultural anthropology, and the history of religions, including Hume (for the rational and empirical foundations), Dumézil (for the discovery of patterns of myth and social structure capable of cross-cultural comparison and historical modulation), and Lévi-Strauss (for the integration of social structuration with the fundamental logic of human thought as articulated in systems of dual classification). Then, with a little help from Kant, Dumont, Wheatley, Boas, and Geertz, Smith formulates his own theory of society, religion, and thoughtfulness, and applies it to Ezekiel's visions of the new temple in Jerusalem.

Smith finds that Ezekiel's visions accord with the model of the temple-state as honed to perfection during the previous three or four thousand years of ancient Near Eastern civilization. This model consists of two systems of social stratification governed by the notions of power and purity. A king occupies the apex of a system with power to organize labor, the authority to tell people what to do, and the ability to get things done. Thus power is executive and filters down through a hierarchical stratification of control in which all members of the society have their place. All power is derived from the king who is sovereign, and whose power determines that he be regarded as the locus of the sacred. Purity is the notion that governs a second system of stratification concerned with the order and stability of the society as an organic unit of human activity and social well-being. Priests preside over a system of temple sacrifices designed to rectify things that go wrong or get out of place. At the apex of this system in which everyone and everything has its proper place, the high priest represents sanctity or holiness. The two systems are merged in such a way that everyone knows his or her place in relation to both authority (power) and purity. But the two systems also work as binary opposites, in that the king is highest in power, lowest in purity (by virtue of his function as warrior and "executioner"), while the high priest is highest in purity, but lowest in power.

The importance of Smith's work is enormous, not only as an explication of the social logic invested in the Jerusalem temple of Greco-Roman times, but also as an application of a social theory of religion that calls for the construction of axioms by careful attention to description.

Jewish Reconfigurations of the Temple-State

Jewish literature of the hellenistic age reveals an overwhelming fascination with the image of the temple at Jerusalem, as well as a deep concern for its fate in the cross-currents of the political and cultural histories of the times. The temple was understood on the ancient Near Eastern temple-state model, and that model was assumed as the right way for Jews to imagine themselves structured as a people whose destiny was storied in the epic of Israel. But most knew that the Jerusalem temple-state was in serious trouble, and many felt that the trouble was due as much to the Hasmonean dynasty (unclean priests) as to the occupations of the Seleucids and Romans (foreign power). Thus there were many attempts to research the epic, analyze the recent social history, identify the core loyalties that defined Jewishness, and rethink the shape of Jewish society. The temple-state model loomed in the background as the ideal standard by which to judge the current state of affairs and imagine what must happen to secure a Jewish future.

However, depending upon where a Jewish intellectual stood in relation to the plural forms of social life characteristic for the times, and in relation to judgments about the political and cultural state of affairs, the temple model itself came under scrutiny. Many reconfigurations of the temple model were produced as one of the ways in which Jews seriously engaged the questions of their place in the larger world and their destiny as a people. One might illustrate the variety of temple and social reconfigurations by reference to the conclusion to Ben Sira's poem in praise of the *hasidim*, the organization and ideology of the Qumran community, Philo's projection of the temple liturgy onto the structure of the cosmos, the daring meditations on Jerusalem and the land of Israel in the first century B.C.E. Psalms of Solomon, the cosmic order of wisdom liturgy in the Wisdom of Solomon, the tragic view of the epic's end in Josephus and the apocalypse called 4 Ezra, and so forth. Three other characteristics of the thinking and literature of the time (in addition to this basic fascination with the temple image) are also best understood as intellectual labor in the interest of temple-state reconfiguration (i.e. rethinking the social shape of Israel).

The first characteristic is the presence of ideal figures, sometimes decked out in the most extravagant, bigger-than-life imagery. Many of these have traditionally been understood as "messianic" figures and taken as evidence for a widespread Jewish expectation of "the" messiah, a promised king in the line of David. However, recent attempts to actually document such an expectation have failed. I refer, among other studies, to the Princeton Symposium published as *The Messiah* (1992) with James Charlesworth as editor, and a collection of papers edited by Jacob Neusner in *Judaisms and Their Messiahs* (1988). A better designation for this phenomenon, studied from a slightly different perspective, is *Ideal Figures in Ancient Judaism* (1980), the title of a set of studies edited by George Nickelsburg and John Collins. My own view is that these figures functioned as symbols for a social construct. Instead of describing the structure of an imagined society as a whole, and detailing the complex interrelationships among its various layers, fabrics, and boundaries, these Jewish authors worked out the essentials of the society they idealized by projecting a single anthropological image. This agrees with the way in which abstractions were achieved in Hebrew thought, and especially with the way in which single figures (such as Adam, or Jacob-Israel) were storied as individuals but understood as social symbols. If so, it is of extreme importance to notice that the fantastic portrayals of human figures in this literature condense and combine the attributes that belonged to the social roles of structural significance for the temple-state model and its epic history: king, priest, prophet, and the patriarchs. The stories of the patriarchs were appropriate for this purpose because they were understood to be about the covenants that were to guarantee the eventual establishment of the temple-state in Jerusalem.

A second characteristic of this literature is the way in which the story of Israel was treated as an etiological epic for the temple-state in Jerusalem. In this case, the questions raised by the troubled times had to do not only with the significance of the founding events for the shape of the temple-state in Jerusalem. They were also about what went wrong to account for all of the disasters befalling it. Epic revision is a perfectly understandable mode of mythmaking. It consists of a search for the elements essential to the promise, ideal, or logic of a people's history (as epic) and society (as culture). This ideal is frequently found toward the beginning of the history, or in some golden age of the past. This ideal image can be set in contrast to the present state of affairs as a standard for judgment, instruction for repair, or as a projection of hope for future resolution. One might think, given the traditional Christian interpretation of the Hebrew scriptures and the customary view of Jewish messianism at the time of Jesus, that the golden age of David and Solomon would automatically have been everyone's ideal image of theocracy. There were a few flirtations with that era of the epic as ideal. The author of Chronicles took a turn at portraying David as the ideal king. The Hasmoneans thought of themselves as recapturing the extent of his kingdom. And the notion of a Davidic messiah did pop up again in the Bar Kochba resistance to Rome. But most intellectuals looked elsewhere, for the Hasmoneans had tarnished the Davidic ideal. And besides, a realistic assessment of the time made the warrior-king model look silly. None of the kings of recent history fit the ideal model. The foreign kings were wrong because they were foreign (Ptolemies, Seleucids, Herodians, and Romans). And the Hasmoneans were wrong because they were first and foremost (illegitimate) high priests who had then proclaimed themselves as kings as well. What were Jewish intellectuals to think and do? The answer for most was to look for the promised ideal elsewhere in the epic.

Ben Sira imagined the covenants with the patriarchs as the foundation for the ideal temple-state governed by a high priest *without a king*. And he wanted very much to see Simon II's priesthood as the realization of that ideal. He did acknowledge that, according to the epic histories, Israel had had three "good" kings, David, Hezekiah, and Josiah. But each of these were important for reasons other than their royal power. In Sirach's view, their kingdoms were part of the history of struggle on the way to the Second Temple; they were not the ideal. Philo zeroed in on the life and writings of Moses where he found the constitution for the diaspora synagogue as a perfectly proper way to be Jewish and worship in God's cosmic temple. David is only mentioned twice in twelve Loeb volumes of Philo's works, and one of those occurs inadvertently in a scriptural citation. Qumran found the ideal in the archaic priestly codes in Leviticus and then focused on the prophets as a wedge driven between the sorry histories of the kings and the present temple establishement, a wedge of divine oracles that assured an eventual purification of the temple system. The Psalms of Solomon are a precious documentation of some group of pious Jews who were forced to reconceptualize the shape of Jewish society in Palestine by painfully relinquishing the Jerusalem temple to their past, putting a "king" in the place of the high priest, and then portraying this king as a teacher of Torah wisdom! Is it any wonder that the Jews had had their fill of kings and finally found a way to imagine living without one? One can trace the moves from Second Temple Judaism to Rabbinic Judaism as a marvelous revision of epic history. Not David, the king with power, nor Aaron, the performer of sacrifices, but Moses, the teacher who understood what God really wanted, captured the Jewish imagination. Philo had idealized Moses as prophet, priest, and king. But he was "king" by virture of "legislating" the law (a wonderful twist on the hellenistic concept of the king); "prophet" by virtue of receiving the law as revelation from God and seeing the meaning of history from creation to the land (a very clever subversion of both Greek and Jewish notions of the prophet); and "priest" by virtue of writing the five books as textual mystagogue for the instruction of Jews of all times wherever their synagogue might be (thus preparing for the notion of rabbis as priests).

A third important feature of Jewish thought toward the end of the Second Temple period was a heightened concern for purity. According to the archaic model, the laws of purity were articulated in the temple system of sacrifices, and Leviticus appears to have been a basic handbook. What happened was a resignification that dislodged the significance and observance of these codes from the system of sacrifices. None argued against the temple liturgy, leaving it in place as a very important actualization of Jewish presence in the world. But all developed alternative and substitute ways for thinking about purity and being a pious and observant Jew. Ben Sira used life-wisdom to turn torah and the observance of temple sacrifices into an all-encompassing ethic. Philo "spiritualized" the "special laws" by using allegory to develop a Jewish ethic of intention and behavior that could be lived even in Alexandria. And the Pharisees actually produced a small code of rituals that anyone could observe at home (prayers, fasting, washings, tithing, and family taboos). These counted as standards for Jewish purity and became the basis for the later Rabbinic elaborations. These are remarkable developments. They should not be misunderstood as quests for personal piety, religious experience, or salvation. They were the products of intellectual labor in the interest of redefining Jewishness and Jewish society in the pre-shadow of the temple's demise.

The result was that Jews decided for purity and against power. After the destruction of the temple, as the shift was made from Pharisees and priestly scribes to the rabbis, it was not forgotten that the notion of purity was rooted in the temple-state model. But the model was now located in an imaginary world. In the place of the priests and their sacrifices, which now took place only in an imaginary temple, teachers (rabbis) would preside over the laws of ritual purity and so make possible the sanctification of the life of Jews who gathered in diaspora synagogues. How did they do that? By *halakah*, an elaborate translation, codification and application of temple practices into codes of daily conduct. In the process of this intellectual activity, documented in the *Mishnah* (200 C.E.), the torah written by Moses was also transformed from epic into domestic "law." Purity, not political power, would focus the imagination and define the practices of diaspora Judaism.

The Concept of the Polis in the Greco-Roman Age

The ancient Near Eastern temple-state was not the only model of society haunting intellectuals during the hellenistic period. The Greek *polis* (city-state) was also firmly in mind, an ideal state where a *demos* (citizens) had freedom and autonomy to govern themselves by legislating their own laws. In the minds of some intellectuals, the polis might have room for a "king," but only for a philosopher-king whose wisdom gave guidance for wise legislation. This model, born during the classical period, played an extremely important role in shaping society during the Greco-Roman age. Cities were founded everywhere in the wake of Alexander as the vehicle and expression of hellenistic culture. Thus hellenistic culture was a culture of the city. But there was a problem. The cities founded in its name did not fit the ideal model. To the peoples of the Levant, the hellenistic polis was a vehicle of colonial imperialism taking control of disenfranchised natives. The *demos* of these cities consisted of foreigners (Macedonians, principally, but also other "friends" of the Ptolemies and Seleucids), and the power to govern was in the hands, not of the people, but of tyrannts who ruled by force. Even intellectuals in the several school traditions of Greek philosophy could see that. So something had gone wrong.

The response of the philosophic schools was a major shift in focus, away from the classical model of the "democratic" city-state, and toward the imagination of an ideal kingdom. Treatises were written on the topic of "kings" (good) and "tyrants" (bad). The ideal king would be the embodiment of (moral) law (an *empsychos nomos*). As for the law *(nomos)*, traditionally understood as "convention" rooted in democratic legislation, it was now imagined as ideally rooted in *physis*, the "natural" order of the *cosmos*. And as for "virtue" *(arete)*, the Greek ideal of personal character achieved by learning and discipline, it was now defined as living "in accordance with *physis*." An older mimetic hierarchy of *cosmos/polis/anthropos* was transformed to become *physis/nomos/arete*. An assessment of real society (where tyrannts governed cities and empires) forced the elision of the *polis* in the archaic model and put the ideal *anthropos* (as *arete*) in direct relation to the "natural order" of the cosmos. This encouraged the reduction of all images of sovereignty to symbols of personal virtue. As the Stoics said, "Only the wise man is king." Or, as Epictetus said, the Cynic's staff was his "scepter." Thus the language of rule or kingship came to be used as a metaphor for personal self-control. The term *king* no longer had to refer to an actual ruler, and *kingdom* no longer had to refer to a political domain. "King" became a metaphor for human being at its "highest" imaginable level, whether of endowment, achievement, ethical excellence, or mythical ideal. "Kingdom" became a metaphor for the "sovereignty" manifest in the "independent bearing," "freedom," "confidence," and self-control of the superior person, the person of ethical integrity who could "rule" his "world" imperiously. Of course, no one was fooled about real kings and their real power. Stoics knew that real kings were dangerous, and that an outspoken philosopher could be banished or executed. The author of the Wisdom of Solomon knew that the righteous were being killed by the rulers of the world. And the Maccabean historians, fully aware of the problem with despicable rulers, had to turn their heroes into martyrs in order to find some way to ascribe them honor and eulogize their virtue. Real kings were tyrants; real kingdoms had no soul; and real power was brutal. So pensive people looked to the cosmos on the one hand, and turned inward on the other, to find a way to survive with integrity in a world where violence had become banal.

The Greek analog to the Jewish notion of purity was honor. Honor and shame provided the codes that structured society in layers and governed one's place in the whole. During the hellenistic era an important thing happened to the notion of honor. Honor was tied to virtue, and the supreme example of an individual's virtue came to be the noble death. The concept of the noble death can be traced back to that of the warrior who "dies for his country." Then, from the late classical period and through the hellenistic period the concept was applied to philosophers (Socrates) and teachers as the ultimate display of their virtue. Thus the tyrant's power had become the standard for testing the integrity of virtue, even though the standard for judging virtue itself was the "law of nature" *(nomos tes physeos)*. Note the logic of the noble death. It is the logic of martyrdom, the one who "dies for" personal integrity, a philosophy, a people, land, or righteous cause. Note also that endurance unto death at the hands of those in power was not considered weakness. It was the ultimate display of "sovereign" strength. As the sayings went, "Living well is to practice dying"; "Your cross will come to you."

Thus it was that the political machinations of the time had broken the archaic and traditional social systems of the Levant and forced a rethinking of power, honor, and purity. Every traditional culture, with its land, people and social institutions had been disrupted. The suddenly expanded horizons of the world, now ruled by a few kings from the great cities of the Eastern Mediterranean, were no substitute for the smaller, organic societies that had sustained a fully-orbed life for their people. Peter Brown and Jonathan Z. Smith have emphasized the entrepreneurial nature of social and religious experimentation resulting from the fragmentation of traditional societies. Associations, cults, networks among households, schools, shrines, and enclaves document the interest in living in closer-knit, smaller societies. So the philosophers were not wrong in their assessment of the larger scene as problematic for human well-being, and in their attempt to understand how one might nevertheless become a citizen of the world (a cosmopolitan). Their contribution to the emergence of Christianity is basic. They introduced an ideal king into the city-state model of society, expanded its horizons to cosmic proportions, and transferred the whole to what Philo called the noetic world (from *noesis*, "thought," "intelligence"), an ideal archetype that should be the pattern of the world "below," a world known only to the mind, yet held to exist as the fundamental order of ontological reality. From the Greek point of view, an ideal king had to be in the picture to counter tyranny, the inexplicable curse that troubled actual societies. It was the tyrants of this world who had caused all the trouble.

The Early Christian Notion of the Kingdom of God

Early Christians were fascinated with a social vision they called the kingdom ("rule" or "sovereignty") of God. It was their own social vision, undeveloped in its first occurances in the earliest layers of the "teachings of Jesus," but soon to become a distinctive concept that merged the social anthropologies fundamental to both the Jewish and the Greek cultural traditions. On the one hand, it was rooted in the Jewish notion of theocracy and the concept of the people of God as a family, and on the other it drew upon the Greek notion of the individual living in accordance with nature, participating in a "kingdom" that was, in effect, an order of things prior to, displaced from, and in contrast to the kingdoms of the world. This vision created its own attraction, combining as it did the heady notions that any individual could "belong" to the kingdom and so become a "child" of God. This combination of individual egalitarianism with the paternalistic notion of divine sovereignty was a winner, especially when experienced in the formation of groups that found themselves, quite by surprise, no longer defined along traditional lines.

At first it was enough to think of individuals catching sight of the kingdom and behaving in ways that manifested a call to alternative life-styles (as in Q and the Gospel of Thomas). But it was not long before the kingdom of God became a self designation for some groups within the Jesus movements. And then, two big ideas commended themselves. The first was that some of these groups began to think of themselves as the right way to represent the contemporary form of "Israel." That was a very large claim, and it introduced one of the major tasks for early Christian intellectuals. This task was to read the Jewish scriptures and revise the epic of Israel so that it could end with Jesus and the Christian's kingdom. That task was not completed until the fourth century. The second big idea that occurred was an expansion of the horizon of their God's kingdom to encompass all other kings and their kingdoms. That idea was audacious, for it had the effect of introducing a conscious critique of the Roman empire when compared with the small and unlikely social formations of the early Christians. It also had the effect of imagining Jesus as the "king" of the kingdom of God.

The Myth of Jesus as King of the Kingdom

The story of mythmaking in the early Jesus movements, or how Jesus the teacher became Jesus the king of a cosmic kingdom, is a very difficult and complex chapter of Christian beginnings. There are, however, several mythmaking moments that can be identified, and in each case a social logic to the myth can be seen as its rationale. One such moment is the way in which the people of the Q tradition manipulated the voice and contents of the "teachings of Jesus." They did this by attributing additional sayings to their founder-figure and rearranging the collections as instructions for the kinds of "kingdom school" they were becoming. Another is the emergence of the *christos* myth in the congregations known to Paul. Here the logic of martyrdom commended itself as a way to justify the claims they were making about themselves as a form of "Israel" though with mixed ethnic constituency. And a third moment is the invention of the "gospel story" by Mark in order to justify a Jesus movement in the wake of the Roman-Jewish war (66–70 C.E.). These and the many other myths that various early Christian groups produced do make sense in relation to the experiments in social formation these movements represented.

The poem in Philippians 2 about Jesus as Lord is clear documentation that the congregations known to Paul had actually entertained the daring thought of allegiance to a king whose kingdom was destined to subsume the kingdoms of the world. The martyrology basic to the myth made it possible to imagine a post-death destiny and role for Jesus, now imagined as the heavenly sovereign. These congregations then became a network of social units, destined later to challenge the Roman order. The speed at which this conceptual change took place, from alternative life-style to alternative society, the complexity of the conceptual and mythic logics that had to be packed into the new self-understanding, and the extravagance of the claims implicitly made, all bear witness to the attraction of the new social formations and vision. The combination of the two big ideas, constituting both the new form of "Israel" as well as the ultimate kingdom, must have been very heady indeed. And Jesus was now the Lord of this kingdom, a kingdom imagined to encompass the whole world. Is it any wonder that the common feature of the many early "christologies" destined for approval by the fourth century "church" were terms of sovereignty? Christ, Lord, Son of God, Son of David, and the Great Shepherd were all royal titles. Kingship was the common denominator. Jesus had become the king of the kingdom of God.

What about Jesus as priest? During the formative period, Jesus was not mythologized as the great high priest. The book of Hebrews is the only evidence for an attempt to imagine Jesus as the heavenly high priest. This myth was viewed by the "orthodox" with great suspicion during the next three centuries. And as it turns out, it is still an anomaly in the New Testament, for scholars do not know where to place it in any of the many early Christian traditions about which there is some knowledge. That may seem strange, given the fact that the temple did begin to appear as an appropriate image for the Christian kingdom, given the fact that Christians did want to lay claim to the Hebrew epic which was an etiology of the Jerusalem temple, and given the incidence of sacrificial terminology in the myths and rituals of the early *christos* cult. But much of the sacrificial terminology used to explicate the effects of Jesus's death for others, though derived from and intended to allude to the sacrificial temple cult, actually served to elaborate another notion of sacrifice altogether. As discussed earlier, the fundamental logic of the *christos* myth (or *kerygma*, as in 1 Cor 15:3–6) was a martyrdom, understood on the Greek model of the noble death, not on the model of a temple sacrifice. However, the language of temple sacrifice had been used metaphorically by hellenistic Jewish authors of the Maccabean histories to interpret and apply the Greek concept of the noble death to the Hasmoneans. In these histories the Maccabees were portrayed as dying for the law, and their deaths at the hands of Antiochus IV Epiphanes were regarded as "sacrifices" for the cause of redeeming the law, the people and the land from his tyranny. In the case of Jesus's death, the language of sacrifice was used to imagine that he had been "faithful" to God's plan for his kingdom and so had "died for" the people who belonged to the kingdom of God. Thus the basic ingredients of this "sacrifice" for the kingdom were politics, virtue, and vindication, not the priestly rectification of wrongs that needed to be set right.

That introduces the question of what happened to the notion of purity. In some ways this question is the most difficult of all, namely why early Christians rejected such a fundamental concept. Part of the answer is that some did not. Peter, the Jerusalem "pillars," some of Paul's Jewish-Christian "opponents," and the entire Jewish-Christian movement that lasted for centuries, all accepted purity codes much on the Jewish model. Part of the answer is that the codes of purity shifted when interpreted by the teachings of Jesus (as in the Gospel of Matthew) and the concept of holiness changed when applied to the new congregations of *christos* (as in Paul). But the debate with the Pharisees in Q and the pronouncement stories of the Gospel of Mark, as well as the issues of law, ritual, piety, table fellowship, and the circumcision of the Gentiles in Paul and other early literature, together with the long history of *adversus Iudaios* literature characteristic for patristic theologies, are more to the point. As the pronouncement story in Mark 2:15–17 lets us see, eating with tax collectors and sinners was just what the Jesus movement was about. Yes, they were unclean. But it was all right to be "unclean." The Jesus people were the "clean unclean." And as the congregations of *christos* concluded, they, including their gentile members, were fully "justified" not to demand that they all live like Jews. So the Christian "kingdom," of mixed and spirited constituency, was bound to be in trouble with its ethical codes. Jewish codes of purity would not do, and the Greek standards of virtue and honor were not enough. The vision of the kingdom of God apparently called for another kind of standard. Paul took a stab at it with his "law of *christos*" and "mind of *christos*"; Mark turned discipleship into a mimetic following of Jesus to the cross; and it wasn't long before the "witness" supreme was located in the stories of the martyrdoms of the apostles and bishops of the flock. Loyalty to another sovereign was the real code, a sovereign not of this world. And the sovereign? Jesus the Lord, or Christ the king, a symbol of the kingdom in which purity was subsumed in the concept of his rule.

It is important to note that early Christians symbolized Jesus and conceptualized his kingdom by merging Greek and Jewish thought, even while carving out a place for themselves that was bound to compete with both Greek and Jewish culture. The mythology of Jesus as cosmic lord, the preferred epithet for God in the Septuagint, was de facto a revision of the Israel epic of astonishing affront to Jewish sensibility. The collapsing of purity and power in the conception of divinity was a challenge to Greek conceptuality as well. The historical significance of the early Christian turn to symbols of sovereignty, in contrast to the Jewish turn to symbols of the priestly teacher, and in contrast to the Greek symbols of personal virtue, all as responses to the breakdown of societies in the Greco-Roman age, is therefore very great. It was this fascination with sovereign power that predisposed Christians to cozy up to Constantine, and that set the pattern of relationship between the scepter and the staff for the next one thousand years.

Purity, Power, and Innocence in the Gospel of Mark

Mark set Jesus in opposition to the Pharisaic laws of purity and the sacrificial system of the temple cult. He also portrayed Jesus and his message without recourse to the Greek notions of virtue and honor (except for the honor implicitly attached to his noble death). And he did not pick up on the notion of righteousness as developed in the *christos* cult. In Mark's depiction, Jesus represented power, sheer power, the power of God in confrontation with the power of the Jewish high priest, the power of the Jewish king, and the power of the Roman empire. Jesus's power was pure, but it was a kind of purity other than that assumed by the temple system. Jesus was pure, not because he resided at the pinnacle of priestly activity, but because he was the (royal) son of God. By virtue of an anointing with the holy spirit from God, Jesus was out to rout the unclean spirits who were in control of the worldly kingdoms. This was a new notion of purity, a perfect union of sovereign sacrality and priestly holiness. As such it violated both the temple-state model's bifurcation of purity and power, and the Greek ideal of sovereignty grounded in personal virtue. If one set the temple-state model in the background in order to locate where such a combination of purity and power might reside, one could only imagine it at the level of the divine itself where God above, both pure and powerful, ruled over both the king and the high priest in the world below. Thus divine power and purity collapsed in the singular figure of the Christian's king. That invention was bound to have consequences.

How and why Mark achieved this characterization is a very important question. That is because his narrative, the first one to be written, became the basis for the other New Testament gospels. It therefore marks the moment when the Christian gospel was composed. It created the picture of Jesus and Christian origins that everyone still entertains. I have told the story of Mark's mythmaking in *A Myth of Innocence* (1988). It has to do with the way in which Mark combined earlier Jesus traditions with the essential logic of the *christos* myth by using the wisdom tale of the innocent righteous one. It was the wisdom tale that provided the pattern for his composition of the passion narrative. In the martyrology of Paul's *kerygma*, the death of Jesus was purposefully not placed in an historical setting where motivations other than those of God and Jesus would have to be supplied. In the transition from the *kerygma* to the narrative of the passion, however, where the "tyrants" were named and motivations had to be spelled out for everyone participating in the event, the questions of innocence and guilt were unavoidable. Apparently, Mark did not mind. This means that Mark's gospel introduced the notion of innocence to the characterization of Jesus as the man of power and purity. Jesus became the Christian symbol of a social anthropology in which power, purity, and innocence implode in the moment of a violent crucifixion.

Briefly, Mark took the sign of power implicit in the miracle stories and displayed it as the exponent of purity in a cosmic battle between good and evil. He therefore preferred exorcisms over healings, for they could be used to define Jesus's exercise of power as legitimate, that is, pure, setting up the contrast between unclean spirits and the holy spirit that Jesus brought into the world. Mark then combined this notion of power with that of Jesus's authority taken from the pronouncements stories where Jesus always had the last word. The formal combination of miracle story with pronouncement story is absolute and programmatic in the first action of Jesus in the synagogue at Capernaum, and in the first set of five stories in Mark 2:1–3:6. In this set of five incidents Jesus encounters those in charge of a world gone wrong and exhibits his power and purity. His weapon is now his word, and the leaders in league with the temple establishment make the point by charging him with blasphemy (Mark 2:7).

One can trace the escalation of this conflict in the design of the first five stories, and then throughout the gospel. In the story of Jesus's first appearance in the synagogue (Mark 1:21–28), the scribes are not present, but they are mentioned by the people as those whose authority was not like that of Jesus. At the healing of the paralytic (Mark 2:1–12), the scribes are present and murmur about blasphemy. In the next story about eating with tax collectors and sinners, the detractors are identified as the "scribes and Pharisees" and are brought to silence (Mark 2:15–17). The Pharisees question the disciples in the next story about fasting (Mark 2:18–22), then finally address a question to Jesus himself in the story about plucking grain on the sabbath (Mark 2:23–28). In the last story of the set, another combination of miracle and pronouncement story, Jesus directly confronts the Pharisees with his program and the Markan plot is set. The Pharisees go out to hold "counsel with the Herodians against him, how to destroy him" (Mark 3:1–6). From that point on various combinations of Jewish leaders show up from time to time in order to develop the narrative theme of the plot to destroy Jesus and take it to its conclusion.

That the man of power gets killed has always been seen as the problem of Mark's story. However, such a view overlooks several points. One is that the story time does not end with the plotted time. The story will end in an apocalyptic reversal when the son of man and the kingdom finally come with power. This solution to the problem was achieved by setting the gospel story in the larger context of an apocalyptic view of history. Another observation is that the crucifixion is viewed as a violence perpetrated in the city that thereby sealed its own destruction. This was achieved by relating the crucifixion of Jesus (30 C.E.) to the destruction of the temple (70 C.E.) and casting both as the first two battles in an elongated apocalyptic scenario. And a third point is that Jesus is portrayed in the passion narrative as the innocent victim of the first precipitating encounter. This was achieved by studied allusion to an old Jewish story of the righteous one who is persecuted unjustly. For Mark, Jesus's crucifixion was not a sign of powerlessness, not an event of redemption, and not the end of the story. It was only the first in a series of violent reciprocities. Because they killed him, God would destroy the temple, and Jesus would return as the son of man "seated at the right hand of power" (Mark 14:62). No wonder the high priest tore his clothes when Jesus said that, and called it blasphemy. He was right. Power, purity, and innocence had been collapsed in the single figure of Jesus as the son of God who, from Mark's perspective, had every right to violate the temple and challenge the sovereignty of the Second Temple state.

If we place Mark in the 70s of the first century and do a bit of social sleuthing to determine the troubles faced by the Jesus movement for whom he wrote, the strategy is clear. Mark entertained an apocalyptic imagination of the world in order to salvage a social experiment in confusion and trouble. Note that by Mark's time the temple had been destroyed, though not by God. It was the Romans who, according to Mark's story, were innocent of the crucifixion of Jesus. Thus we can see the viciousness of Mark's narrative plot in which the destruction of the temple serves as the sign for Jesus's innocence and God's vengence upon the Jews. Thus also the historical implausibility of the plot that imagined the reasons for the crucifixion of Jesus linked to the destruction of the temple forty years later. The mythic frame was a compensation for the failure of a social program that had not materialized and the honor of a founder-figure who should have taken the world by storm, but did not. Not yet.

Innocence and Power in Contemporary Christian Imagination

I have gone to some length in the effort to analyze the narrative symbol at the core of the Christian imagination. I have done so by unpacking it in reverse, that is, by showing how it was put together in the first place. I regard all of the cultural backgrounds, conceptual elements, mythic motifs, social motivations, imagistic facets, literary intertextualities, and layers of interpretive nuance as integral to the extremely dense symbol Mark created. I know that Christians have subsequently reshaped and redressed the symbol many times, starting with Matthew's toning down of the dramatic apocalyptic edge of Mark's story, and that some may see that fact as a reason to discount the importance for contemporary times of the Markan variant of the Christian gospel. I also am aware that the Christian and cultural contexts at the turn of the twenty-first century are so much different than those of the first that it is difficult to imagine how some of the facets integral to the symbol at its conception could possibly retain their power. I am thinking, for instance, that our general acceptance of a modern view of the human social enterprise with its orientation to individualistic anthropologies, social democracies, and critical, scientific thinking, makes it very difficult to grasp the cognitive significance of the symbol's fundamental aspects. It may be difficult, for instance, to imagine that a personal mythic figure could function as a symbol of a collective, social unit and its culture. The categories of sovereignty, hierarchy, purity, and honor are also problematic for moderns as factors to be used to theorize the structure of a human society. And yet, who will say that an analysis of Mark's portrayal of Jesus is irrelevant for coming to terms with a contemporary society where Christians want to exercise power?

My own suspicion is that the Markan symbol of the Christ is still very much a part of both the Christian and the American mind. I also think that the Christian gospel has profoundly affected American culture, and that the "hero" in American imagination owes much to the figure of the Christian's Christ. In any case, I would like to present a profile of the American hero in comparison with Mark's portrait of the Christ as a reflection on the construal of power in the contemporary American imagination. The Gospel of Mark came to mind as I read *The American Monomyth* by Robert Jewett and John Lawrence (1977; 1988). According to Jewett and Lawrence, the American hero is super clean and possesses superior power. According to Mark, Jesus was super clean and possessed of superior power. My question was whether the hero and the Christ are related in some way.

In the first edition of their book (1977), Jewett and Lawrence traced the profile of the American hero from the popular novels of the late nineteenth century (such as *Uncle Tom's Cabin* [1868], *Buffalo Bill Cody* [1869], and *The Virginian* [1902]); through the radio serials of the 1920s and 1930s ("The Lone Ranger," for example); the comics of the 1940s (Superman, for instance); and the dime western; to *Playboy,* TV serials (with focus on "Star Trek"), and the cinema of apocalyptic in the late 1970s (such as *Jaws, Earthquake,* and *The Towering Inferno).* Interwoven are vignettes from the daily life of American politics and the articulation of American values by those who momentarily had the public's ear (and then its eye). In the second edition (1988), the list of examples was expanded by including chapters on "Saintly Shootists in a Pop Religion of Death" and "Monomythic Politics: From Star Wars to Olliemania." As one can see, the list of American folk heroes is difficult to place in a single category of fiction. It encompasses real life figures as well as fantastic creations and includes folk heroes and film stars as well as presidents.

The scene is set in the wilderness, whether the dark eastern forests, the wild western expanse, the urban jungle, or the strange and frightening world of galactic adventure. The story opens on a small group of huddled humanity in trouble with some paradisiac vision. This is sometimes cast as the little house on the prairie, sometimes as an enchantment with the pristine beauty of the mountain man's terrain, and sometimes as an edenic enclosure in or near some city, an enclave surrounded by the fright and ugliness of the rest of the world. They are there to find a better life than was possible in the tarnished civilizations they left behind. But they have no plan. The paradisiac vision is not working, and as for the city, the only model available for thinking about society, it is the place where the worst evils always cluster. So troubles come, whether in the form of having to cope with the wild without, or the sad discovery of conflicts within. Recourse to democratic institutions fails, trust in the law turns to suspicion, and the stage is set for the entrance of the hero.

The hero, for his part, arrives untarnished by the history of troubles. He is selfless, chaste, unencumbered by social entanglements. He is a loner, highly charged with confidence, skill, and impeccable perception. He is able to discern the root of the problem, to locate the source of evil, and give immediate chase. Fortunately for the outcome, the hero also has his hands on the latest technology of destruction. From guns to lasers, he can be trusted to use his power for good, for the people's cause is right and the hero is pure. He is the incarnation of altruism, an essentially faceless figure, and even violence at his hands is therefore justified. His shots are straight and his conscience clean.

To take only one well-known example, the good ship *Enterprise* of the series "Star Trek" is on a five-year mission to explore the galaxy. The galaxy is the new frontier, and the old westward-ho and shoot-out plot are accordingly transposed. Unbelievable power is in the hands of two incarnations of goodness, Captain Kirk and Mr. Spock (a sort of Adam III and Mr. Techne). There was an interdiction against interference in any other culture happened upon, in keeping with the high purpose of the mission. And yet, in every episode the captain and the crew encounter an alien culture, put it to the test, find it wanting, and demand its transformation. Resistance ends in violence, and the trekkies scream for more.

In the Gospel of Mark, Jesus suddenly appears in the world with great authority and power. The world is troubled, full of human illness and governed by ineffectual worldly powers. Jesus's power derives from the spirit that God has given him, a spirit which, were the reader not told, might not be recognized as pristine, pure and thoroughly divine. Immediately he announces a new world order called the kingdom of God. He will be the king and he marches into the land to do what has to be done. He enters Galilee, then Capernaum, then the synagogue at Capernaum, and there he confronts the unclean spirit at the heart of the old world's problems. He casts it out, not with a gun, but with a zap nonetheless. The unclean spirit cries out, "What have you to do with us, Jesus of Nazareth? Have you come to destroy us?" The implied answer is, "Yes, indeed." The people respond by saying, "What is this? With authority he commands even the unclean spirits." They are fascinated because of the unbelievable concentration of purity and power in the person of Jesus. Later, as the target of his power turns from the demons to the civilization that housed them, we learn that Jesus is not only the man of power and purity, but that he is innocent as well, innocent of the destruction he has caused and will cause, innocent by virtue of his completely altruistic motivations for the people's cause.

There is not a great deal of difference in the story of Jesus and that of the Virginian, or the Lone Ranger, or Captain Kirk, except that Jesus is divine and that he does get killed. To be sure, those differences have always kept the two stories apart in the American imagination. "Don't confuse the Spirit of God with firepower," is the response; "and don't confuse the sinlessness of the savior with the hero's dedication to his mission. White horses and silver bullets are one thing; sacrificial lambs another. Let's not talk about purity and power in the same breath. Purity belongs to religion and power to politics. So let's just say that the Christ is the Christian's savior, and the popular hero a projection of the can-do of the people. The Christ must die in a mission that first fails in order to save his people. The hero has to win in order to destroy his enemies. The American hero has to do with the dominant popular culture; Mark's story has to do with a powerless movement concerned only with personal salvation. So how can both stories be related?" Thus the difference that makes a difference between these two stories, otherwise quite similar, in the mind of most Americans, comes to focus on the death of the Christ.

But can the fact that Jesus gets killed be the redemptive feature that makes the Christian myth a constructive and helpful story for Christians living in a hero's world? What if we notice that Mark Part I (the appearance of the man of power in Galilee, Chapters 1–8) and Mark Part II (from the transfiguration through the passion narrative, Chapters 9–16) are actually quite separable scenarios, and that, given a changing social history, now one and now the other may come into more prominent and timely focus for a people? Even the sequence between power and powerlessness, or victimage and victory, or violence and the peaceable kingdom, can shift depending upon the application of the myth to a social situation and the way in which the righteous ones identify themselves with Jesus, whether as victim or victor. The apocalyptic moment, for its part, also can shift its correlation with social history depending on the nation's perception of its purity and power. For much of our history the United States has cultivated a millennial mentality as if, in this land and people the kingdom has come, is rightly coming, with power. Recently, however, America's failures to fulfill its missions have precipitated a sense of lost power, and the apocalyptic vision has been relocated into the future. When that happens, the tragic, redemptive, anti-hero scenario of Mark Part II and beyond finds its fascination. Thus, both martyrdom and the destruction of the enemy, whether executed by the righteous nation, the foreign power, or God, can vindicate the righteous cause.

It is also the case that, as Scott Johnson wrote in the *Los Angeles Times* (Opinion, May 7, 1985), "The image of American innocence is central to our country's consciousness," and that "Even our failures . . . seem merely to persuade us that, like all messiahs, we may be at times too good, too eager with our help, and so become the victim of an undeserving or ungrateful world." Note that, in the shift to an apocalyptic frame for either a reading of the gospel or a re-imagination of the hero, the sign of failure and the sign of victory are identical. The sign is a violent destruction in which victim and victor are simply factors of opposition in an equation of double inversion. The inversions depend on how one assigns the values of purity and innocence. Thus both martrydom and the destruction of the enemy, whether executed by the righteous nation, the foreign power, or God, can vindicate the righteous cause. As the embarrassing line left hanging from the Vietnam War has it, "We had to destroy them in order to save them." With such a symbol imagined at the beginning of the Christian era, and such a sign projected into the future for an eventual vindication of the righteous kingdom, Christians and Americans win either way, violence notwithstanding, as long as the man of power, purity, and innocence leads the way. Does it make any difference whether that man is the Christ or the American's hero? It is the concentration of power, purity, and innocence in a single anthropological figure and symbol that marks America's mythological mentality and signals to the rest of the world our danger. If so, the so-called redemptive feature of the Christian myth only accentuates America's affair with the heroic. It is that obsession that seems to be the problem whenever we run into trouble with the use and abuse of power and seek to address it.

Whether a myth's function is to provide a model for social construction, or a constructive escape from the messiness of life in the real world, neither the American hero nor the Christian's Christ appear to be helpful symbols for our time. They do not provide a helpful model for taking responsibility for problem solving of the kind required for the social democracies we are trying to construct. They frustrate our coming to terms with post-modern intelligence about the irresponsibility of laying blame on or hoping for help from external saviors and authorities. And they keep us from thinking clearly about power and powerlessness as factors to be considered and addressed in the construction and maintenance of societies wherever we may encounter them. The myths may have set an agenda for naming a problem, but they have not helped to solve it. Neither looks to the social arena for help or hope. Both encourage personal reenactment. The reduction of either mythic figure to an individualistic symbol for personal assessment or reenactment can only frustrate the social analysis called for in our time. We need to understand much more clearly the many structural arrangements of power required in a society that wants to balance powers, limit greed, control predation, negotiate interests, celebrate difference, mourn loss, appreciate the everyday, and enjoy one another's foibles. Yes, and delight in the privilege of living in a beautiful and fragile world, so fragile in fact, that the marvels of the human enterprise might be measured, not only by our efforts not to destroy one another, but by our efforts not to destroy the ecology of the natural world that supports us. If so, the time has come for a cultural critique that includes taking a hard look at the myths of the hero and the Christ.

CHAPTER SEVEN

Christ and the Creation of a Monocratic Culture

Introduction

One of the defining features of western Christian culture has been a predilection for monism. Preference for the singular over the dual and the many comes to expression, for instance, in the ranking of monotheism over polytheism, the "problem" of the one and the many, and the concepts of one faith, one church, and one Christian world. Because the world has finally been recognized as multicultural, and the Christian mission to convert the whole world to the one true faith is hardly possible, mono-thinking has become highly problematic. Some would say that Christian and western mono-mentality is actually dangerous in our pluralistic, global age. Christian thought has found it very difficult to accommodate difference, appreciate plurality, and accept negotiation as skills necessary for the construction of societies. The question is whether we can be more precise about the reasons for such a mentality.

I want to explore the genesis of those reasons at the beginnings of Christianity. To set the stage for my deliberations, I shall have to begin with some traditional clichés, knowing that in the course of the chapter each will have to be revised. I refer to commonly held generalizations used to distinguish the Semitic, Egyptian, Hellenic and Roman cultures that collided and merged during the Greco-Roman age. My thesis will be that the particular form of monotheistic thinking characteristic of early Christian thought resulted from a cross-cultural merger of mythologies in the course of forming groups that were experimenting with novel social ideas. Mythologies of divine agency in the interest of a particular people, characteristic of Semitic cultures of the ancient Near East, were combined with concepts of cosmic power and order taken largely from the hellenic traditions of philosophy. Thus the domain of a single God, attached specifically to a certain people and their land, was expanded cosmically to universal horizons. The reasons for this development were related not only to the fact that the people of this God's concern, whether Jews, Samaritans, Christians, or some other combination of Semitic and gentile peoples, were dispersed throughout the Greco-Roman world. It was also the case that traditional ways of imagining the world were inadequate to conceptualize the newly experienced multicultural world. Meeting the challenge of constructing a coherent universe by putting together bits and pieces from different cultural traditions must have offered its own intellectual satisfactions. The problem was that the expanded universe included many peoples and their gods who were not beholden to the Jewish and Christian God. And this God had a rather stern streak to his character, demanding exclusive loyalty and obedience to a strict code of ethics governed by the concepts of divine justice and righteousness. It was this combination of a particularistic God with the notion of a universal scope for his legitimate domain that created the conditions for the peculiar mythology we now recognize as Christian.

In order to imagine this God taking charge of the Greco-Roman world, moreover, early Christian mythology was cast in decidedly monocratic modes. This monocratic mythology militated against Christians coming to terms with the pluralistic social and cultural world in which they lived. Other peoples found ways of accounting for cultural difference that did not demand uniformity. Christians developed the notions of *message, conversion, paganism,* and *catholic,* all of which implied that all other peoples should worship and obey the one true Christian God. Both the logic of this mythology and the social reasons for its emergence need to be grasped in order to understand its original attraction and evaluate its continuing effect throughout western history. I shall try to keep both the conceptual and the social dimensions in mind as I proceed. I want to develop the thesis in four stages: (1) The building blocks of a monocratic mythology; (2) the genealogy of a monocractic worldview; (3) the mentality of a Christian culture; and (4) the history of a Christian civilization. At the end I shall list several reasons why I think Christian monocratic mentality obstructs critical thinking about contemporary social and cultural issues.

The Building Blocks of a Monocratic Mythology

In the traditional imagination of Christian origins, the significant moments usually focus on the person of Jesus as viewed through the gospel story. For the critical scholar and historian of religion, however, the gospel story presents many more questions than answers about the emergence of the new religion. Instead of thinking that Christianity started all of a sudden as a human response to the divine appearance of an incomparable personage and his miraculous destiny, as the gospels have it, the critical scholar tries to account for the gospel story itself as one among many different myths of origin that emerged in the movements that claimed Jesus as their founder. This mythmaking activity took place in the course of social experiments whose energies must be explained primarily as interest in responding to their social and cultural circumstances. Only at the end of about 300 years can the historian catch sight of a comprehensive system of mythology and social construction that resembles the institution of religion we call Christianity, the religious institution that has played such a role in shaping western culture. If we let these first 300 years define the period of Christian origins, instead of thinking that everything significant must have happened during the life of Jesus, four building blocks can be identified that structured its mythic system. These are the concepts of God, Christ, the church, and the Bible. In every case, the attributions of singularity and unity characteristic of mono-thinking are characteristic if not fundamental for the concept.

God.   To imagine a single deity, patronymic hero, or event at the beginning of the world is not peculiar to Christianity. All peoples usually do. A first father of the gods, heroes, kings, and world was in fact a customary image for the peoples of antiquity, whether projected as the lord of a pantheon, chthonic hero, or cosmic power. But, as everyone knew, these powers were intimately related to a particular people and their place on the earth. A particular people was known as an *ethnos* ("tribe," "nation," from which in the English

155

language we get "ethnic"), and every *ethnos* had its own gods and particular culture. The Greeks made a game of describing the new gods they encountered as they moved from place to place in the multicultural world of the eastern Mediterranean. Herodotus presents an excellent illustration of this kind of interest in other cultures. As long as there were many peoples untroubled by the fact that there were other cultures in the world, it did not seem strange that there were many father-gods. Even the Jewish attempt to reduce their own mythologies to a monotheistic concentration did not require a denial that other peoples had other gods. The rub came when armies marched, peoples merged, cultures clashed, and the domains of the gods changed hands, as happened in the wake of Alexander. It was then that the way a god was treated in relation to the other gods required rethinking. Both Jews and Christians of the first centuries took for granted the polytheistic world in which they lived, though they may have called the gods of some other peoples demons. One can trace the Christian denigration of the gods to demons from Paul (Cf. 1 Cor 8:5–6; 10:20–22), through Clement of Alexandria (Cf. *The Exhortation to the Greeks*), to Theodosius I (and the rationales of his bishops for the many pogroms instituted against the so-called pagan religions). This was not the only way of treating other gods. Most people looked for the ways in which their gods and the gods of other peoples were similar, and thought of each as a manifestation of the same divine power. A common practice was to combine the names or attributes of two deities. One could also list the names of many gods for other localities that exercised functions similar to one's own, then say that the name of one's own deity was the true name of the god. The Christian God did not assimilate. Christians emphasized the particularity of his activity in the sending of his son, and the incredible concentration of purpose in his plan to establish his righteous kingdom. There was no room for compromise in the minds of these early Christians. Their audacity was not merely the claim to be the only ones to know the one true God, but to make of his domain a universal canopy destined to encompass all peoples. As the *christos* hymn in Philippians 2 put it, a bit prematurely to be sure, ". . . every knee should bend . . . , and every tongue confess that Jesus *christos* is Lord, to the glory of God the father" (Phil 2:10–11). It was the universal scope of a particularistic god imagined by a *people* unconnected to any particular land or *ethnos* that eventually spelled intolerance. Where did such *audacious* ideas come from?

The Christ.   One of the embarrassments for Christians has always been the conceptual contradiction between a monotheistic claim and a dualistic or even a triune image of God. This conceptual oddity got started with the elevation of the man Jesus to divine status as the Christ and son of God. As we have seen, recent studies of this process during the first one-hundred years of Christian mythmaking picture a spotty history of colorful images of Jesus against a rugged social landscape marked by very different kinds of groups. There was no uniformity to the views about Jesus, and it is impossible to trace a monolinear history of the one Christian church from Jerusalem to Rome as Luke wanted his readers to imagine. There were schools, movements, enclaves, associations, households, congregations, and cults. In every case of mythmaking focused upon the figure of Jesus, the attributions can be understood as roles appropriate for the founder of the movements that various groups had produced. Many were energized by grandiose claims to represent what most of them called the kingdom of God, an idealistic social order of universal scope and ultimate destiny. These social experiments were eager to claim divine authority for their teachings, ideals, and movements, and they gravitated toward myths that attributed divine wisdom and authority to Jesus as their founder. The social roles of teacher, prophet, sage, and messiah gave way to myths of cosmic and apocalyptic destiny. This was all in the interest of imagining that their views of the kingdom of God were right and destined to be actualized. Human features were combined with godlike functions in the single image of the historic man of cosmic destiny.

One of the more important myths, common for the times, was that of the son of the high father god destined to inherit the father's kingdom. This myth was easily pressed into service by some early Christians. It granted Jesus divine generation and made it possible to imagine his appearance in the world, his importance as a founder-figure, and his destiny as a cosmic king. The reasons for the emergence of this mythology are easily seen. In order to imagine how their claim to be the new people of God could be true, the connection between Jesus, the founder of their movements, and the God of universal domain, had to be close. The result, however, was a conceptual confusion created by the composite image of a god-man held to be a singular manifestation of the high creator-God. If the Christian imagination of their God as the one true God was audacious, given the multicultural world in which they lived and the fact that they were actually only an insignificant minority movement, the Christian view of Jesus as the Christ and son of God might be called *fantastic*. We can now begin to see not only the conceptual extravagance that these early Christians were willing to entertain, but their incursive sense of presence in the world. To say that their Jesus was the *only* son of God, as in the Gospel of John (John 1:18), or that there was "no other name under heaven given among mortals by which we must be saved," as in Peter's sermon in Acts (Acts 4:12), is more than monomania. It turns an exclusive claim to ultimate justification into an absolute and universal principle of judgment about the rest of humankind. These conceptual contradictions in the development of Christian theology seem to be related to the extravagant claims of a people who thought of themselves as the only representatives of a superior and uncompromising social vision.

The Church.   Though we usually take the concept of the church for granted, and think that the notion of the one true and universal church was a natural development rooted in that concept, nothing of the kind was thinkable at the beginning. What we now know is that many different movements, groups, and congregations formed in the wake and name of Jesus, and the term *ecclesia* ("gathering," "assembly of citizens," *church*) began to be used in only one type of gathering. This happened among the Pauline congregations oriented to a cult of the cosmic *christos*. During the time of Paul, moreover, the term was used only for an individual local congregation. It was not used to refer to all of the congregations together as a single entity or of a social organization that bound them together as a network. That soon happened, however, as the use of the term in the Gospel of Matthew (Matt 16:18; 18:17), the letters to the Colossians and Ephesians, and the letters of Ignatius shows. Eventually the term *ecclesia* was used to describe the network of congregations over which bishops presided and so became the name of an organization that thought of itself as the caretaker of orthodoxy. The many other forms of Christian persuasion now had to compete for official recognition by reaching agreements with the church on matters of practice and belief. How in the world did such an idea get started?

New Testament scholars point in two directions. One partial analogy is the way in which associations *(collegia)* and cults formed networks of hospitality for travelers. The other model was that of the network of Jewish synagogues in dispersion throughout the Roman world. We cannot be sure that Christians were consciously following either model. But the similarities of the *ecclesiai* to the synagogue model suggests that a common social anthropology must have been involved. There is much evidence for a pervasive early Christian social anthropology of a type similar to Jewish concepts of the people of God. Thus the notion of the one church must have been closely related to the notion of being one *people (ethnos)*. The problem in this case was that belonging to a *people* had always been a matter of ethnic extraction and loyalty to its cultural tradition. The early Christians were *not* an *ethnos*. They were of mixed constituency and some even emphasized that fact. And despite their claims upon Jewish cultural traditions, Christians were decidedly *not* being Jewish in most of their ways. So what about the early Christian claim to being a *people* when they were not? What about their sense of presence in the world, calling themselves the assembly of citizens? What about their creating a network of local congregations on the model of the diaspora synagogue and calling themselves the Israel of God? If early Christian theology was audacious, and the early christologies were fantastic, what adjective shall we use to describe the claim that underlay this emerging concept of the church? Scholars are now using the term *fiction* to describe the early Christian claims to being a *family* of *brothers* and *sisters*. Paul used the hyperbole *new creation* to express the obvious fact that Christians were not a normal *ethnos*, but a new way of constituting the "Israel of God" (2 Cor 5:17; Gal 6:15–16). Are not these stunning expressions of a most amazing social notion? Why not call such a social posture *imperious*?

The Bible. The Bible was a Christian creation of the fourth century. Christians normally do not think of the Bible as the product of Christian mythmaking activity, but as the record of the history it recounts. At most, the Bible is thought to *contain* some myths, but not as a whole to *be* a myth. I have followed the process of the making of the Christian Bible in *Who Wrote the New Testament?* (1995). I came to the conclusion that the final selection and arrangement of these writings to form the Christian Bible was designed to create an epic charter for the church. *Epic* refers to an account of a people's past, usually with a focus upon their land, temple, or illustrious ancestors that give the people identity. Epic frequently delves into the remote past, as far back as the precedent-setting events of the culture or even the creation of the world if possible. It must link up the ancestors with the gods and sweep through all history to end with the contemporary social formation of the people as if it were exactly what the gods had in mind from the beginning.

The Jewish scriptures were the epic of Israel, a "history" that was supposed to end in the establishment of the temple-state in Jerusalem as the capital city of the land of Israel and the center of worship of the one true God who would attract even the gentiles to gather around. When Jerusalem and the temple were destroyed in the Roman-Jewish war of 66–73 B.C.E., the ending of the epic was thrown into confusion. Christians eventually took advantage of this confusion and read the history in such a way as to suggest that Jesus as the Christ (now understood as "the Messiah"), and the church as the new Israel, had been the proper goals of the story of Israel all along. They needed to do this because, without an epic history of their own, Christians could only claim to be a novelty, and novelties were not thought of as good news in late antiquity. They had, as a matter of fact, been criticized by the Greeks and Romans for thinking they were a new kind of people on the basis of a brand new revelation. Much of their earlier literature did sound that way. At first, everything important was said to have started with Jesus. That was the way the gospels read, Paul preached, and Luke's history sounded. Most of the early writings had found it helpful to imagine Jesus in roles that were reminiscent of this or that role of historical importance for the people of Israel. But it was not until the fourth century when the bishops made a selection of early Christian writings, attached them to the Jewish scriptures, and made some arrangements in sequence, that the Bible as a whole emerged as the Christian epic. Thus the church was exactly what the God of Israel had had in mind from the creation of the world.

A slight problem was that, on closer inspection, and read as a whole, the Jewish scriptures were still more the story of God and the Jews than the average reader found comfortable. As Marcion said, to read the Old Testament as the story of the Christians' God one would have to conclude that he changed his mind, destroyed the Jews for not obeying his law, then offered salvation to the gentiles without demanding that they keep his law. Since that did not make sense, Marcion said that the God of the Old Testament could not be the same as the Christian God. That caused consternation for Justin Martyr and other second-century theologians. So various schemes had to be devised in order to interpret the Jewish scriptures some other way. "Look," these Christian scholars said, "the story shows that the Jews never did understand, much less obey, what God wanted of them. They forced God to punish them, didn't they? And as for God changing his mind, that can't be right. Don't you see that he was trying to get the Jews to tell the gentiles about him all the time?" This is the way Justin Martyr read the Old Testament. His favorite device was to use an allegory of the *logos*, a curiously faceless mythic figure popular with certain Jewish and hellenistic philosophers of the time. "The *logos*," Justin said, "could be discerned hiding behind and speaking through the enigmatic words of God and the prophets throughout the Jewish scriptures. This mysterious *logos* was in reality God's son, the Christ, trying to get the Jews to listen. The Jews never did hear the voice of God's son or understand the deeper meaning of God's instruction to them. That is why God finally sent his son, Jesus the Christ, and why the Old Testament is really the story of the Christians' God."

So the Jewish scriptures became the Christian epic. But notice that in order for the "history" of the Jews to be read as the Christian epic, it had to be in *textual* form, and the text *had* to be read as an allegory with the "true" meaning "hidden" until discerned by the Christians. Only in this way could the Bible take its place as integral to the Christian mythic system. The astonishing thing about this fiction is that the Bible has been accepted as a true account of the history of Israel by all peoples converted to Christianity wherever the church has spread. And this historical fiction has succeeded in suppressing all other histories of the peoples, because this is the only history that is said to be true, that tells of salvation for those who convert. It has served, as a matter of fact, as an account of the prehistory of western civilization and thus as the monolinear outline of all human history. Thus an implausible allegory has served as the history of humankind and canceled out the importance, often the memory, of the indigenous histories of all other peoples converted to Christianity. What shall we call this kind of cultural conquest, the acquisition of an epic not one's own, laid down as the only history of value for coming to know the one true God and belonging to his people, a particular history that counts as universal? Shouldn't we call it *arrogant*?

The Genealogy of a Monocratic Worldview

I have used the terms *audacious, fantastic, imperious,* and *arrogant* to describe the claims implicit to the four building blocks of Christian mythology. I want now to offer a kind of apology for these early Christians by suggesting that they may have had their own good reasons for thinking the way they did. The apology can begin by observing the clash of cultures that characterized the Greco-Roman age. In the wake of Alexander peoples were dispersed, temple-states were broken, city-states were misused as means for colonial conquest, cultural institutions were fragmented, and social life as traditionally lived in every land and district of the eastern Mediterranean was penetrated by the successive overlay of several foreign powers. No ancient culture survived the collision intact. This does not mean that everyone experienced the Greco-Roman age as a social crisis or thought of it as a cultural tragedy. Energies were unleashed that we might call creative, entrepreneurial, and adventuresome. The basic institutions of production, marketing, festivals, education, and travel continued to work. And people moved freely to take advantage of the opportunities for making a better living in some other city. But the bursts of intellectual energy documented by the production of literature during this period, and the emergence of experimentation in the formation of clubs *(collegia)* and other associations that flourished in this time, tell us that the clash of cultures had taken its toll, and that the burgeoning of social and intellectual experimentation was driven by a desire to salvage some fragments of traditional cultures, reconceive the world that was now multicultural, and reconstruct society to allow cross-cultural intercourse and enhance individual integrity. One can imagine both the frustration and the exhilaration called forth by attempts to make coherent sense of life in a pluralistic and multicultural world, a world for which the traditional philosophies, theologies, cultures, and ethics were no longer adequate.

Erik Peterson devoted several studies to the development of monotheism as a social and cultural consequence of the Greco-Roman age (1926, 1935, 1951). The important ingredient had to do with the location and conceptuality of political power. It was not a "religious" reflection upon the nature of "one God" that was critical, but the notion of a single ruler *(mia archon)* that eventually produced the concept and terminology of a monotheistic monarchy. Peterson traced the history of this concept from Homer through Plato, Aristotle, the pseudo-Aristotelian writing called "On the World," the Isis aretalogies, Philo, and early Christian writings to show that the models used at each juncture to imagine the worlds of the gods and the cosmos were taken from the several political systems under review at the time. Of some importance for the picture characteristic for the first Christian century was the Persian model with its "hidden" sovereign and fully empowered satrapies who functioned as the sovereign's agents throughout the domain of his power. As I read Peterson, the intellectual problem of imagining a single ruler and god was called forth by social and multicultural fragmentation and driven by the desire to reimagine a comprehensive order on the (inadequate) models of older organic social arrangements.

The early Jesus movements and the first congregations of Jesus *christos* attracted people who were fully aware of the inadequacy of traditional social arrangements and who were eager to experiment with new ideas and new ways of living together. As discussed in Chapters 5 and 6, they were all driven by what might be called a social vision, the outlines of which are formally quite similar. The earliest and most common name for this vision was the *kingdom of god (basileia tou theou*, "domain," "sovereignty," "reign of god"). Though vague and capable of many different elaborations, this term gives us a clue to the basic ideology of the Jesus movement, and to the reasons people had for being attracted to it and investing themselves in it. We might call it the vision of a society alternative to the *status quo,* one based on a theocratic model to counter the tyrannies of the Alexandrian successors and the harsh, soulless practicality of the Roman imperium. This agrees with other terms soon to be used by these groups, such as the Israel of God, the people of God, the temple of God, or the assembly of God. A theocratic vision also explains why the many mythic roles ascribed to Jesus in various groups, such as Christ, Lord, son of man, son of David, and son of God overlap at the point of attributing royal authority or kingship to him. And as for the universal horizon of the new social vision, it was rooted in the desire to encompass the many cultural traditions and the fragmented social realities in a new conceptual arrangement of the whole. No wonder these groups were bubbling with excitement. They were experimenting with ethnic mixes, fictive families, forums for disenfranchised intellectuals, revisionary histories, displaced cultural artifacts, novel ethics, hybrid philosophies, personal transformations, new calendars, feasts, and festivals—all energized by a social vision called the *kingdom of God.* It was, in effect, an exhilarating way to say good-bye to the past and take up its shards for creative re-arrangements.

In a sense, the extravagance of the Christian system of mythology that I have underscored can be explained by the social and cultural circumstances of this experimentation. The constraints customary to a person's placement in a traditional, fully orbed and working society had lost their sanctions. For daring individuals with sensitivity to issues of identity and ethics, power and justice, social well-being and cultural constructs, persons willing to entertain new thoughts and ways, the sky was apparently the limit. Caution on our part is called for, however, in that much of what strikes us moderns as fantastic about the early Christian myths was actually quite in keeping with the worldviews of the ancients. Notions we might find incredible, but which were common coin of the times, included such things as the cosmos penetrated by divine powers; a hierarchy of the powers and gods; a continuum of gods, heroes, and divine men; divine appearances, revelations, and maps of the heavenly world; miracles, magic, and cults of divine presence. The extravagance of the early Christian myths did not lie in notions such as these, but in the stretch created by the odd combinations of mythic images from different cultures used to imagine a universe fit for the Christian fascination with its new social order. Even from the point of view of intelligent non-Christians of the time, the intellectual bricolage characteristic of early Christian mythmaking did not always succeed in fitting together disparate myths to create a coherent mythology. There were many rough seams, embarrassing intellectual incompatibilities, and grotesque combinations of images along the way. Examples would be the unavoidable suggestions, unintended by those who first dared a combination of images to rationalize some other persuasion or practice, that God had sent his son *to be* crucified; that Jesus's crucifixion was a *sacrifice;* that the one who came to be the messiah and king of Israel ended up as the *lord of all* peoples *because* the Jews killed him and God transformed him into a cosmic king; that the spirit of the transformed Jesus, the spirit of God, and the physical spirit that held the cosmos together according to Greek thought were one and the same thing; that imitating Jesus's martyrdom was the way to personal salvation; and so forth. The problem was that the social vision itself was so vague and idealistic from the beginning, so out of touch with reality, that its elaboration only made the matter worse. The cosmic dramas needed to imagine the inauguration of the kingdom of God announced by Jesus his Christ and son eventually filled the horizons of all time and space, pushing everything that could not be merged with the all-encompassing mythology to oblivion. Thus the gap between the mythic world imagined by Christians and the real world in which they still actually lived became unbridgeable.

We might, however, want to give these early Christians credit for trying. And we might want to appreciate their adamant refusal not to give up on questions of social justice and personal significance. But the costs to the integrity of the human mind and spirit were enormous. Not only was the vision hopelessly idealistic to begin with; the kingdom of God soon had to be imagined either as a heavenly spiritual realm in contrast to the earthly kingdoms, or else its establishment on earth had to be deferred until the end of history and its apocalyptic denouement. That robbed temporal existence of its current significance for the Christian. And as for the church, which did have temporal significance as the guardian of the vision, it hardly provided a place to work out a social experiment to match the productive societies of the Greco-Roman imperiums. And so the concerns for social justice and personal well-being that generated the original vision had to be redirected. The church would settle for the age-old role of playing priest to the kings of the Roman imperium and its successors. It would eventually make a place for the rulers of this world in its divine cosmology. And as for the church as the representation of the kingdom of God on earth, there was little more to do than make sure that every Christian finally arrived at the real (spiritual) kingdom in the sky. The relentless focus of divine obligation on the individual, the introspective conscience of the west, and the notion that religion is primarily a matter of personal experience and piety, are all aberrations of the human capacity for constructing sane societies. They are aberrations created by the incredible extravagance of the Christian system of myth and its ritualization in the church. Thus there are limits to the apology I offer for the mythmaking of the early Christians. As a remarkable response to a particularly challenging moment of human history, the invention of the Christian mythic system can be appreciated. But as a cultural legacy, suppressing all other views and so creating the monocratic mentality of western civilization, the scholarly assessment will have to be much different. It is time we asked about the inherent logic of the Christian myth and the effective difference it has made in the history of western civilization.

The Mentality of a Christian Culture

The Christian fascination with the single and singular image, whether of God, the kingdom of God, the Christ, human history, or the individual person, has always been held in tension with the less comfortable acknowledgment of its opposite. The individual person created for a blissful destiny might actually become a lost soul. Peripheral vision catches sight of human histories untouched by the gospel. The Christ, both human and divine, is ultimately neither fully human nor fully divine, and his destiny is marked by violence. The kingdom of God is never actualized by the kingdoms of this world and its Christ-king must struggle to the end against the forces of hell. And as for God, there is always evil to contend with, if not the prince of demons himself. These oppositions create a series of ranked pairs that define a particular form of dualism characteristic for Christian thought. Ultimately, the dualism is overcome in the imagination of victory for the Christian symbols and the banishment to outer darkness of their troublesome opposites. Thus monocracy wins. But for the meantime, a kind of dialectic pertains that calls for a radical event of transformation to shift from the one to the other. Thus the inculcation of the Christian mythic system has created a peculiar mentality capable of accepting opposition, conflict, and violence in the interest of protecting a monocratic ideal. I should like to analyze the logic of the four building blocks of Christian mythology in respect to this observation. What we find in every case is a built-in double dialectic. Two oppositions define the complex dualistic images. One opposition is internal to the image itself; the other occurs in the relation of the image to its setting or the larger world in which it operates.

The Christian concept of **God** is rife with internal tensions. These are sometimes grasped as the difference between person and being, agent and cosmic spirit, or transcendence and immanence. This tension may derive from the merger of a Jewish theology, where a "jealous god" exercised agency in the interest of a particular land and people, with a Greek notion of the *arche*, the first principle of cosmic being. But however derived, and however understood as an interesting intellectual puzzle capable of teasing a long line of western philosophers and theologians, this internal tension is always matched by some external opposition to God located in his creation, his human creatures, or the demonic spirits that share with him the control of the world. This opposition has given the Christian drive for a monocratic solution great impetus and energy.

The **Christ** is also a composite figure defined by an internal tension between the human and the divine. This was not a problem for antiquity, however, until the importance of the Christ for personal salvation came under review. This external relationship of the Christ to Christians was extremely tensive, offering a model for imitation on the one hand, while standing over against the Christian as lord on the other. Each pole of the relationship, the one anchored in the humanity of the Christ and offering the possibility of the *imitatio Christi*, the other rooted in the divinity of the Christ and offering a vindication that only God could give, canceled the other out. A complete *imitatio Christi* was impossible; an ultimate vindication would have to wait. This deferral of a resolution to the dialectic of Christ as lord and savior has given the Christian conscience a great desire for cleansing and release.

Christians have never been able to agree on the proper location for the spiritual kingdom of God, whether in heaven as a present reality, or as a reality only to be realized at the end of time. And its relation to the other spiritual domain, this one called hell, is also very fuzzy as the many notions of after-life and purgatories show. As with the Christian concepts of God and the Christ, however, the tension that counts in this case resides in the relation this mythic image sustains to its external oppositions. The kingdoms of the earth are not the kingdom of God, though they "should" be; the **church** dare not claim to be the kingdom of God, though it claims to administer the rule of God; and the Christians invited into the church get to the kingdom only by making a long and lonesome personal journey that ends beyond one's lifetime. The gap between the Christian notion of the kingdom of God and the realities of the human societies we construct has given the Christian desire for well-being a decidedly personal and otherworldly focus.

In the case of the **Bible,** the internal tension is clearly between the Old and the New Testaments; the external tension between the biblical epic and all of the other histories of the world. In order to work as the Christian epic, the church's charter, and as the story of salvation, both tensions, the internal and the external, must be overcome in the reading. A single story has to be traced through all of western history from the beginning of time until the end of the world, and a single set of events, unfortunately missing from all other histories of the world, needs to be marked as the acts of God. It is not always seen that the Christian significance of the so-called Christ-event requires the Christian interpretation of the Jewish epic as precursor and preparation. And it is hardly ever acknowledged that the Christian interpretation of the Old Testament requires an allegorization that is forced and illogical. Christians seldom admit that at the level of Jewish myth and history the Jewish epic is clearly *not* a story in search of a Christian ending. And at the level of the Christian allegory of the Old Testament the logic breaks down in two distinct ways. The first is, as Justin Martyr knew full well, that the details of the gospel *story* of the Christ could only be discerned here and there throughout the Old Testament, and that these snippets of allegorical significance do not hang together as a coherent narrative theme. This means that the Christian allegorization of the Old Testament was forced, or rather that the Old Testament could not really be read honestly as an allegory of the gospel at all. The second logical infelicity had to do with the christological significance of the supposed allegory. As Justin also knew, the significance of the "deeper meanings" encoded in the Old Testament texts was *prophetic*. The significance of Jesus as the Christ could only be established by noting that he had "fulfilled" these unconnected prophecies and expectations of his coming. That means, however, that the Christian allegory of the Old Testament is only possible in retrospect. Thus it is an allegory "in advance" of the story that makes it an allegory. That is no allegory at all. It is a trick that the exegete plays on himself at the expense of his own intellectual integrity. So what was a poor Christian exegete and theologian to do? The answer was, as Justin expressly said, to realize that the deeper meaning of the words and deeds of God in the Old Testament, where the allegory of the coming Christ resided, *could not* have been grasped by the Jews. The deeper meaning could only be located, and this is the terribly embarrassing part, in the mind of God. To deny the logical contradictions inherent in such an allegorical enterprise has required a long history of entertaining mystification at the expense of reason in the Christian quest for a monocratic construction of both cosmos and history.

No wonder the resolutions to the double dialectic inherent in the Christian mythic system, one having to do with the internal logic of the system, the other with its application to the real world, require the imagination of dramatic events held to be unique and thought capable of resolving the opposition by destroying or transforming the negative term. The unfortunate consequence of such a resolution to such a problem is that the event invariably must be radical and violent, destroying the opposition in order to position the victor as absolute. Note that the pairs are ranked and that only those on the monocratic side of the dualities are thought to be worthy of victory. For the Christian, the events of paradigmatic significance are the crucifixion and resurrection of the Christ and the apocalyptic ending to personal, human, and world histories. These paradigms serve as the model for the ultimate solution to the problems of duality, opposition, and conflict. Is it possible for such a far-fetched mythology, and such an extreme solution to conflict, to penetrate an entire culture and determine its mentality? The answer is yes.

The History of a Christian Civilization

The history of western civilization and the spread of Christianity are largely parallel stories. The correlation has been true of the Roman era missions (fourth to sixth centuries), the encounter with Islam (seventh to ninth centuries), the crusades (eleventh and twelfth centuries), the period of European empires (twelfth to fourteenth centuries), the so-called age of discovery (fifteenth to seventeenth centuries), the era of colonization (eighteenth and nineteenth centuries), and the modern period of globalization (twentieth century). The customary rationale for the spread of Christianity is rooted in the concept of *mission*. The idea is that Christians naturally want (or at least should want) to take the truth of Christianity to all those who live in ignorance of the one true God and the salvation he offers through his son Jesus Christ. One problem with this rationale is that the notion of mission is *not* natural to the religions of the world and thus cannot be taken for granted in application to the Christian religion. It is exceptional, as a matter of fact, and much in need of explanation. The usual appeals to the New Testament only work as long as the notion itself remains unexamined. This is true of the so-called "mission speech" of Jesus (Luke 10:1–12); the "missions" of Paul; the twofold "mission," one to the Jews and one to the gentiles; the "great commission" (Matt 28:19–20); and Luke's "history" of the spread of Christianity from Jerusalem to Rome. None of these texts can be used to *explain* the attraction and spread of early Christianities. All of these texts are curious rationalizations after the fact of the spread of this or that Christian movement for reasons other than a missionary motivation. None can be used to clarify the reasons for the later emergence of the Christian concept of *mission*. None can anchor the notion of mission firmly in the logic of the Christian mythic system.

And when we try to correlate the notion of mission with the subsequent history of the spread of Christianity, it doesn't work. One can hardly claim that Christians have always been motivated with a passion to bring enlightenment and salvation to every human being. Since Constantine, the ebb and flow of Christian influence has followed the expansion and contraction of political spheres of influence friendly to the church. The so-called Christian missions since the age of discovery have always taken place under the shadow of what we might call the canopy of the political influence and interests of a Christian nation. A variety of interests can be identified for the expansion of western civilization to encompass the other peoples of the world. The one interest that does not appear to be primary is a concern for the spiritual well-being of the natives. The pattern has been that Christian missionaries have *followed* in the wake of the explorers, traders, generals, colonists, and provincial governors of the western nations. Why? The answer must lie elsewhere than in the Christian notion of mission with its implicit claim to altruistic interest in the salvation of the unenlightened. It must be found in the logic of the relationship that Christianity has sustained with the kings of western civilization.

A remarkable change in the history of the early churches took place during the time of Constantine and Eusebius. By conscious design, the emperor and the bishop decided to work together in the construction of a religious institution that would have the official blessing of the state. Christendom can be dated from that time, an arrangement between the scepter and the staff that still haunts us. One way to understand what happened is to see the Constantinian revolution as a reconstitution of an ancient model of civilization most clearly exemplified in the Near Eastern temple-state. As discussed in Chapter 6, Jonathan Z. Smith has analyzed this model in *To Take Place: Toward Theory in Ritual*. The model consists of two hierarchical systems of difference, one of power located in the king, and one of purity located in the high priest. This model had been unworkable since the time of Alexander, and the designs of Constantine upon the Christian churches could hardly have been motivated by an interest in recreating antiquity. But the model of an empire centered in a temple and a palace must have continued to resonate and the result of the liaison struck by these two leaders was formally similar. The Christian bishops would guarantee purity and pray for the emperor; the emperor would guarantee protection and the exercise of executive power. And so Christianity changed its ways. Signs of the new status were basilicas, liturgies, interpretations of the eucharist as a willing sacrifice, priests in charge of sacred places, temples constructed in Palestine, pilgrimage, cults of the martyrs, creeds, monks, other-worldly pieties, and with Augustine what Krister Stendahl has called the introspective conscience of the west. Christianity was no longer a religious association experimenting with a theocratic vision of an alternative society. It was now the religion of a priesthood in charge of the purity of the people and their loyalty to the state.

What happened to the kingdom of God? What happened to cultural critique? What happened to the Christian vision of an alternative society, to the monocratic mythic system, to the figure of Christ the cosmic King? Well, it does seem as if the second and third century displacements and deferrals of the kingdom of God to spiritual and eschatological locations above and beyond the world left a personal Christian piety in its place. The bishops now had the oversight of Christians in preparation for a kingdom to come in some other time and place. That required a priestly role in the interest of purity. And the churches were no longer enclaves fostering the imagination of an alternative to the Roman empire or constantly calling for the critique of the Roman order. That meant that the stage was set for the earthly king and the heavenly king to join forces in the control of a theocratic society. Both would rule over the same domain, the emperor in charge of making the society work, the Christ in charge of the culture. And both the bishops and the emperor would agree on models of centralized power and canon law. It is true that the agreement required frequent adjustments and negotiations, but no adjustment from that time until now, not even the modern critique of the kings, or the view of religion as only a private affair, has succeeded in dislodging the model from the western mind. Outwardly, the model takes the form of a balance between power and purity that many Americans think requires the separation of church and state. But at its core the model is monocratic, one that needs the Christian God to guarantee the right of those in power to rule with authority. This monocratic model does not have to surface for articulation and debate in order to be at work. Indeed it dare not be surfaced for critical review. It works at the level of unexpressed and unexamined assumptions common to the culture, informing attitudes, values, and patterns of thinking that are regarded as self-

172

evident. It creates what the French have called a mentality. It is a mentality in deference to a Christian mythology.

One other thing happened when Constantine made the Christian churches the official religion of the Roman empire. Christians were no longer a minority. They finally had status as legitimate citizens of the Roman empire, and they had more than just legitimacy. They had the power to say what all citizens of the Roman empire should believe, how they should act, and how they should worship. It was this transition that spelled danger for all non-Christians, for the erstwhile "persecuted" minority now had the power to persecute. And they did. It took a while to work out the rationale for pogroms against the pagans, but when they did find the reasons for thinking it the right thing to do, they said they had to do it because they were guardians of purity under the monocratic canopy of a Christian empire. It is this pattern of thought, not a Christian theology of a mission to the needy, that one can follow down through western history. The clients of the kings are the first to move into a new territory, then the Christian missionaries come. The rhetoric is enlightenment, but the reality is the demand that the people convert. The underlying logic is conformity under the canopy of a monocratic rule. The result is that the indigenous peoples are forced to accommodate an alien culture. The story has been told again and again. The gods of the other peoples die or are reduced to folk heroes or demons. The local shrines are replaced by Christian churches. And the biblical epic consigns the indigenous histories to local legends, if allowed rehearsal at all. Becoming a Christian means learning a new history, one that requires the acceptance of a fictive lineage in order to be accepted by the new monocracy. What a strange mental gymnastic demanded of those who convert. But that is only half the problem. The other half is that converting may not be enough. That is because the demand to convert is driven not only by the monocratic ideal of conformity, meaning that everyone should be obedient to the same authorities, but by the underlying notion of opposition basic to the Christian myth. Other people who are not Christians are invariably ranked lower than the Christians who bring them the message of salvation. Until they convert the other people are thought of as pagans, outsiders, ignorant, and ungodly. And even after converting, the onus of being different may still determine second-class status for many generations. This has been the story of Christian imperialism right up until our time, a story that is now in need of critical review. The question is whether Christianity has any resource for revamping its mythic system, for coming to terms with the many cultures of today's global world, for existing comfortably within the social democracies of our time that have wrested themselves free from a monocratic mythology.

Conclusion

In conclusion I would like to share one paragraph from the epilogue to my book *Who Wrote the New Testament?*, cited with only minor changes:

> A multicultural world groping toward the construction of smaller social democracies, each connected to a land charged with ethnic histories, linked together only in the interest of a global economy and a balance of world powers, is not how the Christian epic was supposed to end. The epic is part of a mythic system and set of ideals that run counter to the way in which the world is actually working. The Christian myth is based upon a worldview that is universalist in scope, monolinear in historical imagination, a singular system in organic conception, hierarchical in the location of power, dualistic in anthropology, and which has to have miracles, and other dramatic or divine moments of rectification in order to imagine the adjustments that humans have to make when life and social circumstances change or get out of control. These features of the worldview assumed and projected by the Christian mythic system are no longer helpful as ideals in our multicultural world (1995, p.306).

Where, then, does that leave us? It leaves us, I think, with the challenge of starting some frank discussions of the effective differences religions make in the ways we structure our societies and celebrate our cultures. I have suggested some reasons why I think the effect of Christianity has not always been good. We are being called upon to revise radically the monomania of western Christian mentality in order to appreciate difference, accept critique, celebrate plurality, negotiate compromise, and march with trumpets blaring whenever we catch sight of the tremendous investments common people make in the human enterprise of making sure a society works. Some Christians *might* find it possible to rise to that challenge. But if they do, they will have to find some way to revise the monocratic mythology and cultural mentality of a very long Christian history. It no longer fits the world in which we live.

CHAPTER EIGHT

The Christian Myth and the Christian Nation

The legacy of the Christian myth lies hidden in the cultural constraints created by Christianity in the long history of its civilizations. The hidden constraints of the Christian myth have seldom been acknowledged, because the cultural manifestations of the myth are so obvious, traceable, familiar, and appreciated. They are obvious because a manifestation is a material or social product of the intersection where the myth and human energies of social formation come together. Thus the outlines of the myth can easily be traced through the mosaics of the fifth century basilicas in Italy; the architectural history of monasteries, schools, churches, cathedrals, town halls, palaces, and state buildings in Europe; the history of rituals, public processions, and Christian "missions" from the fourth to the twentieth century; the history of western music, art, theatre, literature, and philosophy. For each of these manifestations the canopy of Christian myth has been taken for granted as the frame of reference for cultural shifts and has generally been thought of as the matrix or sounding board for generating new thoughts and helpful enlightenments. The constraints imposed by the canopy of Christian mentality, on the other hand, have not been so obvious or easy to describe and trace.

The fact of constraints upon the human capacity for experimentation in the quest for knowledge and social well-being has sometimes been acknowledged, but it has seldom been seen as the result of the canopy of Christian mentality. That is because the notion of a canopy created by myth has not been a concept until recently. Instead, the way we have traced the history of those moments in which new thoughts and discoveries have made advances in knowledge has been to take it for granted that the "advances" had to be made in struggle against contemporary systems of thought. It has not always been acknowledged that the entrenched mentality was a variant of the myth's persistence and power. Many of the major modulations of western thought have such a moment of daring and dangerous discovery. The Magna Carta comes to mind, as do Petrarch, Copernicus, Galileo, Zwingli, John Locke, da Vinci, Darwin, and others. It has been understood, of course, that the price paid for thinking freely has often been ostracization, defrocking, excommunication, or worse. It has also been obvious that these reactions are due to a combination of two major factors: (1) that new thoughts threaten the privileges of those invested in the status granted by the dominant social and cultural structures; and (2) that the defensive rationalization of those privileges can often be made by appeal to the Christian myth.

One might have thought that the western history of intellectual enlightenments, social revolutions, scientific discoveries, and industrialized technologies would have outgrown an archaic myth-ritual system created in a bygone age of cultural clash and experimental social formations. That, however, has not happened. It has not happened primarily for three reasons. The first is that the Christian myth was ritualized, institutionalized, and granted access to imperial power and privilege as the religion of state for the entire history of the western kings and their kingdoms. The myth became the script for Christian ritual and its cultivation by the institutions of the church honed the Mass to perfection, determined the shape of cultural constructions (starting with the cruciform structure of imposing cathedrals that provided employment for workers and craftsmen and design challenge for artists and architects), and etched the story of the Bible into the imagination and sensibilities of entire populations.

The second reason for the permanent entrenchment of the Christian myth is that it was "canonized" in the form of a written text. Stories written into texts are difficult to change, and in this case there were taboos against doing so. To make matters worse, for the first one thousand years only the literate elite could read the texts, and they happened to be the priests of the Christian church. They controlled the pictorial exegeses which were displayed for the masses. And when the texts were printed and read in the languages of the peoples, the priests and preachers learned about "hermeneutic," the learned skills required to apply the archaic languages of the sacred texts to contemporary systems of faith and morals. Thus the etching has been fortified by an imprinting, a pedagogy of training by repetition.

The third reason for the persistence of the Christian myth has to do with its capacity to generate a certain kind of thinking. This capacity is a result of structural features accidental to its formation, but obvious to any who meditate upon it and attempt to determine its logic. Because the Christian gospel functions as the foundation story for Christianity and its cultures, it is assumed to have a logic, i.e. reasons why the story goes the way it does. But the logic assumed to be there does not agree with the logics of any critical or constructive thinking that humans have been able to bring to its study. Christians have decided that the logic lies in the mind of God, that it is a "theo-logic." Thus the relation of the Old Testament to the New, the relationship of the divinity of the Christ to the notion of one God, the relation of the divinity of Jesus to his humanity, the logic of his death as a "sacrifice," for example, soon became the conceptual issues that generated systems of thought called theologies and philosophies. These systems of thinking were often developed as "apologies" for the Christian myth and its institutions, but they did not always feed back into the hermeneutical enterprise of helping priests and people understand the logic of their faith. Instead, theologians and philosophers found themselves attracted to the logical contradictions of their systems of thought and developed signs and signals for playing the abstract game of dialectic. The problems to be solved were: the one and the many, reason and faith, power and purity, nature and culture, the real and the symbol, the thing-in-itself *("Ding an sich")* and human epistemologies, history and spirit, and so forth. With the western intellectual preoccupied with the game of dialectic, and with the game of dialectic rooted ultimately in the conundrums created by the Christian myth and ritual, no wonder the Christian myth has never been critically examined.

The mythic world has been forced to alter its shapes and valencies in keeping with modulations of cultural mentality caused by changes in social circumstances and intellectual adventures. But it has been able to do so without losing its power as myth to arbitrate the constraints on human activity and thinking. One can trace the mythic transformations in the imagery and style of its depictions from the heavenly good shepherds of the Byzantine mosaics, and the sculptured majestic Christs of the Romanesque period, through the madonnas, saints and Christian knights portrayed with the s-curve sways of the Gothic period, the crucified Christs, resurrected Christs, and ascending Christs of the baroque period, to the use of depictions and symbols suggestive of the "spiritual presence" and "cosmic powers" of the divine agents of the Christian myth in the modern period. These changes in focus and style correspond to changes in social histories and thought, but the changes in the way the mythic world is imagined have not called its mythic functions into question. Thus the resilience of this myth is truly amazing.

Tracing the way in which the Christian myth has been established, recognized, and manipulated in the history of the United States is a bit more difficult than following its manifestations and effects through European history. There are several reasons for this. One is that the social formation of the new nation in America was founded on political thought engendered by the Enlightenment, not by direct appeal to the Christian gospel or epic as charter. The principles of both the American and the French revolutions were "freedom" (from monarchial and autocratic rule), "equality" (of all citizens under the law, or equal access to justice), and "fraternity" (or the recognition of common stake in the well-being of the people or class of people as a whole), based on the "laws of Nature and Nature's God" as Thomas Jefferson phrased it in the Declaration of Independence. James Madison's Preamble to the Constitution of the United States put the formation of "a more perfect union" (fraternity), the establishment of "justice" (equality), and the securing of the "blessing of liberty" (freedom) in the hands of WE THE PEOPLE OF THE UNITED STATES. Both Jefferson and Madison included "religious liberty" among the freedoms intended, even though the primary focus was on freedom from monarchial rule. Since these are the documents that attended and rationalized the events of the birth of the nation, and since they appealed to collective human capacities for social formation on the basis of natural law, there was very little need or chance in immediate retrospect to credit the Christian myth with the founding of the "Christian nation."

The second reason for the difficulty in tracing the function of the Christian myth in American history has to do with the constituency of the peoples and their many religious traditions that came together in the American colonies. The mix of peoples in the United States was quite different from the social demography of any given European nation, and by the time of the Revolutionary War there had already been a vigorous and convoluted history of social engagements not only among the thirteen colonies, but with England, France and other European nations, as well as other peoples in the "new world" from France, Spain, Africa, the Caribbean, and the North American continent ("native Americans"). Thus there was not only "denominational" conflict, there were issues of how to relate to peoples of different ethnic traditions who were not Christian at all. It has sometimes been suggested that the multiethnic and multicultural mix of peoples in the United States of America is similar to that of the Greco-Roman world at the time of Christianity's origins. The problem with this situational similarity and its intended glorification of the "fulfillment"of the "Judeo-Christian tradition" in the "manifest destiny" of the new "Christian nation," is that the first century Christians were a minority and developed mythologies to justify gaining a place within their multicultural world, while the Christians in the United States, though splintered by family quarrels, were and have been in the majority in their multicultural world. Thus the Christian myth in America has been a mythology that assured Christians of their superior status and dominant place. So how was it, we might ask, that the Christian majority reconciled the Christian myth with the humanistic principles of the new nation and eventually imagined the "constitution" of the nation to be "Christian"?

The answer is by means of many rationalizations over a long period of time. The story of the Christian myth in America is one of mythmaking by default, as is the story of the various interpretations of the Constitution in American history. The Christian myth was already in place in the Christian institutions that brought it with them from Europe. It did not have to be invented. What happened was a process of reconceptualizing both the Constitution and the template of the Christian myth in application to many moments of social change, crisis, and rationalization called for by the social histories of the peoples. In due course the two myths of origin converged but could not mesh.

The standard account of history has assumed that the United States was from the beginning and continues to be a Christian nation. It is possible to follow some of the expressions of that assumption throughout its history. There is the account of the pilgrims who fled "religious persecution" in Europe and colonized New England as puritans. That was clearly before the revolutionary war, and much more to our credit as a nation with religious purpose than stories of the land grants in Virginia and the Carolinas where plantations were developed for profit. The Great Awakenings of the eighteenth century, the first in New England, the second in the Virginias, and both spreading out to the west and south, have also often been rehearsed as signs of a basic Christian religiosity and piety. As for the "founding fathers," it was taken for granted that they read and studied the Bible, as indeed they did, even though mainly to reduce its system to the "pure Deism" Jefferson wanted to find in the teachings of Jesus. Francis Scott Key could praise ". . . the Pow'r that hath made and perserved us as a nation" for the victory of the States in the War of 1812 and the triumph of the Star Spangled Banner "O'r the land of the free and the home of the brave." Samuel Smith, a Boston minister, had no trouble when composing "My Country 'Tis of Thee" in 1831 thinking of "Our fathers' God" as the "Author of liberty" and "Great God, our King." By the time of the Civil War, the author of the Battle Hymn of the Republic could discern the "truth" of the Christians' God and Christ in the victories of the Union army as its soldiers "marched on," ready to "die to make men free." With the expansion westward, the circuit riders and other evangelists of American church history come to mind, eventually meeting up with the Spanish padres of the vast southwestern territories. It does not need emphasizing that this standard account is woefully inadequate as history and completely oriented to Protestant interests. Left out of account are the Catholic missions in the Southwest, the French and Spanish Catholic influence in New Orleans and the early South, as well as the many immigrant waves of different people and religions throughout the nineteenth and twentieth centuries, and large portions of American history filled with vigorous activities hardly touched by Christianity at all.

Every Christian denomination has its own history of origins and engagements with the ebb and flow of Christian religiosity in the United States. This level of Christianity's presence in American history set the scene for the media's pulse on the fate of church development and membership after the second World War. The burning question was whether the American people really believed in God and went to church. The churches were important to the society because their teachings aimed at inculcating virtues of responsibility, hard work, honesty, integrity, and tolerance. And of course the churches are to be credited for supporting social values such as family, loyalty, honor, citizenship, and patriotism. As for their influence, one thinks of the recognition of the God in whom "we trust" on our bank notes (!), and the theological addition to the pledge of allegiance to the flag in 1954 of ". . . one nation, *under God*, indivisible, with liberty and justice for all." The problem is that these observations about the Christian churches and their desire to be the religious, ethical, and righteous leaven within society are not the whole story of the legacy of the Christian myth or the social history of the people of the United States.

The Christan myth has been repeatedly used as divine mandate and argument for two distinctly contradictory public policies. On the one hand it has been called upon to undergird the high purposes of nation building, including a constructionist approach to the "original meaning" of the Constitution, the articulation of ethical values for the society, the inculcation of personal virtues for its citizens, and the legislation of laws designed to insure the moral integrity of the nation such as blue laws, prohibitions, and punishments for crime. On the other, however, it has been appealed to in the course of our history to justify policies and practices that violate the virtues and ideals espoused by and for the Christian nation. Two examples of the history of violations come immediately to mind. One is the history of slavery and the treatment of the black peoples among us. The second is the history of the westward expansion and the treatment of the land and native Americans. Both of these stories can be read as thematic streams of American history, starting with a problematic encounter at the beginning, moving through episodes that correlate with major shifts in America's social history, and coming to the end of the twentieth century without resolution. A brief review of the way in which mythmaking has occurred in one of these histories can illustrate the real·legacy of the Christian myth in American social formations.

The story of the Christian nation that included Africans among its many peoples can begin with the observation that they were imported as slaves to work the plantations of the South. The first boatload of African slaves landed in Virginia in 1619, one year before the *Mayflower* arrived in Cape Cod, and 100 years after the start of the African slave trade in the middle Americas and the Caribbean. The Spanish colonialists had depleted the native Indian work force, and the Catholic bishop in Chiapas prevailed upon the Spanish crown to allow the importation of Africans as slaves for the missions and plantations in the new world. The request was granted and the trade began, eventually to expand into the North American colonies. By 1750 there were approximately 250,000 African slaves in the colonies, and by 1860 a census counted 4,441,830 in the United States. When Thomas Jefferson wrote the Declaration of Independence in 1776, combining contemporary French thought with what he understood to be the biblical basis for a free and enlightened society, the fundamental truth held to be self-evident was that "all men are created equal." It was a grand concept and a serious statement of tremendous consequence for the history of the United States. But it did not apply to African-American slaves. Jefferson himself was a slave owner, as was James Madison. And though Madison let it be known that he was troubled about the institution of slavery, neither he nor Jefferson nor the Congress of the United States expressed having conceptual trouble over conflict between the practice of slavery and the principle of equality. Part of the reason for this was that the principle of equality in its French derivation had never intended an application to ethnic anthropologies. Even in France the slogan of "equality" pertained only to the bourgeois, not to the peasants. And in the Declaration of Independence, "equality" was a high-sounding argument based on "the Laws of Nature and Nature's God," but in support of a revolution at the level of governance and law in the interest of economic freedom from England. Slavery was the institution that made possible the southern plantation, and it provided the economic foundation for the wealth of the new nation. Thus it apparently never occurred to the "fathers of the country" that slavery was wrong because it violated the principle of equality. But by stating that equality was grounded in "creation," and counted as a "law of Nature's God," Jefferson unwittingly invited subsequent interpretations that were quite different.

As questions were raised about slavery by French humanists and English pietists, abolitionist movements increased during the eighteenth century. In America, this resulted in forcing a discussion about the legality of slavery and how the new federation could govern a union of states both "slave" and "free." As tensions over this issue increased, and the institution of slavery had to be defended in the South, history shows that the Bible became an important argument and ideology. All through the south, the rhetoric found in sermons, newspapers, essays, and interviews was the same. "The Bible said" that slavery was ordained by God. From the Old Testament the proof text was Genesis 9:20–27, God's curse on Ham, one of the three sons of Noah, interpreted to say that Africans would be slaves of the other peoples of the earth. From the New Testament the proof text was from Paul's letter to the Colossians in which he enjoined wives to be subject to their husbands and slaves to obey their masters (Col 3:18–22). The standard homiletic throughout the Bible Belt interpreted this to say, "If a wife is to be subject to her husband, *how much more* a slave." What could the abolitionists say? All they had in their quiver were abstract principles about the "fatherhood of God" and the "brotherhood of man" to argue for the morality of the constitutional statement about "equality" in the Declaration of Independence. And so the debate about slavery took place in the United States Congress over doctrines concerning the admission of newly formed states from the territories of the Louisiana purchase as to whether they would be allowed to be settled by slave owners. The Missouri Compromise (1820), the doctrine of popular sovereignty embedded in the Kansas-Nebraska Act (1854), and South Carolina's Act of Secession (1860) that occasioned the Civil War (1861–65) were driven by desires for political and economic privilege and power, not issues of Christian morality grounded in the Christian myth as charter or in the statement about equality in the constitutional papers.

As the Civil War quickened, however, Lincoln found it necessary to think through the consequences of a war for the sake of the Union

185

(fraternity) in relation to the issue of slavery that had sparked the secessions. The result was the "Emancipation Proclamation" of January 1, 1863, in which the slaves then held by citizens of southern Confederate states "in rebellion" against the United States were declared "free" by the United States. This joined the principles of union (fraternity) with freedom (liberty) in a brand new way, for the freedom envisaged was clearly that to be accorded to African-Americans who had been slaves. This "act of justice," Lincoln wrote, was "warranted by the Constitution upon military necessity." This is hardly a strong indication that considerations of the right to equality (justice) had played a significant role in his deliberations. At Gettysburg, however, ten months later, when Lincoln thought to honor the Union soldiers who "gave their lives that the nation might live," the "new nation" was said to be "conceived in Liberty, and dedicated to the proposition that all men are created equal." That is mythmaking in action. Jefferson's reference to equality, which had to do with bourgeois legal and economic freedoms, was now redirected to encompass the social anthropology of a nation divided over principles of democracy, states rights, and federal jurisdictions. If we put that together with Julia Howe's "Battle Hymn of the Republic" (1861), in which it says, "As He (Christ) died to make men holy, let us die to make men free," the convoluted mergers of Christian myth and the Constitution of the United States are obvious. What about the South? What about the God who ordained slavery? What about the Bible?

One year after the war (1866), the white supremacist Ku Klux Klan emerged as the undergound resistance movement to the Reconstruction of the South, and the era of intimidation, lynchings and burnings began. Apparently the Christian myth and Bible would continue to be read and applied to the social situation in a way quite different from that of the Battle Hymn of the Republic. The social situation *was* different, devastatingly so. The foundations and structures of an entire way of life cultivated to perfection during the preceding 200 years of social and cultural formation had been destroyed. When the reconstruction period ended ten years later in 1877, Jim Crow laws were enacted throughout the South. The rule was "separate but equal," or "equal, but separate." Thus the legal principle of equality was given token acceptance even though the social principle was not. And the fiction of supporting the *principle* of equality actually resulted in the construction of a social system that refused to allow freed blacks full participation in the civil rights of white society for the next 70 years. Lynchings continued as ritualized exorcisms of the danger blacks represented to the Christian purity of whites. Plantation owners were no longer in control of their slaves and thus were awash in a social chaos that frightened the white woman and threatened the manhood of the white male (Harris, 1984; Singleton, 1987). As Rebeca Felton, a southern white woman from Atlanta, wrote in her letter to the Boston Transcript, 1897:

> When there is not enough religion in the pulpit to organize a crusade against sin; nor justice in the court house to promptly punish crime, nor manhood enough in the nation to put a sheltering arm about innocence and virtue—if it takes lynching to protect women's dearest possession from the ravening human beast—then I say lynch, a thousand times a week if necessary.

In the meantime blacks found ways to keep their dignity despite the humiliations of this demeaning social system. They did this by turning the Bible into a charter for liberation, by creating music that sang in the face of oppression, and by going to war for America as Americans. Yet another reading of the Christian myth emerged, this one reaching back into the Old Testament to pit the God who ordained freedom against the God who ordained slavery. When the black troops returned to America after the second World War, accustomed to high praise and medals of honor, Jim Crow finally became unbearable and ridiculous even in the eyes of enlightened whites. Rosa Parks refused to sit in the back of the bus and the demonstrations against segregation and for civil rights began. The 1950s mark a major turning point in the social history of the United States. The concept of equality had been enriched by adding human respect and civic value to the notions of equality under the law. The administration of justice in the South was now a matter of concern and scrutiny throughout the rest of the United States. The blacks had found a way to let the rest of America know that something was wrong with the system. Martin Luther King had a dream, and the liberation movements of the 1960s carried the wave of reform to "theologies of liberation" for blacks, women, gays, native Americans, impoverished Latin Americans, and the poor in the United States and beyond.

Since the civil rights movement of the 1950s, and especially after the Supreme Court decision in 1954 to desegregate the public schools in America, the goal has been "integration." Some progress has been made in the restructuring of social and legal systems called for by the principle of equality rooted in enlightenment anthropology. Voting rights, jury rights, welfare rights, affirmative actions based on equal oportunity rights, work place rights, open housing, educational programs, and more have been instituted. Christians have responded, some wanting to be involved and to give Christianity the credit for humanizing advances, others, however, by digging in their heels to stop the slide of a Christian nation into social decadence and immorality. This resistence to the liberation movements of the 1960s is now talked about as a "culture war" or a "third Great Awakening" of evangelical Christian religiosity. It is not clearly acknowledged in public forum that a continuing deeply ingrained resistance to the Civil Rights movement and civil liberties legislations has also been driving this resurgence of Christain thinking. In contrast to other accommodations of the Christian myth to the social interests of the dominant classes in western cultural history where the myth has simply given its blessing to such enterprises as colonialism (as "mission"), capitalism (as "Protestant ethic"), and the "taking of the West" (as "manifest destiny"), the rise of the Christian right in America as a political movement is a clearly articulated merger of Christian myth and new politics.

What about integration? What about equality? Well, the track record is not good. Despite some obvious and helpful changes in the domain of politically correct attitudes and behavior on the part of persons in public, legislation intended to guarantee integration, such as open housing, or school busing, has not worked. Gated communities, white flight, and private schools have left inner city schools crowded with blacks and poorly supported. As for the welfare system, it has come under attack because, as they said, "The black woman" (who for 250 years, we should remember, exemplified a work ethic that kept both black and white families together and provided for their sustenance) "is lazy, content to produce children just in order to receive more welfare." The workplace left the inner city, and for blacks the highly touted American dream turned into a nightmare.

Many ironies result. White politicians now preach "family values" to the blacks whose families once were separated and sold by slave owners. Affirmative action initiatives, set in place to rectify the consequences of the long history of inequalities, are now being used by whites to claim discrimination. Racial profiling has finally been seen as wrong, but only after prisons were crowded with young black males. Words like "liberal," originally overloaded with positive connotations, have been tarnished beyond recognition by the mantras of preachers and politicians wanting to "conserve" American "morals" in the face of democratic programs thought to be dangerous. And there is the phenomenon of violence committed by Christian crazies: the burning of black churches, pro-lifers killing abortion clinic doctors, and hate crimes by white Christian supremacists against blacks, Jews, and gays. It surely has become clear to all with a modicum of social sensibility, that a combination of Christian virtue, political power, and conservative mentality appealing to the Constitution for rationale is fully capable of taking back, or wanting to take back, all of the social justice programs set in place during the last half of the twentieth century. The confusions created by the conceits, deceits, and dishonest political rhetorics in the United States of America are directly related to the inadequacy of the Christian myth to provide the American experiment with programs and policies of legitimate rationale.

And as for the "equal protection" clause of the 14th amendment to the constitution, adopted July 28, 1868, an amendment purposefully enacted with the African-American in mind, it has been used by the Supreme Court of the United States to hand the presidency of the United States to a southern Christian conservative who thinks of Jesus as his model political philosopher. This president immediately nominated a right wing Christian lawyer to the post of attorney general who has said, "We have no king but Jesus" (Pollitt, 2001). An article by Vincent Bugliosi explains that the Court had never accepted the equal protection argument in any case brought before it by blacks or in cases having to do with discrimination, and that accepting the argument in this case clearly violated both the intention and the legality of the application of the law. Those who followed the events of the presidential election in 2000, and especially the post-election political and judicial fracas in Florida, will understand the motivations confirmed by that Supreme Court ruling (December 12, 2000). Bugliosi concludes that ". . . the real equal protection violation [in this case] took place when [the Court] cut off the counting of the undervotes" (2001). Equal protection? Equality? Integration? As Jimmy Carter explained the reasons for writing an account of his childhood in Georgia, "We need to recognize that the racial issue has not been dealt with" (2001). That means that something is terribly wrong in America. If "American" means living here in this land and taking part in its life and work, the African-American is the most American of any other immigrant people, but the least recognized as worthy of equal rights and equal protection under the law. Even at the height of the civil rights activity when Ralph Bunche, a brilliant black American with stellar credentials in international diplomacy for the United Nations, asked the Congress of the United States to declare lynching illegal, the request was refused.

As for the way in which the Bible has been viewed, a change took place in the last half of the twentieth century that relates to the theme of social integration. I refer to the public and political rhetoric of the Bible as the charter for the "Judeo-Christian tradition." The concept of a "Judeo-Christian tradition" intended a rapprochement between Jews and Christians. It also commended itself to African-American Christians with their orientation to the Old Testament and their desire for alignment with "mainstream" religions in America and with religious and political concepts of tolerance. Religious and political leaders regularly appeal to the Bible and that tradition as the epic heritage that guides us as a nation. The problem with this notion is that it amounts to an overlay of myth upon myth, for only by reading the Christian Bible with sentimental naivité and overlooking two thousand years of persecution, can a Judeo-Christian tradition even be imagined. The intention has been noble, namely the appeal to biblical authority as the basis for a Christian tolerance of other religions. This intention might be considered harmless, for it served quite well as long as Christians were in the majority, as long as those who were graced with tolerance accepted their place as minorities, and as long as the sentiments were shared only at the level of attitudes toward Judaism, black Christianity, and other religions. But that circumstance has run its course. The confusions about religion and society at the turn of the twenty-first century, as well as the long list of reasons to be troubled about social and political issues having to do with multiethnic relations and cultural conflict, as well as quality of life, environmental policies, social securities, economic justice, and equality under the law, indicate that an appeal to the Bible will not be enough to call for clarity of purpose as we struggle with our social formations.

It is time to recognize that the Bible is not a document calling for equality. The Christian myth calls for conversion and obedience. It projects a global vision, but that vision is completely inadequate for the purpose of imagining the future of a multiethnic, multicultural world. There is no place under the canopy projected by the Christian myth for all the peoples of the world who are not Christian. Christian mentality was rendered uncritical and uncreative by the fact of one thousand years of Christendom. The total control of the mythic imagination during that period, and the fact that the world of the imagination encompassed the very horizons of human experience and thought made it possible to think that the Christian myth was about the majesty of an all inclusive vision for the redemption and well-being of humanity. But the history of the western Christian nations since the ages of discovery and enlightenment has proven otherwise. And now, a critical analysis of the origins, logic, and legacy of the Christian myth shows why it is not working to help Christians think about equality and take guidance for human relations and policies at the beginning of its twenty-first century. Social problems will not be solved by preachments, conversions, and violence. The imagination of external saviors, apocalyptic judgments, and divine sovereignty runs counter to the social visions now required. And the history of biblical authorizations in America runs from wars in the interest of political powers, through lynchings in the interest of exorcising difference, to atrocities in the interest of white supremacy. To proclaim, "We have no king but Jesus," sounds like an even balance between church and state, a democracy on the one hand and a deep religious piety on the other. But it has no value for clarifying procedures in the interest of democratic legislation, or constraints against the mendacity of self-serving political ploys. The Christian myth is simply not adequate as a mythic imagination for the social formations that need to be constructed in order to assure human well-being in a multiethnic, multicultural world. It cannot be used to celebrate the high moral purposes of the American experiment in nation building, and it cannot be used as the major theme for the history of that experiment.

In recent times a number of culture historians have taken note of this fact. A stunning essay by Russell Banks, University Professor of the Humanities, Emeritus, at Princeton University, begins with a reference to Derek Walcott's observation, "Either I'm nobody, or I'm a nation," which Banks understands as ". . . a claim that our essential, individual identities depend upon our ability to view ourselves as a people. If so," Banks continues, "then We the People require a tale that in a plausible way describes and dramatizes our origins. Without it, we will separate ourselves first from our antecedents and then from one another, and, like a deracinated family, We the People will perish." He then shares with his readers some conclusions he has reached after many years of wondering about what a truly American literature might look like. His quest finally came to focus upon the story of slavery in America and the way in which it has affected all of our structures of human relations. The essay ends with the following sentences:

> I take it as a given that our best and most ambitious fiction writers are those whose sense of purpose is guided by a desire to participate in the making of a national literature. My hope is that this ongoing, 200-year-old project will provide us a truly democratic literature, one that has at its center the historical and moral facts of creolization and that therefore both honors our people's highest standards for our treatment of one another and does not in the process lie about our tragic failure to meet those standards.

There is no indication in his essay that Banks has been worried about or critical of the way in which the Christian myth has functioned as the standard for the story of nation building in America. His insight is therefore all the more telling, namely that the real story might well draw upon "our people's highest standards for our treatment of one another," as well as tell the truth about our failures, for it suggests that this would be possible without having to appeal to the "Judeo-Christian tradition" for legitimacy or guidance. Others also have been thinking about the American story, wondering whether the treatment of African-Americans and their response to that treatment should not be seen as its theme. Ken Burns, for instance, has been telling the story of the American people in his documentaries, one of which is the history of *Jazz*, another the history of *The West*. As in the essay by Banks, neither of these histories comes to focus at any point on the legacy of the Christian myth. But both expose the white (Christian) American attitudes toward peoples imagined as "other." *The West* explores the circumstances, motivations, and behavior of encounters with native Americans in the quest for land and expansion. *Jazz* documents the response of African-Americans to slavery and the series of demeaning social systems and circumstances created to keep them in their place. This response is more than a theme for the telling of the story. It correlates with Banks's observation about where "our peoples's highest standards for our treatment of one another" can be found. Jazz brings to expression a fundamental characteristic of the African-American. It is an ability to experience oppression without violent response or obsequious loss of dignity. This has been accompanied by an amazing capacity to peer deeply and knowingly into the reasons for structures of unjust power without being overwhelmed by them. Jazz turns out to be a way of transcending circumstances fully acknowledged as human hurt. To celebrate such moments by singing the blues is a cultural creation of tremendous significance. What if we recognized the African-American capacity for thinking about, understanding, and responding to social structures as an example of the human resources among us that we have not tapped for social solutions? What if we recognized that Jazz, in the view of Wynton Marsalis, is what "democracy is all about"? What then? Why then we might be getting ready for another round of social formation and mythmaking with real people, real issues, and real dreams in view.

EPILOG

O ur challenge at the beginning of the twenty-first century is to come to terms with the world in which we live. We need to analyze our myths, cool our rhetorics, and rank our social interests. It is actually quite possible to imagine a multiethnic, multicultural world which is just, productive, interesting, rewarding, and worthy of celebration. That we have not done so is largely a result of our preoccupation with inadequate myths. This book is about the inadequacy of the Christian myth for rationalizing the social experiences of the modern world, and especially the American history of tragic failure to engage other peoples as human beings and work out equitable agreements for living together. In the last chapter a second myth came under review, that of the myth of the Constitution as a founding document for the "Christian nation." That myth had to be described because of its intertwined history with the Christian myth in the interest of bringing the legacy of the Christian myth to a conclusion. What we have learned from tracing the history of reinterpretations of the Constitution is that the ideal of equality has easily been scuttled time and time again by those in power, and the Christian myth has often provided the rationalization. A third set of myths support the institutions and fictions of a capitalist economy. This study has not touched upon them, but they also would need to be surfaced for critical analysis if the next round of social formation is to be driven by critical thinking and cultural critique.

It won't be easy. Critical thinking demands more than we have thus far invested in our public debates and political programs. An example of the way in which the Christian myth continues to dominate thinking and discourse at the turn of the twenty-first century in the United States is the emergence of a system of thought called "creationism." When one considers the knowledge scientific research has achieved about the natural history of the earth, its flora and fauna, about the evolution of the human species, and about the function of myths in human societies, preference for the account of creation in the Bible as an alternative "scientific theory" is a stunning reminder of the power of the Christian myth to continue to control the human imagination. How is this possible? And how should we describe such a merger of systems of thought? Has the myth been forced to accommodate scientific thinking? Or has scientific thinking been scuttled by the preference for another accounting of the world? Has the resistance to the scientific account been fed by intellectual issues, aesthetic values, loss of divine agents, moral anomie, cultural decay, or by fright at the thought of losing the senses of "meaning" and "salvation" that the Christian myth seems to guarantee? Perhaps there is yet another explanation. Could it not be that, in the minds of many, the Bible is still the bulwark against threats to the Christian desire for supremacy?

The mythmaking called for by the social and cultural circumstances at the beginning of the twenty-first century could start with some honest talk about social interests. Why not find a way to imagine alternatives to the vortex of personal, private, and special interests with which Americans seem to be obsessed? Why not create a forum to discuss the kind of world in which we would like to live? There are after all many models of social democracies to consider and many combinations of social and cultural resources to think about. Mythmaking could take the form of focusing attention upon the human resources available for constructing a social democracy and the reasons why a social democracy might commend itself as an appropriate societal and political experiment. Mythmaking of this kind might prove to be a very exciting intellectual adventure with constructive consequence for social formation. The larger horizon of the mythic canopy might well begin to fill with human histories and agents instead of divinities. These human agents might well begin to symbolize amazingly strong, resilient constructive and humanizing capacities once thought of as fragile and innocent victims when confronted by the forces of fear, greed, predation, and sovereignty. The very intellectual activity called for in order to wrest free from older mentalities beholden to the gods and cowed by fears of penal consequences would actually count as mythmaking. To refocus imaginary concentration on the forces thought to generate and sustain social interests is exactly what mythmaking is about. Equality might turn out to be more important as a real goal than as a mythic rationalization. Real equality might actually make it possible for everyone to feel good about themselves in a society where everyone was equally cared for. And the Christian myth? What would be wrong with admitting the poverty of its social logics? One could then go on to consider the many beautiful and profound cultural accomplishments that have taken place under its canopy in the long history of the western nations, bewonder them, and wonder how to use them now that the Christian mystique gives way to a truly wondrous aura of human creativity? In some such way the forum America now needs might become a quest for a social vision adequate to address the social histories and circumstances of our time. If the quest for a new social vision were driven by social interests that are encompassing of others, and if it enhanced the full range of human capacities for rewarding a full spectrum of occupations and performances, and if it sought to imagine how truly satisfying it might be for everyone to realize equality, justice, well-being, and honor in a world in which they are available for all peoples, I would say that the study of religion in our time may finally be worthwhile.

ANNEX

The Christian Origins Project

The Proposal

In 1995, at the annual meeting of the Society of Biblical Literature in Philadelphia, Merrill Miller and Ron Cameron convened a consultation on the topic "Ancient Myths and Modern Theories of Christian Origins." The purpose was to explore scholarly interest in the formation of a seminar to pursue that topic in detail. Papers had been prepared by Mack and Cameron, and responses were ready by Jonathan Z. Smith and John Kloppenborg. Miller presided, the room was full, and a large number of scholars expressed interest in the project and asked to be considered for membership in the seminar.

Miller and Cameron had been talking about such a project for two or three years and had shared their ideas with a number of colleagues in the fields of Biblical and religious studies. Thus there were several of us who had been conversation partners while the plans took shape, and I was pleased when they asked me to write a paper for the consultation. Chapter Three is a revised version of that paper. Its purpose was to make the rationale for the project as clear as possible, for we thought it important to assess the general reaction and degree of consent to the proposal among colleagues in the guild. I therefore underscored the point about our "Christian origins" project being different from the quest traditional to New Testament studies. Not only had New Testament scholars always assumed that the decisive events lodged in and around the person and life of the historical Jesus, this assumption had to be joined by a second, namely that these events revealed to his first followers, the disciples, his role in the inauguration of a new religion. And thus a third assumption has been required, namely that the announcement of these events having happened was sufficient for belief, and that belief was sufficient for conversion to the Christian religion. Since none of these assumptions could be supported by the New Testaments texts and the state of New Testament scholarship, and none can be supported by contemporary studies in the way new religions and movements start and grow, a reconception of Christian origins was called for. Scholars in the history and sociology of religion do not account for social formations and their myths (or ideologies) by appeal either to a single cause ("origin") or to the priority of persuasion ("belief") in matters of social attraction, conversion, commitment, and cultural change.

We need not have worried. The proposal to refocus the quest for Christian origins from Jesus to the investments made by early Christians was hardly questioned. Recent scholarship had already succeeded in identifying many disparate social-textual locations from the first one hundred years, and thus had begun to question their social dynamics. Early Christian texts without canonical status had taken their places on our desks and required explanation. Neither the Lukan history nor the trunk and branches model worked for organizing early Christian data. These texts and layers of texts not only indicate many social locations; they indicate groups of different formations, teachings of divergent purposes, and myths that, though incompatible with one another, can be seen as appropriate for their particular locations. As for the different kinds of social formation, studies have begun to identify features of movements, schools, "voluntary" associations, households, hospitality networks, synagogues, and mystery cults in various combinations among early Christian groupings. Thus the questions confronting New Testament scholars are: how to account for them, how to treat them, what to look for now that the framework for placement, comparison, and interpretation can no longer be a developmental history of elaboration based upon a single, fundamental persuasion about the significance of the historical Jesus. To engage all of these texts and questions requires that the shift in perspective be radical, away from a fascination with the single origin, linear development assumption (i.e. the gospel story and portrait of Jesus), and towards a recognition that different myths were generated for different reasons in different social locations. And so, with most of our colleagues agreeing with us about the state of New Testament studies, the reasons for making the proposal were quickly perceived and well received, but the method we proposed for examining the fact of many different groups and mythologies did create some problems. We had in effect tried to set an agenda without saying how to approach it or where engaging it might lead.

As this proposal was shared and discussed with colleagues during the course of the next year, two persistent questions revealed the difficulty some were having with the conception of the project. One question was that, if the new map consists of disparate loci of different moments of mythmaking and social formation, how can we still regard them all as "Christian," and how can we account for the fact that all of them appealed to Jesus as their founder? This question was serious because we were hoping eventually to be able to say something about *Christian* origins. But the question also assumes that, if all early Christian groups claimed Jesus as their founder, and if we still regard them all as "Christian," no matter how diverse, the quest for Christian origins has to say something about the person they all viewed as their founder. It is easy to see that this question derives from the traditional view of Christian origins and is simply another way to rephrase the reasons for the original quest of the historical Jesus. Three observations can be made in answer to it. The first is that the use of the term *Christian* in the phrase "Christian origins" and the frequent reference to "early Christians" are matters of convenience, not capable of being definitional. The second is that the appeal to Jesus by all of the groups we intend to study does raise the question of mutual recognition among these groups and the importance each attached to the name of their founder-figure. But that becomes a datum in need of the kinds of explanation we hope to achieve by asking about the reasons for and interests in the social formations and mythmaking under review. Thus the more important observation is that the many views of Jesus are mythic and that each mythic view corresponds to a particular group's way of thinking about itself. The proper questions to ask of these many myths are, therefore, why these groups would have wanted to create Jesus myths at all, and how those myths related to the activities of these early

Christians. Only by placing all or many of these myths at some intersection of social formation and discursive activity can proposals for the reasons be suggested.

A second question is closely related to the first, but more sophisticated in its perception of the problem. If all of these groups and their myths turn out to be different instances of a common phenomenon, and the common feature cannot be traced to the influence of their founder-figure, what may the common phenomenon have been? This question is in fact quite interesting, once one sees that the common feature does not have to be, indeed cannot have been, anything that the historical Jesus actually may have done, experienced, or represented. The question, rather, is what all of the myth-making about Jesus may have had in common when investigated in relation to the various social formations in which each myth was generated and in relation to the challenges of the Greco-Roman world. If the seminar can make some proposals in answer to this question, it will have succeeded in offering an explanation for Christian origins that has little to do with the historical Jesus and much to do with the reasons people had for investing themselves in the social experiments that thought of Jesus as their founder.

The Seminar Plan

Thus it was decided to address these questions at the second consultation by examining a particular practice (meeting for meals) and a specific site (Corinth). This consultation was at the annual meeting in New Orleans. Stanley Stowers, Brown University, was asked to present a paper on the meal text in Paul's letter to the Corinthians in light of the work he had been doing on Greek "sacrifice" *(thusia)* and its social and political functions. Hal Taussig, Chestnut Hill College, was asked to present a paper on the ritualization of the meal in Corinth. The papers were excellent examples of what might be learned by focusing on the intersection of a social formation and its mythic rationale, but it soon dawned on the presenters and conveners of the consultation that the question of "origins" did not automatically surface. It was too easy, apparently, to bypass the question of the dynamics between social formation and mythmaking, to assume that we knew why these Corinthians had formed such a group and were eating together, and why the *christos* myth was already accepted. We simply overlooked these questions and moved on to the more interesting task of describing more fully their practices. Thus a strategy would be needed to focus the work of our seminar on the questions of attraction, social formation, and mythmaking.

The strategy question was hotly debated within the steering committee and among other members of the seminar. There was general agreement about the state of New Testament studies and the goals of the seminar project, but little wisdom on how to proceed. All were clear about dispensing with the quest for the historical Jesus. Everyone thought that the fact that there were many different groups of early Jesus people and *christos* people had to be explained. All emphasized taking a "social description" approach to the study of these groups. Using a wide-angle lens that opened out onto the Greco-Roman world was taken for granted, as was the care that had to be taken in selecting analogues for comparison with early Christian practices. Most were ready to consider my notion of locating the intersections of "social formation" and "mythmaking." And all were eager to be freed from the monolinear Lukan model of the first chapters of Christian beginnings. The problems had to do with our texts, determining which might provide adequate data for the kinds of reconstruction thought necessary, and which groups were best to "visit" if we really wanted to challenge the traditional paradigm, draw a new map, and render an explanatory account of Christian beginnings.

The proposal was accepted that we make a short list of "sites" for consideration, and work on a plan to "visit" them with my redescription project in mind. In the meantime, a decision was made to use the third (and last) consultation at the meetings in San Francisco, 1997, to "visit" two early "sites" as a test-case for the proposal. The sites were the social-historical settings for Q and the Gospel of Thomas. Several members of the seminar had worked on these texts; both texts had already been assigned by New Testament scholars to the "Jesus movements"; and each had played an important role in challenging the dominant paradigm of Christian origins. If we were able to turn these texts into sites on a new map of Christian origins, the seminar project could be launched.

The San Francisco meeting was a stunning success. Willi Braun surprised us by arguing that the "school of Q" could be compared to

(1) those who made collections of the Greek Magical Papyri, (2) the Epicurean "school," and (3) the pre-rabbinic priestly-scribal associations that Jack Lightstone has described. William Arnal developed a strong argumentation for scribal deracination as the social situation and motivational impulse for the Q people. Ron Cameron demonstrated the "intellectual labor" involved in "working" with the sayings of Jesus in the Thomas tradition, i.e. he put the text of Thomas squarely within a "school" setting. And Arthur Dewey analyzed the mode and method of memorization that produced the curious tenor of the sayings of Jesus in Thomas. Not having worked together before as a scholarly seminar, we were barely able to respond to these papers, much less to press the presenters on the agenda of a Christian origins project. We all knew, however, that the project had begun. The expertise of a scholar trained in New Testament studies *could* be brought to focus on the question of the social interests, practices, and rationalizations required to render a new account of Christian origins. It was now possible to form a seminar under the auspices of the Society of Biblical Literature and plan a six-year schedule of work.

The plans were laid to visit (1) the so-called First Church in Jerusalem, (2) the "pre-Pauline" congregations of the Christ, (3) Paul and the Corinthians, and (4) the Markan "community," leaving two meetings unscheduled while we tested our pace. These social-textual locations ("sites") were selected for two reasons. One is that they were certain to offer a range of social and discursive differences with which to work. The other is that each has been pivotal for the traditional view of Christian origins. If renewed investigation can show that the traditional interpretations of these sites are problematic, that they cannot be made to fit the traditional scenario of a gospel account of Christian beginnings, the need for an alternative explanation and a different history of the whole will become clear. Thus the aim of the seminar's plan is to open a few windows onto that history and offer explanations in keeping with theories of social formation and mythmaking. If that can be done, an alternative account of Christian beginnings will begin to take the shape of a new "map." The new map will not paraphrase the Lukan story line, or provide an alternative master narrative. It will consist in identifying several moments of mythmaking in diverse social, historical, and geographical locations. The new map will pinpoint these moments as data in need of more explanation.

The Seminar's Accomplishments

In 1998 the seminar visited the site of the Jerusalem "pillars" by focusing upon Paul's description in Galatians 2. In 1999 the attempt was made to locate the site for the first use of the term *christos* in the "pre-Pauline" congregations from whom Paul must have learned about the designation. In 2000 the seminar visited Corinth and asked about the social models that were taken for granted by the Corinthians and by Paul. Major papers were produced and distributed in advance for each session by members of the seminar. E-mail was used to register responses and engage in debates throughout the year. Debriefing memos were written after each session. And discussions at the meetings began to surface questions of serious issue having to do with method and theory. A first volume of papers with extensive introductions and commentary is planned to cover the work of the seminar for the sessions on Q and Thomas, Jerusalem, and the pre-Pauline *christos* question. This and other volumes will appear in the Symposium Series of Scholars Press.

In retrospect, there is no question about one important result of this work of the seminar. It has succeeded in problematizing the customary imagination of Christian origins. The notion of a "first Church in Jerusalem" was thoroughly analyzed and found wanting. The texts traditionally used as a basis for the notion were scrutinized. Strong and persuasive alternative readings argue for the fictional constructions of mythic events in Jerusalem on the model of diaspora perspectives on the epic and mythic importance of Jerusalem. The "reports" of Paul and the narratives of Luke both use the diaspora perspective to great rhetorical advantage. Thus these constructions can be accounted for as claims upon the mythic importance that Jerusalem had for diaspora Jews and early Christians. Though the "pillars" in Jerusalem with whom Paul held conversations may have been "Jesus people," there is nothing in Paul's report that describes their relationship to the other Jesus peoples of whom we have some evidence, or explains why they were there. The few features that can be extracted from the report by inference and deduction all point to a strikingly different interpretation of the importance of Jesus than anything available to us elsewhere from the first chapters of Christian beginnings. In no case can the construction of a "Christian" persuasion and congregation be put upon these "pillars." Thus the emergence of a Christian congregation in Jerusalem in the immediate wake of the gospel story of Jesus needs to be deleted from the traditional imagination of Christian origins. There is absolutely no evidence for it.

The question of the first use of the term *christos* could be phrased quite precisely. That is because *christos* does not occur in the early Jesus traditions such as Q and Thomas, and in Paul it was already and oddly used as a name, not as an attributive (or as a title as happened later in Mark's gospel). In order to explain these curiosities, Merrill Miller produced a set of papers on the uses of the terms *messiah* in Jewish literature of the period and *christos* in early Christian literature. The conclusion he came to was that the first use of the term in some "pre-Pauline" Jesus school was not "messianic," could not have been "messianic," and makes no sense at all when pushed back into the life of the historical Jesus, as has usually been imagined. Miller's studies will be included among the seminar papers planned for publication.

Putting these two sessions together with the work accomplished in the third consultation on Q and Thomas, the seminar has demonstrated that the traditional (Lukan) imagination of Christian origins cannot be right. It not only has no documentation upon which to build, the very texts traditionally thought to support it read better another way. That other way is in support of the mythmaking engaged in by other groups in other locations. Thus the project's theory about the importance of mythmaking for different social formations has received some confirmation.

Less progress was made, however, on the description of these sites for the purposes of drawing a new map of Christian beginnings. That is because the seminar has not yet found a way to bring comparisons and redescriptions to a satisfactory conclusion, or to devise the theory required for the explanations it seeks. These tasks are new, difficult, and demanding. Nevertheless, some observations can be made about the seminar's discourse-in-the-making that bode well for the future of the project. As an example, the seminar has begun thinking about the relative merits among several social formations of the Greco-Roman time for comparison with various early Christian formations. Schools, associations, cults, synagogues, and households are all in the picture and under discussion in relation to the variety of self-designations that early Christian groups used for their collective identities.

The seminar has also made some important observations about the *experimental* and *reflexive* nature of most early Christian group formations for which we have some evidence. These groups were *experimental* in that the marks of novelty, discussion, debate, and changing configurations of both social formation and mythology are features shared by all of the sites available for investigation. They were *reflexive* in relation to their social and cultural contexts. "Reflexive" means that they positioned themselves within and over against the larger social and cultural worlds by rendering critical judgments about their cultures of context and their relationships to them, and by seeking liaison with other groups and social institutions. This resulted in the critique, borrowing, rearrangement, and resignification of various practices and ideas from that larger world context. Most early Christian groups do not appear to have formed enclaves to encourage personal withdrawal, private meditation or individual transformation. They were actively engaged in forming groups and in carving out a place for themselves as social units within their larger social and cultural arenas.

Another observation has to do with a mythmaking strategy in common among all of these groups, namely an appeal to the epic of Israel. The many attempts to claim alignment, precedence, promise, and theological linkage with the epic of Israel are not coherent when lumped together. But the purpose of the strategy is similar from group to group, and this provides us with a clue to the social projects driving these experiments. The social project must have been both reflexive and cross-cultural by design. The project was to reimagine and reinvent the collective (in this case, "Israel") in a form appropriate for the larger human horizon of the Greco-Roman age. They were able to do this in embryo by tinkering with the Greek models for households, schools, and associations. Note that the Israel epic provided what might be called the primary resources for mythmaking both in regard to the founder-figure Jesus and in application to the identity of a group as a way of being "Israel." In both applications appeal to the Israel epic softened the otherwise sharp edges of the claim to novelty and the fact of experimentation.

Also in keeping with normal modes of mythmaking, all of these groups entertained views of the world that included the expanded horizons of what we have come to call the *cosmos*. This would not be a remarkable feature were it not for the fact that these were small, experimental associations with very questionable claims to any social or intellectual tradition from which an appropriately rationalized cosmic imagination might have been automatically taken. That cosmic speculations energized early Christians can only mean that they wanted to imagine themselves taking their place in the larger scheme of things, often in the very center of that scheme.

Thus, a terminology appropriate to the project has begun to surface, including semi-technical terms to describe features of the *social formations* and *mythmaking* under review (such as *experimental, reflexive, fictive,* and *collective*). This suggests that the seminar is already producing a discourse to support its collaborative efforts in historiography. However, it has also begun to raise very serious questions about the use of *attraction* as a self-evident term for the *social interests* and *motivations* that need to be ascertained if we want to render an *explanation* as well as an *account* of these early social experiments. And the question of the relation between social formation and mythmaking has produced an important second-level discussion of social theory and religion.

The Quest for Social Theory

The need for social theory has increased as the project has developed. The scenario of Christian origins now in the process of being redescribed as a new map of experimental social formations and mythmaking requires theoretical confirmation and explanation. The customary "explanations" for Christian origins assume a certain view of human history (that it is open to divine interventions) and a certain anthropology (that mystifications and second-hand reports of revelations are automatic and sufficient modes of persuasion and belief). What can be put in their place to account for the human energies and social interests that were obviously driving this cluster of social experiments?

The "social approaches" to early Christian groups and texts characteristic of New Testament studies in our generation have relied heavily on (1) Weber's views on charisma and cultural change, and (2) the quantitative, social-scientific study of religious groups in America. Not surprisingly, when applied to early Christianity, neither the Weberian tradition nor the social-scientific approach has produced a critique of the dominant paradigm of Christian origins: Jesus remains in place as the charismatic founder-figure; early Christians are still cast as believers in the miraculous events of Jesus's appearance; early Christian groups are described as worshiping congregations (i.e., "churches"); and the main attraction for Christianity's success is thought to be its offer of "personal salvation" (See Mack's response to Rodney Stark, 1999). Since these features of the dominant paradigm are no longer applicable to the material evidence critical scholars have as data for Christian origins, it means that another approach to social and anthropological theory is called for.

The three academic traditions of greatest potential for social theory, including a social theory of religion, have not been entertained by New Testament scholars: those stemming from Durkheim, Marx, and cultural anthropology. The Durkheim tradition has seldom been invoked, much less pursued and applied. The few applications of Marxist theory have been spotty, belabored, and anachronistic ideologically. And the rich resevoir of ethnography available to historians of religion and cultural anthropologists has rarely been recognized, much less touched upon to explain early Christian phenomena.

Recently, however, Jonathan Z. Smith has traced critical moments in the development of social theory from Durkheim through Dumézil, Lévi-Strauss, Dumont, Wheatley, and others, calling upon ethnography to provide data for a social theory of religion. The move from social theory in general to a theory of religion in particular is possible with Smith because of a profound and critical investment in what might be called a rational (or intellectual) social anthropology. Smith has applied his social theory to early Judaisms and Christianities in two important books: *To Take Place: Toward Theory in Ritual* (1987); and *Drudgery Divine: On the Comparison of Early Christianities and the Religions of Late Antiquity* (1990). Smith's work is foundational for the Christian origins project of the seminar. My own work on early Christian texts has consistently been an attempt to apply Smith's intellectualist theories of myth, ritual, religion, and social behavior to early Christian groups and their thinking. In doing so, the need to account for social and cultural change has become critical in order to account for the emergence of new formations. It is the fact of changing formations that has determined the use of *social formation* and *mythmaking* as technical terms, both of which are intended to be taken as gerunds, i.e. concepts of dynamic processes.

Starting with the observation that all early Christian groups focused their attention primarily upon themselves as social formations, the question naturally arises as to whether that interest in social formation can be understood as a sufficient motivation or generator for the phenomenon itself. Is interest in social formation an interest common to all human social formations? Can it be spelled out or defined with precision? Is it basic to "the human enterprise" of creating societies? Can it explain the phenomena of myths and rituals (i.e. what modern scholars have identified as "religious" phenomena) as well as other systems of signs and patterns of practices that appear to have more immediate relevance to social constructions and processes? These questions demand having another look at Smith's social and intellectual anthropology, his data base in ethnography, and his debates with cultural anthropologists on the best ways to test and refine theory.

In the meantime, however, the question of the relationship between social formation and mythmaking has been receiving much attention among seminar members. The study of this intersection has as one of its goals not only to construct a profile of the social situation, and a reading of the text as a distinctive literary creation contemporary to that social situation, but to work out the connections between them. These relationships included those features of the social situation which may have called for or generated the text, and the way in which the rhetoric of the text may be understood to have addressed the situation. In order to control the description of an early Christian social location, comparison with models, groups, and practices current in the social worlds of the Greco-Roman age is required, and that move puts us in touch with chapters of the human story for which we do not usually need extra explanatory theories.

And yet, even in these cases of social experimentation drawn from the Greco-Roman world, the relationship between social formation and mythmaking will not be clear without attention to theories of each as human constructions. Thus their descriptions are not yet *explanations* of why and how a given combination occurs, of why the people were thinking and acting as they were, in what they were interested, and what the effective difference might be of each factor of social construction and mythmaking.

Differences in the way in which members of the seminar viewed this relationship between social formation and mythmaking already surfaced at the session on Q and Thomas. Then, in the summer of 1999, a special conference was arranged at the University of Vermont to discuss whether members of the seminar might want to develop a second track to focus on a discussion of social theory, one that would not endanger the concentration of effort on site descriptions. Since members of the North American Association for the Study of Religion had become interested in the Christian Origins Project, they invited us to meet with them and/or under their auspices for the purpose of holding theoretical discussions. Two such meetings have taken place (in 1996 and 1999), and others are tentatively planned. Several members of the seminar have been asked to prepare papers or statements that address the theoretical underpinnings of the project, and a formal presentation on theoretical issues in the application of the terms *social formation* and *mythmaking* was made by Willi Braun and William Arnal at the meeting of the seminar in 2000. The reader will find my own response to this quest for social theory in chapters 4 and 5 of this book.

Thus the seminar is poised to make a significant contribution both to early Christian studies and to studies in the theory of myth and social formation. This is remarkable when one considers the fact that the guild of New Testament studies has never made room for theoretical discussions of religion and society. It is of course much too soon to tell whether the guild of New Testament scholars will want to engage the work of this seminar. But supposing they will, a marvelous chapter of honest intellectual and exciting academic debate can be imagined. The seminar hopes that this debate will take place and that it will clarify issues not only for explaining Christian origins, but for participating in the cultural critique called for by our times.

The proper controls for the further investigation of each of these strategies by the seminar appear to be (1) a wide-angle lens focused upon the many ways in which people responded to the Greco-Roman age, and (2) a social theory of religion grounded in a theory of social interests.

ACKNOWLEDGMENTS

This book offers an account of my work since the publication of *Who Wrote the New Testament?* (1995). My plan at that time was to work on a social theory of religion, for I had been chided by colleagues for not spelling out the theory that informed my interpretations of the Gospel of Mark *(A Myth of Innocence,* 1988) and the document Q *(The Lost Gospel,* 1993). And then Merrill Miller and Ron Cameron swept me into their orbit of planning for a seminar on redescribing Christian origins under the auspices of the Society of Biblical Literature. I was soon fully engaged with their schedule of assignments, topics, and seminar sessions and found myself bouncing back and forth between early Christian studies and studies in the sociology and history of religions. My work has taken the form of numerous call and response papers, e-mail letters, debriefing memos, university and conference lectures, and commissioned essays. In keeping with Sartre's dictum about recognizing the thrust of one's projects only in retrospect, it finally occurred to me that I had been getting ready to make a statement about the making, logic, and legacy of the Christian Myth.

All of the chapters in this book draw upon earlier drafts of papers and lectures written for various occasions. All have been revised and rewritten in keeping with the theme of the book.

1. "The Historical Jesus Hoopla" draws upon a lecture given to a workshop for high school teachers in Vejen, Denmark, and a paper students asked me to write at the end of a course on the teachings of Jesus which I taught at Claremont.

2. "The Case for a Cynic-like Jesus" draws upon an essay-lecture that I rewrote many times for presentation on different occasions. One version of this lecture, given at the 1993 meeting of the Cana-

dian Learneds, was eventually published in the anthology called *Whose Historical Jesus?* edited by William Arnal and Michel Desjardins. Since I think the quest for the historical Jesus misguided, but am most interested in the ways in which myths about him were generated, I reworked this essay to make that point clear and to introduce the reader to another locus and notion of "Christian origins." Exploring this other locus is the major theme of the book.

3. "On Redescribing Christian Origins" is a slightly emended version of the call paper for the first consultation on "Ancient Myths and Modern Theories of Christian Origins" in Philadelphia, 1995. It presents the rationale for the project in which I and members of the seminar on Christian origins have been involved. The original paper was published in *Method and Theory in the Study of Religion* 8/3, 1996.

4. "Explaining Religion: A Theory of Social Interests" is the first of the Larkin-Stuart Lectures given at Trinity College, University of Toronto, in October, 1999. It was also shared with a graduate faculty-student seminar at Brown University, April 2000.

5. "Explaining Christian Mythmaking: A Theory of Social Logic" is the second of the Larkin-Stuart lectures, Trinity College, Toronto, 1999. It was also presented at the east coast meeting of the Society of Biblical Literature, April 2000. This lecture has been substantially rewritten.

6. "Innocence, Power, and Purity in the Christian Imagination" is a reprint of my contribution to a three year project of "Bible and Theology" sponsored by the Lilly Foundation in which I was part of a small subgroup of 12 under the leadership of William Schweiker (Chicago) and Michael Welker (Heidelberg). We were asked to see if biblical scholars and theologians could talk to each other about "power," a major and problematic concept in both the human sciences and the history of religions. The paper presented to the plenary session of the Bible and Theology Project in 1994 has been published in *Power, Powerlessness, and the Divine: New Inquiries in Bible and Theology*, edited by Cynthia Rigby (Scholars Press, 1997). This essay is critical to the development of the present book's theme, and is part of the foundation for the final chapter on the legacy of the Christian myth in American culture.

7. "Christ and the Creation of a Monocratic Culture" is a paper I wrote for a conference on the subject of Christianity's influence on the political history of "western civilization" in Mexico City, February, 1997. Three European, two American, and five Mexican scholars read papers in public forum and met privately for scholarly discussion of Christianity's role in the history of western culture and its spread. The Spanish translation of my paper has appeared in *La genealogía del christianismo: origen de Occidente?* Edited by Herbert Frey (Conuculta, Mexico, 2000); the English text appears here for the first time.

8. "The Christian Myth and the Christian Nation" presents the outline of a research project on the legacy of the Christian myth in American society, culture, and politics. It traces the way in which the Christian myth has been understood and used throughout the history of the United States when that history is viewed as an experiment in social formation and mythmaking.

The description of "The Christian Origins Project" in the Annex is an account of the work of the seminar on "Ancient Myths and Modern Theories of Christian Origins." It draws upon a paper written at the request of colleagues in Denmark and discussed at the Universities of Odense, Aarhus, and Copenhagen in the fall of 1999. That paper was written as a succinct "outline" of the seminar's project and its rationale and contained a bit of theory. It was also discussed at a special session of the North American Association for the Study of Religion in November, 1999. Rewritten for inclusion in this book, the chapter deletes the sections on theory and expands upon the work of the seminar during its first five years. It is presented in this book as an invitation to imagine the next steps in an ongoing project in the redescription of Christian origins.

I would like to express my appreciation to the members of the seminar for their critical engagement of my work, and especially to Merrill Miller and Ron Cameron for their leadership of the group. I have learned much from them and from the scholars they have brought together for this project. They and an expanded circle of academics have made it possible for me to continue thinking critically about my own scholarly projects. I am expecially indebted to Engolf Ahlers, William Arnal, Willi Braun, Herbert Frey, Tim Jensen, Jeppe Sinding Jensen, Hans Kippenberg, Luther Martin, Russell McCutcheon, William Schweiker, Jonathan Z. Smith, Stanley Stowers, Michael Welker, Donald Wiebe, Stephen Wilson, and Vincent Wimbush for important contributions at critical moments in my quest for conceptual clarity about the logic and legacy of the Christian myth.

For the encouragement to turn these papers into a book I am endebted most of all to Justus George Lawler who has followed the reception of my work in the field of biblical studies with exceptional critical acumen for fifteen years and who saw that it was time for me to render an account of my work during the past six years. I am deeply indebted to him for his insights and guidance in the production of this book. Without BJ, however, I would not have been able to manage the rewriting required in order to bring these papers together. If my prose is readable and my arguments clear, it is to her credit, for she has been gently persistent with her close readings to make sure my descriptions are accurate and telling.

Apologies are in order for several unavoidable stylistic infelicities. One is the use of "America" and "American" by which I intend a reference only to the people of the United States of America. A second is the use of an italicized and lower case *christos* when referring to early Christian usage before Mark. The exegetical issue is explained toward the end of chapter 5. It is important that the reader *not* think of the traditional concept of "the Messiah" when reference is made to *christos*, the *christos* myth, or Jesus *christos*. Mark was the first to use the term as a title and special designation for Jesus's eschatological role as "king," thus "the Christ." A third infelicity is the use of "early Christian(s)" as a general designation for the Jesus movements and the *christos* groups of the formative period of Christian beginnings. This is a usage of convenience, not intended as definitional.

REFERENCES

Achtemeier, Paul
　1970　　　　"Toward the Isolation of Pre-Markan Miracle Catenae."
　　　　　　　Journal of Biblical Literature 89 265–91.
　1972　　　　"The Origin and Function of the Pre-Markan Miracle Ca-
　　　　　　　tenae." *Journal of Biblical Literature* 91 198–222.

Alsup, John E.
　1975　　　　*The Post-Resurrection Appearance Stories of the Gospel Tradi-
　　　　　　　tion*. Calwer Theologische Monographien 5. Stuttgart: Cal-
　　　　　　　wer Verlag.

Arnal, William E.
　1997　　　　"The Rhetoric of Deracination in Q: A Reappraisal." Ph.D.
　　　　　　　diss., Centre for the Study of Religion, University of To-
　　　　　　　ronto.
　2001　　　　*Jesus and the Village Scribes: Galilean Conflicts and the Setting
　　　　　　　of Q*. Minneapolis: Fortress Press.

Aune, David
　1992　　　　"Christian Prophecy and the Messianic Status of Jesus." *The
　　　　　　　Messiah: Developments in Earliest Judaism and Christianity*.
　　　　　　　Edited by James H. Charlesworth, 404–422. The First
　　　　　　　Princeton Symposium on Judaism and Christian Origins.
　　　　　　　Minneapolis: Fortress Press.

Banks, Russell
　2000　　　　"The Star-Spangled Novel." *Los Angelest Times Book Review*
　　　　　　　(Sunday, July 2, 2000) 1–4. Reprint from *Harper's* maga-
　　　　　　　zine, June 2000.

Bloom, Harold
　1972　　　　*The Anxiety of Influence*. New York and London: Oxford
　　　　　　　University Press.
　1992　　　　*The American Religion*. New York: Simon and Schuster.

Boas, Franz
　1940, 1966　*Race, Language, and Culture*. New York: Macmillan Free
　　　　　　　Press.

Borg, Marcus
　1987　　　　*Jesus: A New Vision: Spirit, Culture, and the Life of Disciple-
　　　　　　　ship*. Harper and Row: San Francisco.
　1994　　　　*Meeting Jesus Again for the First Time: The Historical
　　　　　　　Jesus and the Heart of Contemporary Faith*. HarperSanFran-
　　　　　　　cisco.

Bourdieu, Pierre
　1972　　　　*Esquisse d'une théorie de la pratique*. Geneva: Droz.
　1977　　　　English translation: *Outline of a Theory of Practice*. Richard

Bourdieu, Pierre *(cont'd)*
> Nice, trans. Cambridge Studies in Social Anthropology, vol. 16. Cambridge: Cambridge University Press.

Boyarin, Daniel
> 1990   *Intertextuality and the Reading of Midrash*. Indiana University Press.
>
> 1994   *A Radical Jew: Paul and the Politics of Identity*. Berkeley: University of California Press.

Braun, Willi
> 1995   *Feasting and Social Rhetoric in Luke 14*. SNTSMS 85. Cambridge and New York: Cambridge University Press.

Braun, Willi, and Russell T. McCutcheon.
> 2000   *Guide to the Study of Religion*. New York: Cassell.

Brown, Peter
> 1971   "The Rise and Function of the Holy Man in Late Antiquity." *Journal of Roman Studies* 61 80–101.

Bugliosi, Vincent
> 2001   "None Dare Call It Treason." *The Nation* (February 5) 11–19.

Bultmann, Rudolf
> 1921   *Die Geschichte der synoptischen Tradition*. Göttingen: Vandenhoeck & Ruprecht.
>
> 1963   English translation: *The History of the Synoptic Tradition*. John Marsh, trans. Oxford: Basil Blackwell.
>
> 1961   "Der religionsgeschichtliche Hintergrund des Prologs zum Johannesevangelium." *Eucharisterion* (Festschrift für H. Gunkel), 1–26. *FRLANT* 60. Göttingen: Vandenhoeck und Ruprecht.

Cameron, Ron
> 1990   " 'What Have You Come Out To See?' Characterizations of John and Jesus in the Gospels." *Semeia 49: The Apocryphal Jesus and Christian Origins*. Edited by Ron Cameron, 35–69. Atlanta: Scholars Press.
>
> 1994   "Alternate Beginnings — Different Ends: Eusebius, Thomas, and the Construction of Christian Origins." *Religious Propaganda and Missionary Competition in the New Testament World*. Essays Honoring Dieter Georgi. Edited by Lukas Borman, Kelly Del Tredici, and Angela Standhartinger, 501–25. Novum Testamentum Supplements LXXIV. Leiden: E. J. Brill.

Carter, Jimmy
> 2000   *An Hour Before Daylight*. New York: Simon & Schuster.

Castelli, Elizabeth
    1992   *Imitating Paul: A Discourse of Power*. Louisville, KY: Westminster/John Knox Press.

Charlesworth, James H.
    1992   "From Messianology to Christology: Problems and Prospects." *The Messiah: Developments in Earliest Judaism and Christianity*. Edited by James H. Charlesworth, 3–35. The First Princeton Symposium on Judaism and Christian Origins. Minneapolis: Fortress Press.

Collins, Adela Yarbro
    1984   *Crisis and Catharsis: The Power of the Apocalypse*. Philadelphia: Westminster Press.

Conzelmann, Hans
    1966   "On the Analysis of the Confessional Formula in I Corinthians 15:3–5." *Interpretation* 20 15–25.

Corley, Kathleen
    1993   *Private Women, Public Meals: Social Conflict in the Synoptic Tradition*. Peabody, MA: Hendrickson Publishers.

Crossan, John Dominic
    1973   *In Parables: The Challenge of the Historical Jesus*. New York: Harper and Row.
    1991   *The Historical Jesus: The Life of a Mediterranean Jewish Peasant*. HarperSanFrancisco.
    1995   *Who Killed Jesus? Exposing the Roots of Anti-Semitism in the Gospel Story of the Death of Jesus*. HarperSanFrancisco.

Detienne, Marcel, and Jean-Pierre Vernant
    1978   *Cunning Intelligence in Greek Culture and Society*. Eng. trans. Janet Lloyd. Atlantic Heights, NJ: Humanities Press.

Downing, F. Gerald
    1988   *Christ and the Cynics: Jesus and Other Radical Preachers in First-Century Tradition*. Sheffield: Sheffield University Press.
    1992   *Cynics and Christian Origins*. Edinburgh: T. & T. Clark.

Dumézil, Georges
    1958   *L'Idéologie tripartie des Indo-Européens*. Brussels: Latomus.

Durkheim, Émile
    1912   *Les Formes élémentaires de la vie religieuse*. Paris: F. Alcan (4th ed. 1960).
    1915, 1965   English translation: *The Elementary Forms of the Religious Life*. J. S. Swain, London: Allen and Unwin; New York: Free Press.

Durkheim, Émile *(cont'd)*
1995   English translation: *The Elementary Forms of Religious Life*. Karen E. Fields, trans, with an Introduction. New York: Free Press.

Efroymson, David P.
1979   "The Patristic Connection." *Antisemitism and the Foundations of Christianity*. Edited by Alan T. Davies, 98–117. New York: Paulist Press.

Felton, Rebecca Latimer
1980   *Country Life in Georgia in the Days of My Youth*. New York: Arno Press.

1897   Letter to the Editor of the Boston Transcript.

Fischel, Henry A.
1968   "Studies in Cynicism and the Ancient Near East: The Transformation of a Chria." *Religions in Antiquity: Essays in Memory of Erwin Ramsdell Goodenough*. Edited by J. Neusner, 372–411. Studies in the History of Religions 14. Leiden: E. J. Brill.

Fowler, Robert M.
1981   *Loaves and Fishes: The Function of the Feeding Stories in the Gospel of Mark*. Society of Biblical Literature Dissertation Series 54. Chico, CA: Scholars Press.

Fredriksen, Paula
1988   *From Jesus to Christ*. New Haven: Yale University Press.

Funk, Robert
1996   *Language, Hermeneutic and Word of God*. New York: Harper and Row.

1966   *Honest to Jesus: Jesus for a New Millennium*. HarperSanFrancisco.

Funk, Robert, Roy Hoover, and the Jesus Seminar
1993   *The Five Gospels: The Search for the Authentic Words of Jesus*. Polebridge Press and Macmillan Press.

Geertz, Clifford
1960   *The Religion of Java*. Chicago: University of Chicago Press.

1973   *The Interpretation of Cultures: Selected Essays*. New York: Basic Books.

Gennep, Arnold van
1909   *Les rites de passage*. Paris.

1960, 1969 English translation: *The Rites of Passage*. Monika B. Vizedom and Garielle Cafee. Chicago: University of Chicago Press; New York: Johnson Reprint.

Grabbe, Lester L.
1992   *Judaism from Cyrus to Hadrian.* 2 volumes. Minneapolis:
            Fortress Press.

Gregg, Robert
1993   "Jews, Pagans, and Christians in the Ancient Golan." Slide
            lecture at Claremont, CA: Institute for Antiquity and Chris-
            tianity.

Hanson, K. C
1994   "How Honorable, How Shameful: A Cultural Analysis of
            Makarisms and Reproaches." *Semeia* 68: *Honor and Shame
            in the World of the Bible.* Edited by Victor H. Matthews and
            Don C. Benjamin, 81–111.

Harris, Trudier
1984   *Exorcising Blackness: Historical and Literary Lynching and
            Burning Rituals.* Bloomington, Indiana: Indiana University
            Press.

Hengel, Martin
1974   *Judaism and Hellenism: Studies in Their Encounter in Pales-
            tine during the Early Hellenistic Period.* 2 volumes. Eng-
            lish translation by J. Bowdon. Philadelphia: Fortress
            Press.

Hock, Ronald F., and Edward N. O'Neil
1986   *The Chreia in Ancient Rhetoric.* Volume I. *The Progymnas-
            mata.* Texts and Translations 27. Graeco-Roman Religion
            Series 9. Atlanta, GA: Scholars Press.

Horsley, Richard A.
1985   "Menahem in Jerusalem: A Brief Messianic Episode among
            the Sicarii—Not 'Zealot Messianism.'" *Novum Testamen-
            tum* 27 334–48.

1987   *Jesus and the Spiral of Violence: Popular Jewish Resistance in
            Roman Palestine.* Harper and Row: San Francisco.

Hultkrantz, Åke
1979   *The Religions of the American Indians.* Monica Setterwall,
            trans. Berkeley, CA: University of California Press.

Jewett, Robert, and John Shelton Lawrence
1977, 1988 *The American Monomyth.* Garden City, New York: Double-
            day; New York and London: Lanham.

Johnson, Luke Timothy
1982   "Rom. 3:21–26 and the Faith of Jesus." *Catholic Biblical
            Quarterly* 44 77–90.

Johnson, Luke Timothy *(cont'd)*
1996   *The Real Jesus: The Misguided Quest for the Historical Jesus and the Truth of the Traditional Gospels.* HarperSanFrancisco.

Johnson, Scott
1985   " 'Star Wars' Trusts in Our Innocence, Not Our Nightmares." *Los Angeles Times*, Opinion, May 7.

Johnson, Steven
1993   "Baptism in the Pauline and Matthean Communities." Paper delivered to the West Coast Region, Society of Biblical Literature, Los Angeles, March.

Kee, Howard Clark
1983   *Miracle in the Early Christian World.* New Haven: Yale University Press.

Kelber, Werner
1983   "Apostolic Tradition and the Genre of the Gospel." Paper delivered to a Symposium on Discipleship, Marquette University, April 15–17.

Kelber, Werner, ed.
1976   *The Passion in Mark: Studies on Mark 14–16.* Philadelphia: Fortress Press.

King, Karen
1990   "Gnosticism as Social Criticism." Paper presented to the Gaston Symposium, Unversity of Oregon.

Kloppenborg, John
1987   *The Formation of Q: Trajectories in Ancient Wisdom Collections.* Studies in Antiquity and Christianity. Philadelphia: Fortress Press.
1988   *Q Parallels.* Synopsis, Critical Notes, and Concordance. Sonoma, CA: Polebridge Press.
1992   "The Theological Stakes in the Synoptic Problem." *The Four Gospels.* Festschrift Frans Neirynck. Edited by V. Van Segbroeck, et al., 1 93–120. Leuven: Leuven University Press.

Kloppenborg-Verbin, John
2000   *Excavating Q: The History and Setting of the Sayings Gospel.* Edinburgh: T& T Clark.

Klosinski, Lee E.
1988   "The Meals in Mark." Ph.D. diss., Claremont Graduate School.

Köster, Helmut
1971   "One Jesus and Four Primitive Gospels." *Trajectories Through Early Christianity.* Edited by Helmut Köster and James M. Robinson, 158–204. Philadelphia: Fortress Press.

1982   *Introduction to the New Testament.* Volume 2: *History and Literature of Early Christianity.* Philadelphia: Fortress Press.

Kramer, Werner

1966   *Christ, Lord, Son of God.* Studies in Biblical Theology 50. Naperville, IL: Alec R. Allenson.

Lévi-Strauss, Claude

1949   *Les Structures élémentaires de la parenté.* Paris: Presses Universitaires de France.

1969   English translation: *The Elementary Structures of Kinship.* John Harle Bell, Richard von Sturmer and Rodney Needham. Boston: Beacon.

1962   *La pensée sauvage.* Paris: Plon.

1966   English translation: *The Savage Mind.* London: Weidenfeld and Nicolson; Chicago: University of Chicago Press.

Lightstone, Jack

1994   "The Rhetoric of Mishnah and the Emergence of Rabbinic Social Institutions at the End of the Second Century." Paper delivered to the Society of Biblical Literature section on The Social History of Formative Judaism and Christianity, Chicago.

1997   "Whence the Rabbis? From Coherent Description to Fragmented Reconstruction." *SR* 26 275–295.

Locke, John

1958   *The Reasonableness of Christianity.* Stanford: Stanford University. An abridgement of the essay originally published in 1695.

Mack, Burton L.

1988   "The Kingdom that Didn't Come: A Social History of the Q Tradents." *Society of Biblical Literature Seminar Papers* 608–035. Atlanta GA: Scholars Press.

1988   *A Myth of Innocence: Mark and Christian Origins.* Philadelphia: Fortress Press.

1992   "After *Drudgery Divine.*" *Numen* 39/2 225–233.

1993   *The Lost Gospel: The Book of Q and Christian Origins.* HarperSanFrancisco.

1995   "Cogitations." Unpublished paper written for the steering committee of the consultation on "Ancient Myths and Modern Theories of Christian Origins," Society of Biblical Literature. (Available from the author)

1995   *Who Wrote the New Testament? The Making of the Christian Myth.* HarperSanFrancisco.

Mack, Burton L. *(cont'd)*
1997   "Power, Purity and Innocence: The Christian Imagination of the Gospel." *Power, Powerlessness, and the Divine: New Inquiries in Bible and Theology*. Edited by Cynthia L. Rigby, 241–261. Atlanta, GA: Scholars Press.

1997   "Q and a Cynic-Like Jesus." *Whose Historical Jesus?* Edited by William E. Arnal and Michel Desjardins, 25–36. Studies in Christianity and Judaism 7. Waterloo, Ontario: Wilfrid Laurier University Press.

1999   "Many Movements, Many Myths: Redescribing the Attractions of Early Christianities. Toward a Conversation with Rodney Stark." *Religious Studies Review* 25/8 132–136.

Mack, Burton L., and Vernon K. Robbins
1989   *Patterns of Persuasion in the Gospels*. Sonoma, CA: Polebridge Press.

Malina, Bruce
1986   " 'Religion' in the World of Paul: A Preminary Analysis." *Biblical Theological Bulletin* 16 91–101.

Malinowski, Bronislaw
1922   *Argonauts of the Western Pacific: An Account of Native Enterprise and Adventure in the Archipelagoes of Melanesian New Guinea*. Preface by James G. Frazer. London: G. Routledge.

1948, 1955   *Magic, Science and Religion, And Other Essays*. Boston: Beacon; Garden City, New York: Doubleday.

Martin, Luther
1987   *Hellenistic Religions: An Introduction*. New York: Oxford University Press.

1995   "Secrecy in Hellenistic Religious Communities." *Secrecy and Concealment in Late Antique and Islamic History of Religions*. Edited by H. Kippenberg and G. Stroumsa. Leiden: E. J. Brill.

Marxsen, Willi
1979   "The Lord's Supper as Christological Problem." In *The Beginnings of Christology*. Philadelphia: Fortress Press.

Matthew, Christopher
Forthcoming *Philip: Apostle and Evangelist. Configurations of an Early Christian Figure*. Leiden and New York: Brill.

Mauss, Marcel.
1925   *Essai sur le don*, Paris.

1967   English translation: *The Gift: Forms and Functions of Exchange in Archaic Societies*. Ian Cunnison. With an Introduction by E. E. Evans-Pritchard. New York: W. W. Norton.

1990 English translation: *The Gift: The Form and Reason for Exchange in Archaic Societies*. W. D. Halls. Foreword by Mary Douglas. New York: Routledge.

Meeks, Wayne A.
1983 *The First Urban Christians: The Social World of the Apostle Paul*. New Haven: Yale University Press.

Miller, Merrill
1993 "How Jesus Became Christ: Probing a Thesis," *Continuum* 2/2–3 243–270.
1995 " 'Beginning from Jerusalem . . . ': Re-Examining Canon and Consensus." *The Journal of Higher Criticism* 2/1 3–30.
1999 "The Anointed Jesus." Paper prepared for the Seminar on Ancient Myths and Modern Theories of Christian Origins. Boston.

Muller, Max
c. 1900 *Sacred Books of the East . . . with critical and biographical sketches by Epiphanius Wilson*. New York: Colonian Press.

Neusner, Jacob
1974–1977 *A History of the Mishnaic Law of Purities*. 22 volumes. Leiden: E. J. Brill.
1981 *Judaism: The Evidence of the Mishnah*. Chicago: The University of Chicago Press.
1985 *The Pharisees: Rabbinic Perspectives*. New York: Ktav Publishing House.

Neusner, Jacob, William Green, Jonathan Z. Smith, Eds.
1987 *Judaisms and Their Messiahs*. Cambridge: Cambridge University Press.

Nickelsburg, George
1972 *Resurrection, Immortality and Eternal Life in Intertestamental Judaism*. Harvard Theological Studies 26. Cambridge: Harvard University Press.
1980 "The Genre and Function of the Markan Passion Narrative." *Harvard Theological Review* 73 153–84.

Peterson, Erik
1926 *Eis Theos. Epigraphische, formgeschichtliche und religionsgeschichtliche Untersuchungen*. Göttingen: Vandenhoeck & Ruprecht.
1935 "Der Monotheismus als politisches Problem." Leipzig. Reprinted in Erik Peterson, *Theologische Traktate*, 45–147. München: Kosel Verlag, 1951.

Peterson, Erik *(cont'd)*
1951   "Das Problem des Nationalismus im alten Christentum."
     Theologische Zeitschrift VII 81ff.
     Reprinted in Erik Peterson, *Frühkirche, Judentum und Gno-
     sis*, 51–63. Wien: Herder Verlag, 1959.

Pollitt, Katha
2001   "Dear Larry, Thanks! John." *The Nation*, February 5, 10.

Pomykala, Kenneth
1995   *The Davidic Dynasty Tradition in Early Judaism: Its History
     and Significance for Messianism*. SBL series on Early Judaism
     and Its Literature. Atlanta, GA: Scholars Press.

Priest, John
1992   "A Note on the Messianic Banquet." *The Messiah: Develop-
     ments in Earliest Judaism and Christianity*. Edited by James H.
     Charlesworth, 222–238. The First Princeton Symposium on
     Judaism and Christian Origins. Minneapolis: Fortress Press.

Reed, Jonathan
1994   "Places in Early Christianity: Galilee, Archaeology, Urbani-
     zation, and Q." Ph.D. diss. Claremont Graduate School.

Reimarus, Herman Samuel
1778   "Von dem Zwecke Jesu und seiner Juenger, Noch ein Frag-
     ment des Wolfenbüttelschen Ungenannten." Herausgege-
     ben von Gotthold Ephraim Lessing. Braunschweig.
1879   English translation: *The Object of Jesus and His Disciples, as
     seen in the New Testament*. A. Voysey, ed.
1970   English translation: *The Intention of Jesus and his Teaching:
     Reimarus Fragments*. Charles H. Talbert. Philadelphia: For-
     tress.

Reuters News Service
1996   "Scholars' Inquiry Fuels Search for the Historic Jesus," *Los
     Angeles Times*, Metro. April 6 (Contains citation from Ken-
     neth Woodward, editor of *Newsweek*.)

Robbins, Vernon
1989   *Patterns of Persuasion in the Gospels*. Co-authored with
     Burton L. Mack. Sonoma, CA: Polebridge Press.

Robinson, James M.
1959   *A New Quest of the Historical Jesus*. Naperville, Illinois: Alec
     R. Allenson.

Robinson, James M., John S. Kloppenborg, and Paul Hoffmann, Eds.
2000   *The Critical Edition of Q: Synopsis, Including the Gospels of
     Matthew and Luke, Mark and Thomas, with English, German*

and French Translations of Q and Thomas. Managing editor, Milton C. Moreland. Louven: Peeters; Minneapolis: Fortress Press.

Robinson, James, M., John S. Kloppenborg, and Paul Hoffmann, Gen. Eds.
1996–?   *Documenta Q: Reconstructions of Q through Two Centuries of Gospel Research Excerpted, Sorted, and Evaluated.* Edited by Stanley D. Anderson, Sterling G. Bjorndahl, Shawn Carruth, Robert Derrenbacker, and Christoph Heil. Leuven: Peeters.

Sanders, E. P
1985   *Jesus and Judaism.* Philadelphia: Fortress Press.

Schmidt, Karl Ludwig
1919   *Der Rahmen der Geschichte Jesu: Literarkritische Untersuchungen zur ältesten Jesusüberlieferung.* Berlin: Trowitzsch & Sohn.

Schweitzer, Albert
1906   *Von Reimarus zu Wrede: Eine Geschichte der Leben-Jesu-Forschung.* Tübingen: Mohr.
1959   English translation: *The Quest of the Historical Jesus.* New York: Macmillan.

Seeley, David
1990   *The Noble Death: Paul's Concept of Salvation and Greco-Roman Martyrology.* JSNT Supplement Series 28. Sheffield, England: JSOT Press.
1994   "The Background of the Philippians Hymn (2:6–11)." *Journal of Higher Criticism* 1 49–72.

Sheldon, Charles
1899   *In His Steps: What Would Jesus Do?* Elgin, Illinois: D. C. Cook.

Singleton, Carrie Jane
1987   "Christian Rationalization for Lynching: A Correct Interpretation of the Gospel of Mark." Master's Thesis, Claremont School of Theology.

Smith, Dennis
1980   "Social Obligation in the Context of Communal Meals: A Study of the Christian Meal in I Corinthians in Comparison with Graeco-Roman Communal Meals." Ph.D. diss., Harvard University.
1990   *Many Tables: The Eucharist in the New Testament and Liturgy Today.* Co-authored with Hal Taussig. Philadelphia: Trinity Press International.

Smith, Jonathan Z.

1966   "The Garments of Shame." *History of Religions* 5 217–38. Reprinted in his *Map is Not Territory*, 1–23.

1971   "Native Cults in the Hellenistic Period." *History of Religions* 11 236–49.

1975   "The Social Description of Early Christianity." *Religious Studies Review* 1 19–25.

1975   "Wisdom and Apocalyptic." *Religious Syncretism in Antiquity: Essays in Conversation with Geo Widengren*. Edited by Birger A. Pearson, 131–56. Symposium Series for the American Academy of Religion and Institute of Religious Studies, University of California, Santa Barbara, no. 1. Missoula, MT: Scholars Press. Reprinted in his *Map is Not Territory*, 67–87.

1978, 1993 *Map Is Not Territory: Studies in the History of Religions*. Leiden: E. J. Brill. Chicago: The University of Chicago Press.

1982, 1988 *Imagining Religion: From Babyon to Jonestown*. Chicago: The University of Chicago Press.

1983   "Mythos und Geschichte." *Alcheringa, oder die Beginnende Zeit: Festschrift Mircea Eliade*. Edited by H. P. Duerr, 27–48. Frankfurt: Qumran Verlag.

1983   "No Need to Travel to the Indies: Judaism and the Study of Religion." *Take Judaism for Example*. Edited by J. Neusner, 215–26. Chicago: The University of Chicago Press.

1985   "What a Difference a Difference Makes." *To See Ourselves as Others See Us*. Edited by J. Neusner and E. Frerichs, 3–48. Chico, CA: Scholars Press.

1986   "The Domestication of Sacrifice." *Violent Origins: Ritual Killing and Cultural Formation. Conversations between W. Burkert, R. Girard, and J. Z. Smith*. Edited by R. Hamerton-Kelly, 278–304. Stanford: Stanford University Press.

1986   "Jerusalem: The City as Place." *Civitas: Religious Interpretations of the City*. Edited by P. Hawkins, 25–38. Baltimore: Scholars Press.

1987, 1992 *To Take Place: Towards Theory in Religion*. Chicago: The University of Chicago Press.

1990   *Drudgery Divine: On the Comparison of Early Christianities and the Religions of Late Antiquity*. London: School of Oriental and African Studies; Chicago: The University of Chicago Press.

1992 *Differential Equations: On Constructing the Other*. Thirteenth Annual University Lecture in Religion. Tempe, AZ: Arizona State University.

1996 "Social Formation of Early Christianities: A Response to Ron Cameron and Burton Mack." *Method and Theory in the Study of Religion* 8 271–278.

1998 "Religion, Religions, Religious." *Critical Terms in Religious Studies*. Edited by Mark C. Taylor, 269–284. Chicago: University of Chicago Press.

Smith, Morton

1971 *Palestinian Parties and Politics that Shaped the Old Testament*. Lectures on the History of Religions, New Series 9. New York: Columbia University Press.

1978 *Jesus the Magician*. New York: Harper and Row.

Stendahl, Krister

1963, 1976 "The Apostle Paul and the Introspective Conscience of the West." *Harvard Theological Review* 56 199–215. Reprinted in *Paul Among Jews and Gentiles*, 78–96. Philadelphia: Fortress Press.

Stowers, Stanley K.

1994 *A Rereading of Romans: Justice, Jews, and Gentiles*. New Haven: Yale University Press.

1995 "Greeks Who Sacrifice and Those Who Do Not: Toward an Anthropology of Greek Religion." *The First Christians and their Social World: Studies in Honor of Wayne A. Meeks*. Edited by L. M. White and O. L. Yarbrough, 295–335. Minneapolis: Fortress Press.

Strauss, David Friedrich

1972 *The Life of Jesus Critically Examined*. Translated by George Elliot, Lives of Jesus Series. Philadelphia: Fortress Press. English translation from the German, first published in 1835.

Talmon, Shemaryahu

1991 "The Internal Diversification of Judaism in the Early Second Temple Period." *Jewish Civilization in the Hellenistic-Roman Period*. Edited by Shemaryahu Talmon, 16–43 Philadelphia: Trinity Press International.

Taussig, Hal E.

1990 *Many Tables: The Eucharist in the New Testament and Liturgy Today*. Co-authored with Dennis Smith. Philadelphia: Trinity Press International.

Taussig, Hal E. *(cont'd)*
1994 "The Meals of the Historical Jesus." Paper presented to the Jesus Seminar, Spring.

Taylor, Joan E.
1993 *Christians and the Holy Places: The Myth of Jewish-Christian Origins*. Oxford: Clarendon Press.

Taylor, Mark C., ed.
1998 *Critical Terms in Religious Studies*. Chicago: University of Chicago Press.

Theissen, Gerd
1974 *Urchristliche Wundergeschichten: Ein Beitrag zur formgeschichtlichen Erforschung der synoptischen Evangelien*. Güetersloh: Mohn.

1983 English translation: *The Miracle Stories of the Early Christian Tradition*. Francis McConagh, translator. Edinburgh: T.&T. Clark; Philadelphia: Fortress Press.

Troeltsch, Ernst
1931 *The Social Teaching of the Christian Churches*. 2 vols. London: Allen and Unwin. First published in 1911.

Turner, Victor
1967 *The Forest of Symbols: Aspects of Ndembu Ritual*. Ithaca, NY: Cornell University Press.

Weber, Max
1905 "Die protestantische Ethik und der 'Geist' des Kapitalismus," *Archiv für Sozialwissenschaft und Sozialpolitik* 20, 21 1–54; 1–11.

1971 English translation: *The Protestant Ethic and the Spirit of Capitalism*. London: Unwin.

Wheatley, Paul
1971 *The Pivot of the Four Quarters: A Preliminary Enquiry into the Origins and Character of the Ancient Chinese City*. Chicago: Chicago University Press.

Williams, Sam K.
1975 *Jesus' Death as Saving Event: The Background and Origin of a Concept*. Harvard Dissertations in Religion 2. Missoula, MT: Scholars Press.

Wilson, Stephen G.
1995 *Related Strangers: Jews and Christians 70–170* C.E. Minneapolis: Fortress Press.

Wimbush, Vincent L.
1997 "*Contemptus Mundi—Redux*: The Politics of an Ancient Rhetorics and Worldview." *Power, Powerlessness, and the Di-*

vine: New Inquiries in Bible and Theology. Cynthia L. Rigby, ed., 263–80. Atlanta, Georgia: Scholars Press.

Wire, Antoinette C.
1978   "The Structure of the Gospel Miracle Stories and Their Tellers." *Semeia* 11 83–113.

Wister, Owen
1902   *The Virginian*. New York: Macmillan.

Woodword, Kenneth
1996   See entry under Reuters News Service.

Vaage, Leif E.
1994   *Galilean Upstarts: Jesus' First Followers According to Q*. Valley Forge, PA: Trinity Press International.